Village Matters

Knowledge, Politics & Community
in Kabylia, Algeria

African Anthropology

Village Matters
Knowledge, Politics & Community
in Kabylia, Algeria
Judith Scheele

World Anthropology

Series Editors Wendy James & N. J. Allen
Published in association with
the School for Advanced Research Press

Inside West Nile
Mark Leopold

A Greek Island Cosmos
Roger Just

The Pathan Unarmed
Mukulika Banerjee

Turkish Region
Ildikó Bellér-Hann & Chris Hann

Hinduism & Hierarchy in Bali
Leo Howe

Imagined Diasporas among
Manchester Muslims
Pnina Werbner

Modern Indian Kingship
Marzia Balzani

Melodies of Mourning
Music & Emotion
in Northern Australia
Fiona Magowan

Expressing Identities
in the Basque Arena
Jeremy MacClancy

Village Matters

Knowledge, Politics & Community
in Kabylia, Algeria

Judith Scheele

Fellow of Magdalen College
University of Oxford

James Currey

James Currey
is an imprint of Boydell and Brewer Ltd
PO Box 9, Woodbridge, Suffolk IP12 3DF, UK
and of Boydell & Brewer Inc.
668 Mt Hope Avenue, Rochester, NY 14620, USA

www.jamescurrey.co.uk
www.boydell.co.uk
www.boydellandbrewer.com

1 2 3 4 5 13 12 11 10 09

British Library Cataloguing in Publication Data
Scheele, Judith, 1978-
Village matters : knowledge, politics & community in
Kabylia, Algeria. - (African anthropology series)
1. Communities - Algeria - Kabylia 2. Kabylia (Algeria) -
Social conditions 3. Kabylia (Algeria) - Politics and
government
I. Title
965.3

ISBN 978-1-84701-205-0 (James Currey cloth)

Typeset in 10/12 pt Monotype Photina
by Long House Publishing Services, Cumbria, UK
Printed and bound in Great Britain by
CPI Antony Rowe, Chippenham, Wiltshire

To Saïd

Contents

Illustrations

Glossary

aârouch (Arabic)	political organisation that emerged in 2001 in Kabylia
adrum, iderma (Kabyle)	extended patrilineal family
aït (Kab.)	the sons of, the people of
'âlim, 'ulamâ' (Ar.)	Islamic scholar
amaziɣ, imaziɣen (Kab.)	Berber (lit. 'free man')
amɣar, imɣarin (Kab.)	lit. old man; leading member of the village council
'arsh, 'arûsh (aɛrc) (Ar.)	tribe
axxam (Kab.)	house, household, by extension also close family
bach-agha (Turkish)	highest rank to be occupied by indigenous dignitaries in the French colonial administration
banlieue (French)	suburbs, here mainly the poor suburbs surrounding Paris and other large French cities, generally inhabited by first- or second-generation immigrants
baraka (Ar.)	lit. blessing, benediction; spiritual power or life-giving force held by saints, their descendants, and places and objects associated with them
beur (F.)	second-generation North African immigrant in France
Bureaux arabes (F.)	smallest unit of French military administration of Algeria
caïd (Ar.)	from *qâ'id*, leader; high-ranking indigenous officer in the French colonial administration
cercle (F.)	administrative unit under French military rule
dhikr (Ar.)	Sufi prayer session, based on the repeated invocation of the name of God
douar (Ar.)	lit. round, circle; small administrative unit both in French and independent Algeria
évolué (F.)	member of the French-educated indigenous elite under French colonial rule
jamâ'a (Ar.)	village council
hubus, ahbâs (Ar.)	religious endowment, mainly landholdings
harki (Ar.)	indigenous auxiliary troops in the French army during the Algerian war of independence

hogra (Ar.)	from *haqara*, to despise; lack of respect, corruption
'îd (Ar.)	lit. feast; in Islam mainly the first day after Ramadan and the commemoration of Abraham's sacrifice celebrated by the slaughter of a sheep
ikhwân (Ar.)	(Sufi) brothers
instituteur (F.)	French primary school teacher
khammâs (Ar.)	sharecropper receiving a fixed share of the harvest in wages (originally a fifth)
madrasa, madâris (Ar.)	lit. school; urban Islamic institute of higher education in Algeria
makhzan (Ar.)	lit. storehouse (of taxes); referring to the Ottoman government or their military auxiliaries
maquis (F.)	lit. scrub, bush; guerrilla camp, mainly in the mountains
maquisard (F.)	guerrilla, see *mujâhid*
marabout (from Ar.)	local religious specialist in Kabylia, also used for saint's tomb
médersa (from Ar.)	French-run Islamic secondary teaching institute, or Reformist school in French administrative discourse
mezaour (from Ar.)	village headman in French colonial administration after 1871
mujâhid (Ar.)	fighters on the war of independence on the nationalist side
ouléma (from Ar.)	Islamic reformists, mainly active in Algeria in the 1930s and the following decades
piston (F.)	string-pulling, connections
qânûn, qawânîn (Ar.)	local law codes
saff, sufûf (Ar.)	lit. rank, row; two-fold division in local or regional 'parties'
sénatus-consulte (F.)	first French cadastral survey in Algeria
shahîd, shuhadâ (Ar.)	lit. martyr; nationalist fighter who died during the war of independence, often extended to victims of more recent political events
shaykh, shuyûkh (Ar.)	lit. old man; Islamic scholar, Sufi leader or imam in Kabylia; also village headman under French military colonial administration
taddart (Kab.)	village
tajmaɛt, tijmaɛtin (Kab.)	village council
tâlib, talba (Ar.)	(religious) student
taqbaylit (Kab.)	tribal federation, the Kabyle language; also Kabyle-ness
tifinaɣ (Kab.)	Berber script
trabendo (from Spanish)	illegal import-export business

umma (Ar.)	community of all Muslims
walî (Ar.)	president of a *wilâya*
wilâya, -ât (Ar.)	administrative unit in independent Algeria, roughly corresponding to a French department, also administrative unit used by the FLN during the war of independence
zakât (Ar.)	Islamic alms tax to be paid after Ramadan
zâwiya, zawâyâ (Ar.)	rural teaching institute, pilgrimage site, Sufi centre, in contemporary usage also Sufi meetings

Acronyms & Abbreviations

ALN	Armée de libération nationale
CADC	Coordination des archs, douars et communes
FFS	Front des forces socialistes
FIS	Front islamique du salut
FLN	Front de libération nationale
JSK	Jeunesse sportive de la Kabylie
MAK	Mouvement pour l'autonomie de la Kabylie
MCB	Mouvement culturel berbère
MNA	Mouvement national algérien (former MTLD/PPA)
MTLD	Mouvement pour le triomphe des libertés démocratiques
OAS	Organisation d'action spéciale
ONM	Organisation nationale des moudjahidines
PPA	Parti du peuple algérien
PT	Parti du travailleur
RCD	Rassemblement pour la culture et la démocratie
RND	Rassemblement national pour la démocratie
SATEF	Syndicat autonome des travailleurs de l'éducation et de la formation

Acknowledgements

Special thanks go to Paul Dresch for his patience and good advice; and to the villagers of Ighil Oumsed, and especially Tahar Hamadache and his family, for housing and feeding me, for patiently supporting my curiosity and sharing all their knowledge and contacts with me. I would also like to thank the African Studies Centre at the University of Oxford, the Arts and Humanities Research Board and the Royal Anthropological Institute of Great Britain for funding my research; the *Centre des Recherches en anthropologie sociale et culturelle* in Oran (Algeria) for receiving me in Algeria; the Universities of Tizi Ouzou and of Béjaïa, Djamil Aïssani and the LAMOS, and the *Maison mediterranéenne des sciences de l'homme* in Aix-en-Provence (France) for access to their resources and for their help; the town halls of Chellata and Akbou, the archives and the registry of Constantine, the national archives in Algiers and the French overseas and military archives and their staff; the Grangaud family, Fanny Colonna, Mohand Akli Hadibi, Salma Boukir, and Karima Benatsou for their hospitality and advice; and Morgan Clarke for reading drafts.

Note on Transliteration

Transcriptions of Kabyle follow the transcription suggested by Mouloud Mammeri; for Arabic, they follow a simplified version of the transcription used by Hans Wehr in his *Dictionary of Modern Arabic*. Broken Arabic and Kabyle plurals are indicated in the text. Terms that, in a certain spelling, have come to refer to political groupings or specific categories in French historical and anthropological writings are maintained as such (such as the *Association des oulémas* or the *aârouch*), following local usage. Where a word is used both in Kabyle and in Arabic, the transcription chosen depends on the context.

Introduction

We are here; we will always be here. We won't let them sleep in peace. Even when we have fallen to the ground, a real or an imaginary bullet in our flat chest, we will get up to throw yet another stone into the face of the bad guys in Algiers and elsewhere. The future young martyrs will know what to do. Our photos will be on a poster that other young people will hold up when it is their turn to go and die. This is our history, and it will not betray us. The history that our generation will write with its blood on all the roads and in front of all *gendarmerie* stations.

There are still villages that deserve to be called villages in Kabylia.[1]

In spring 2001, a high school student named Massinissah Guermah was killed inside a *gendarmerie* post in a small village in Kabylia, north-eastern Algeria. This event, which as such was not unusual in a country plagued by endemic violence, often perpetrated by the security forces themselves, led to riots that quickly spread through the region. They were the longest and most sustained in the history of independent Algeria (Roberts 2001; Salhi 2002). The immediate concerns of the rioters were familiar to anyone who had followed the news on Algeria since the 1980s. The main issue was the fight against the *hogra*, a term used to mean corruption, disrespect of citizens by the government, and a general 'lack of morality' among the ruling classes and security forces. The protesters demanded that the *gendarmes* be withdrawn from Kabylia and replaced by locally recruited policemen.[2]

As in riots in Algeria before, government buildings, party offices, shops and institutions, as well as *gendarmeries*, were attacked. However, the riots of 2001 showed certain particularities: they were confined to the Berber-speaking area of Kabylia and hardly spread to other regions in Algeria, where general economic and social conditions were no less conducive to popular outrage. They were also soon followed by the emergence of a peculiar system of organisation or monitoring of the events by village-based 'citizens' committees', which the national and international media ascribed to the re-activation of 'traditional' village committees attested throughout

---

[1] Two e-mails sent by a Kabyle protester to www.kabylie.com in 2002. All translations are my own, unless stated otherwise.

[2] As in many former French colonies, the Algerian internal security forces are divided into two: the police and the paramilitary *gendarmerie*. In Kabylia, the latter are generally perceived to be 'foreigners', whereas the former are more easily accepted.

1

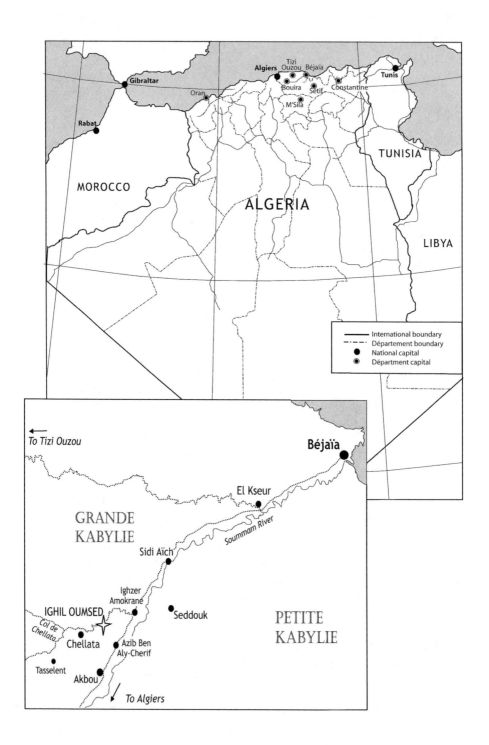

Map 0.1 Algeria and the Soummam Valley

the anthropological and historical literature on Kabylia, and labelled now *aârouch* (a term which up to then had been used to mean 'tribes'). These committees succeeded for several months in channelling the revolt, in organising the region-wide protest movement and in expressing the protesters' anger in a list of claims presented to the government. Alongside claims for a more democratic form of government, for unemployment benefits and justice, this list included demands for the official acknowledgement of the *'spécificité berbère'* of the region and of the country as a whole – although the meaning of the term 'Berber' and the forms in which 'specificity' should be acknowledged were and still are disputed.

Kabylia is a mountainous region east of Algiers (see Map 0.1). It is densely populated, and although it occupies only a small part of the vast Algerian territory, roughly a fifth of the Algerian population count themselves as Kabyles (Chaker 1999). Most of the region's inhabitants speak Kabyle, one of the local variants of Berber, a language that pre-dates Arabic in North Africa and that in one form or another is spoken by a substantial minority in the countries of the Maghreb and the Sahara. Kabylia prides itself on its strong participation in the Algerian war of independence (1954-62); within Algeria, it is the region that looks back on the longest history of emigration to France and French schooling, and that produced the largest number of intellectuals and government officials at independence (Quandt 1972). It is also the region in Algeria that has lived through most political trouble in the post-war period, from an early uprising against the newly established national government in 1963 to the Berber movement in 1980 to the events of 2001 described above; but it is also the part of Algeria that – at least according to official voting statistics, dress and publicly displayed political allegiance – remained least touched by the political Islam that dominated Algeria's political landscape throughout the 1990s.

Yet Kabylia is more than just a geographical area. It is also an ideal, shaped and shared by a variety of intellectual trends and traditions, many of which clearly had an impact on the form taken by the 2001 rebellion. The term 'Kabyle' itself, coined in the years following the French conquest of Algiers in 1830, is of relatively recent origin. 'Kabylia' is notoriously difficult to delimit, and the distinction between Arabs and Kabyles – self-evident as it might appear both in ethnographic accounts and contemporary political manifestos – varies with different historical readings and political contexts, to the point where some writers (such as Lazreg 1983) attribute its very existence to the influence of French colonial ethnography and policy. Ethnographic writing on the area has been rich since the early nineteenth century, and Kabylia is still the area that takes up most space in the anthropology section of mainstream French bookshops. Despite their obvious differences, most of these writings share certain notions of 'Kabyleness', which by now have largely been appropriated by Kabyles themselves, and figure prominently in the various political movements that have succeeded one another in the region. These notions invariably include the democratic tradition of the Kabyles, their lack of religiosity, or rather of 'religious fanaticism', their love of freedom, their settled way of life, their materialism and egalitarianism. Throughout the literature, as well as in everyday conversations in contemporary Kabylia, these qualities are seen as summed up in the Kabyles' attachment to their home village, which is in turn often compared to the primitive *polis* of ancient Greece (cf. for example, Masqueray 1983 [1886]).

Although many of these notions can be traced back to the peculiar colonial context that gave rise to them (Ageron 1979; Lucas and Vatin 1975; Lorcin 1995), their current popularity in Kabylia shows that they are more than just French 'inventions', and that to dismiss them on these grounds would be to misunderstand profoundly, and to lack respect for, local realities. By now, Kabyles have made these notions their own, by adapting them to new intellectual and political developments, and by enriching them with elements from a variety of intellectual strands, such as, for example, the numerous regional Islamic traditions and Algerian nationalism. Thus transformed, these notions and the various and variable idioms in which they are expressed make it possible for those who use them to be part of larger global intellectual trends and traditions. At the same time, they provide a conceptual grid for the evaluation of local activities and political strategies, for the production of community and political legitimacy, and for the expression of social, political, economic and cultural frustration and exclusion, of which the 'events' of 2001 are but one instance. Kabylia therefore constitutes an ideal case study of how ideas that are part of larger, 'global' intellectual complexes develop and are developed (or 'digested') locally, and how these outside complexes, rather than being 'foreign' additions to an already existing locality which would 'falsify' its reality, are constitutive of the very notion of local community itself. This book aims to analyse such a process, through an in-depth study of a medium-sized village in Kabylia, and of the notions of identity, knowledge, political legitimacy and community that are particular to it.

The village

Ighil Oumsed, the village thus studied, is situated in the eastern part of Kabylia, perched on top of a small peak half-way up the southern face of the Djurdjura mountain range, at an altitude of 700 metres (Photo 0.1). From there, it overlooks the Soummam valley, which since time immemorial has been the main land route inland from the important harbour town of Béjaïa. Although, according to villagers and to French archives, the village used to be one of the largest in the area, it is now only of average size due to the population growth in the region generally. According to official statistics,[3] it is permanently inhabited by 1,500 people. Villagers

---

[3] The *Plan directeur d'aménagement et d'urbanisme* (PDAU) of the *commune* of Chellata, established in February 1997.

Photo 0.1
Ighil Oumsed

Photo 0.2
Village
architecture

Photo 0.3
Interior of a
'traditional'
Kabyle house

themselves estimate its size at anything between 1,000 and 6,000 inhabitants. As in any contemporary Kabyle village, its inhabitants speak the local variety of Kabyle among themselves, learn classical Arabic at school and like to watch French satellite television if they can afford it. Levels of schooling vary, as do the professional occupations of the inhabitants, among whom can be found retired workers from the French mines, university teachers, doctors, engineers, school teachers, workers in local factories, mechanics, peasants, petty traders and a large group of un- or under-employed. Every family owns land and engages in some subsistence agriculture, producing mainly olive oil, but most of the villagers' income is derived from outside employment. Emigration to other areas of Algeria, and especially to France, goes back a long way. The first emigrant to take the boat to Marseille is said to have left the village just after the First World War, and there is not a family in the village that does not count one or more emigrants among its members.

The village features varying styles of architecture, ranging from 'traditional' stone houses huddled together around the village mosque, which still conserve the interior that inspired Bourdieu's (1972) study of the Kabyle house to modern concrete villas constructed at a certain distance from the village and surrounded by gardens and parking lots (see Photos 0.2 and 0.3). Since the mid-1980s, the village's only road of access has been paved. The Soummam valley down below is by now densely populated, as much by villagers who have left the cold mountain areas as by 'foreigners' from other areas of Kabylia or from Arabic-speaking parts of Algeria. The nearest town of any importance is Akbou, which can be reached in little more than half an hour by recently legalised private minibuses. The nearest university town and the capital of the *wilâya* (department), Béjaïa, can be reached in less than two hours.

I had been invited to this village by a contact I made through a Kabyle student at a French university and then followed up via the internet. This was not an unusual way to be introduced to the country. French universities are full of Kabyle students, both first- and second-generation emigrants, many of whom have chosen to study subjects related to their own country, and especially to Berber history and culture, a subject that has long been unavailable in Algerian universities. Consequently, most academic knowledge on Kabylia is produced in Paris, from where the only Berber television channel broadcasts, where most of the many Berber websites are based, and where most Berber books are edited or re-edited. To be a local activist thus means to be well connected to France. My host in the village, Arezqi Yennat,[4] had been active in various Berber and other political organisations, and was therefore known within the French as well as the

---

[4] All names have been changed. Members of one family bear the same pseudonym, and the pseudonyms of related families have been derived from the same root, in order to identify the speaker in relation with his or her family background (eg. the Hamlal and the Ihamlalen are distant cousins). The structural relationships between my informants should thus remain intelligible to the reader despite the need to maintain privacy.

Algerian 'Berber scene'. He was very keen to guide a researcher from a university as prestigious as Oxford on her visit to Kabylia. After a first visit in his home village in August 2003, I decided to stay – initially as an honoured guest, and then increasingly as the youngest and most spoiled 'daughter' of Arezqi's family. By the end of my fieldwork, I had spent just over a year in the village, interrupted by short spells in neighbouring villages and in nearby towns and cities. I had also conducted research among the emigrant village community in France.[5]

After my arrival in the village, however, Arezqi, although he generally shared and partly reproduced the discourse on Kabyle identity outlined above, with its emphasis on the 'Kabyle village' as central to Kabyle identity, seemed surprised at the idea that I wanted to stay for a whole year in the village itself, where by definition nothing of interest ever happened – otherwise, why would so many people want to go to the city or even to France, the place where 'real', universally valid knowledge was produced? He was certainly not the only one to be surprised: everybody in the village seemed to know much better than I did what I should really be studying (and where), and they all agreed that my intention to focus on the village, and on the village only, could not result in any serious, 'scientific' work – and that particular village affairs were none of my business, anyway. A 'proper' object of study would have been 'Kabyle culture', or even better, 'Berber culture', as *exemplified* by the village in its more 'traditional' parts and activities, but not the contemporary village itself.

I soon noticed that the villagers' scepticism towards my project was, in a sense, well founded. To try to explain and understand the village in terms only of the village would be to miss the point: the more closely I approached 'village realities', the more all notions of village-ness dissolved, and the village itself seemed to disappear and give way to a loose agglomeration of houses on a hilltop.[6] Even these became increasingly difficult to delimit. How should the village be defined in any case? By its inhabitants? As mentioned above, estimates of the total number of inhabitants by villagers varied hugely, depending on whether they included villagers who lived in the valley, in Algiers or elsewhere: much as the definition of 'Kabyle' could vary according to circumstances, the definition of 'villager' itself was not clear, and there were degrees of village-ness determined according to constantly changing criteria. This was further complicated by the fact that, although there was obviously a physical village in the form of several

[5] During my fieldwork, I conducted interviews in almost equal proportions in French and in Kabyle. The boundaries between languages, especially when speaking to foreigners, are flexible, and many French and Arabic terms tend to be used in colloquial Kabyle. In my fieldnotes, I translated all quotes directly into French. In the following, most quotes are thus an English translation of my on-the-spot French translations of Kabyle. French and Kabyle terms are added when the English term was not available.

[6] Similar problems have been encountered by anthropologists working on villages all over the world, ever since Maine (1876) had established the 'village' as a fundamental category not only of analysis, but also of law and government (for a more detailed discussion of the notion of the 'village', in particular in India, see Dumont 1957 and 1966; Breman 1988 and Kemp 1988; for Central Africa, see von Oppen 2003).

hundred houses perched on top of a hill, a number of imaginary villages existed within this small space, and various degrees of village-ness could be attributed to them.[7] Apparently simple questions about the spatial limits of the village, or the number of inhabitants, or the history, or the main economic occupation of villagers, became thereby part of a never-ending process of renegotiation of the village, and of Kabylia as a whole. This process was in turn part of conflicts or alliances that surpassed the limits of the village, while debates over larger political issues tended to refer back to 'village matters'. In its flexibility and the sheer impossibility to define it once and for all, that existed alongside discourses of apparent simplicity and order, 'village-ness' thus truly seemed to mirror 'Kabyle-ness', this strangely elusive quality that I had come to study. More than anything else, it was this elusiveness, allowing as it did for constant attempts at redefining categories that were central to village – and Kabyle – society, that came to dominate my research.

Rather than a straightforward description, this book is thus an attempt to demarcate, through a detailed case study, the field within which notions of 'village-ness' and other related notions that constitute ideas of 'Kabyle-ness' can be effective. I am thereby aiming to show the continuing relevance of these notions to contemporary Kabyle society and their influence on local notions of political legitimacy as expressed in the events of 2001; but I am also hoping to ask questions that might help to analyse similar cases elsewhere. Chapters 1 and 2 outline the larger intellectual movements that were at play in the constitution of the notion of 'Kabyle-ness' as it is used today, first in France, then in Algeria itself, while giving the historical and intellectual background necessary to comprehend the continuing discourse about Berber identity and the nature of society in Algeria. I aim to show that any separation of the various influences that created 'Kabylia' is futile, and in itself part of a specific intellectual movement; and that several of these intellectual movements, most of which were developed during the nineteenth century, are strikingly similar in their underlying assumptions.

Chapters 3 to 6 constitute the ethnography proper. Chapter 3 attempts a physical description of the construction of the village and the division of its lands, trying to capture the social significance of spatial definitions and boundaries, and trying to explain why these are virtually impossible to fix once and forever. The close relationship between this 'production of space' (Lefebvre 1991) and the production of community is stressed. Chapter 4 is concerned with the history of the village, as it is presented on the one hand by different groups of villagers, and on the other hand by local and regional archives. Special attention is paid to the various leading groups that the village has produced since the beginning of records in the early nineteenth century. I thereby aim to analyse the various ways through which legitimacy – the right to speak or write in the name of the village – has been constructed

---

[7] A similar observation has been frequently made about villages in Britain, see, for example, Frankenberg (1957), Strathern (1981) and Jenkins (1999).

through two centuries of profound economic, political and cultural change, and how the production and control of history in itself were and still are central to the idea of a village intellectual 'elite'.

Chapter 5 shows how villagers interact with the outside world, thereby forging their own overlapping networks of relationships through marriage arrangements, family histories, economic exchanges, migration, education and administrative careers. These networks, rather than being an addition to village life, are essential for its existence, intellectually and culturally as well as economically. Their nature and range have changed significantly over recent decades, and, in many cases, this has resulted in a restriction rather than an opening of village space, with severe consequences for village society. Chapter 6 focuses on the gradual changes that mark the development of the political sphere in the village since the Algerian war of independence, and on the social ramifications and causes of this development. It thus tries to explain the relative success of the Berber movement and the relative failure of the *aârouch* movement in 2001, and the continuities between both movements and preceding political village institutions. I shall argue that, despite variable political rhetoric, the central point of conflict between the various village associations and parties remains the question of their 'representing' the village community, and thereby by extension, of both the nature of the village and that of political representation. Taken together, these chapters aim to describe the village – and Kabylia as a whole – as a place made by outside contacts as much as by its own location, and that can only be understood with reference to the position it occupies within various 'wholes', or intellectual, political, economic and cultural 'world-systems'.

1
Massinissah's Children

Jugurtha is the man who has taken up his uncle Massinissah's slogan 'Africa to the Africans'. In this sense, he is the pioneer of the people's liberation movement. He is the incarnation of the Berber soul and philosophy whose driving force is the constant struggle to take off the straitjacket that any kind of power imposes on society. He is genealogical continuity in the political, cultural and social sense. (Hacène Hireche, quoted by Ourad 2000: 27)

In 2002, the Algerian national football team played, for the first time in history, a French national team (*the* French national team, in fact, that had just won the World Cup, and catapulted France into the never-dreamt-of realms of football paradise). The captain of the French team, Zinedine Zidane, world footballer of the year and Marseille's 'national' idol, was of Kabyle origin. A large number of the other footballers similarly were second-generation Algerian (or West African) immigrants. The team had been heralded by most of the national press and the political establishment as the living representation of France's multi-cultural, but nevertheless distinctively French, identity. For the match, the newly constructed *Stade de France*, situated in one of the notoriously 'Arab' and notoriously 'dangerous' *banlieues* of Paris, was packed with young Algerians living in France and with *beurs* (second-generation North African emigrants).[1] On the balcony reserved for the government delegation, the then French prime minister, Lionel Jospin, was watching. The French president, Jacques Chirac, had once more trusted his political instinct and stayed away.

Even before the match started, trouble announced itself. The French national anthem was shouted down, and the whole stadium seemed to be full of Algerian flags. As soon as the French team was clearly leading, the spectators invaded the playing field, throwing whatever they could find at the official delegation. The match had to be cancelled, and has never been repeated since. The dream of a French Republic capable of turning anybody into a proud Frenchman within one generation had failed, concluded the French media (Dupuis et al. 2002). But what was 'France' to do? No similar incident had ever happened in the history of French (or Algerian) football. Since then, weeks of rioting in the *banlieue* in autumn 2005 and a controversial French law praising the '*bienfaits du colonialisme*' have further

[1] '*Beur* culture' is officially heralded as a vital part of French society and youth culture, although socio-economic realities – the most obvious sign of which is the concentration of most second-generation emigrants in the *banlieue* and the recent (2005) riots that broke out there – often indicate a less successful integration.

confirmed that, even forty years after Algerian independence, the relationship between the two countries was obviously more complex than just that of two independent or even interdependent political powers.

When Algeria achieved independence in 1962, it had been occupied by France for 132 years, longer than any other country in the Middle East or North Africa was held by Europeans. The disastrous impact of French occupation on the Algerian economy, on intellectual life and traditional social networks has been well documented (Nouschi 1961; Launay 1963; Bourdieu and Sayad 1964; Turin 1983; Bennoune 1986), and still haunts contemporary Algeria alongside new structures of dependency that often follow old colonial networks.[2] The impact of this colonial adventure can also still be felt on the Northern shore of the Mediterranean, not least as exemplified by the difficult relationship which the citizens of the *République une et indivisible* are trying to establish with their ex-colonial 'brothers' turned immigrants (Ben Jelloun 1984; Etienne 1989), and by the very hostile French reaction to the Islamist electoral victory in 1991 (Etienne 1995; Burgat 1995).

Independence not only put a definite end to the French dream of empire and international influence, which had already taken a bad blow during the Second World War (Quemeneur 2004). It also forced almost a million French settlers, many of whom had lived in Algeria for several generations, to return to France (Lefeuvre 2004), thereby shattering the project of cultivating an enlarged, invigorated and essentially Mediterranean France, limited to the South only by the Sahara, and of creating a new, better and less decadent society (cf. Bertrand 1921; Llamo 1956). The war of independence was very long (1954–62) and bloody, and it laid open tensions and oppositions not only among the colonised, but also among the colonisers. It precipitated the fall of the Fourth Republic in France. It led to an attempted putsch by French officers in Algiers (Vaïsse 1983), and to the forced departure or violent death of almost a quarter of a million Algerians who had fought on the French side during the war (Hamoumou 1993). It was economically irrational (Eisenhans 1995) and politically controversial (Liauzu 2004; cf. Jeanson and Jeanson 1955; Alleg 1958). Its official 'forgetting' became as fundamental for the French Republic until recently as its mystified memory for the new Algerian republic (Stora 1992). According to Le Sueur:

> The French-Algerian war and the process of decolonisation disrupted France and French perceptions of France on a level not seen since the German occupation and, one can argue, even since the French Revolution. (Le Sueur 2001: 167)

Algerian independence was so disruptive because Algeria and France were not only linked to each other through their long shared colonial past,

---

[2] For a short overview of these, see Aggoun and Rivoire (2004). Officially, roughly a third of all imports to Algeria come from France, which in turns imports 10% of Algerian goods, mainly oil and natural gas. France is the foremost foreign investor in Algeria (Economist Intelligence Unit 2006). To these figures, one needs to add the close economic ties maintained between the two countries through the large number of remittances sent to Algeria by the Algerian emigrant community in France.

but were also essential to each other's most intimate self-perceptions. At the beginning of the conquest, theories about Algerian society were an integral part of the development of a French moral project of society, whose legitimacy depended on the assumption of its universal value. More than anything else, the development of the 'Kabyle myth' (Ageron 1979: 137), which in the nineteenth century projected ideal notions about social and moral organisation debated in Paris at that time on to Kabyle 'primitive democracy' (Lorcin 1995), became central to debates about the nature of good government, of social and moral cohesion, race and nationhood, progress, and the role of religion and science in France (cf. Tocqueville 1988 [1841]; Renan 1873). Algerian independence thus meant more than just the loss of an overseas colony:[3] it meant the end of a certain kind – or rather, ideal – of France.

Today, this ideal notion of France seems long since to have failed in France itself, at least if one believes French apprehensions.[4] Its underlying intellectual and moral paradigms, however, still inform the perception of Algeria in the Western world and partly in Algeria itself (Roberts 2003: 36-7), not least because the vast majority of academic and literary work on Algeria is written or at least published in France and in French.[5] Although other historiographic traditions, such as Algerian nationalist, Islamic reformist or 'Berberist' historiography, are also important, they often echo French historical and moral categories (McDougall 2006). In order to understand both contemporary France and Algeria fully, we therefore need to step back in time and look at the history of the French conquest and occupation of Algeria, of the war and of Algerian independence, in conjunction with the development of social thought in France.

Arabs, Berbers and Kabyles

The southern shore of the Mediterranean has always been important for the various empires and civilisations that successfully dominated the 'Interior Sea' of the Arab geographers – *mare nostrum* to the Romans. It is the history

---

[3] In administrative terms, Algeria was not a colony, but constituted the three southernmost departments of France (without granting full citizenship to the vast majority of its inhabitants). It was intended to be a settler colony (parallels were often drawn with America or Australia, rather than India, see for example Leroy-Beaulieu 1887), yet white settlers remained in the minority, much as in, say, South Africa.

[4] See, for example, the alarm with which especially American influence is perceived in French public debates, as expressed by the mission statement of the *Agence intergouvernementale de la Francophonie* (see www.agence.francophonie.org), or the worry caused by the growing influence of the English language which is readily perceived as one of many signs of 'American cultural hegemony' (see, for example, Cassen 2005). The notion that the identity of France is inherently fragile has become commonplace among British researchers, see, for example, Burke (1989) and McDonald (1989), but also in France, as shown by Braudel's (1986) attempt to (re)define 'France' within an increasingly 'threatening' world.

[5] Out of the 6,976 titles held by the Library of Congress (USA) that respond to the search by the keyword 'Algeria', roughly 4% were originally written in English, about 15% in Arabic, while the remaining 81% were in French.

of these various empires that constitutes the bulk of written history of the lands that were to become Algeria. The history of the population in the area that we are interested in thus represents, just like its agricultural and urban landscapes, a continuous superposition – or mixing, according to which image the historian prefers – of eclectic influences, of Phoenician, Roman, Arabic, Andalusian, Spanish and Turkish origins, on to an 'aboriginal population' named variously Numidians or Berbers. The most lasting of the outside influences is arguably that of the Arabs and especially of the religion they brought with them in the tenth and twelfth centuries, Islam, which over the centuries became part of a distinct North African tradition (or rather a variety of unique North African traditions). Outside these histories of conquest, very little has ever been known about either Numidians or Berbers. This means that both categories lend themselves to historical speculation, and can easily be invested with contemporary meaning. As we have seen in the opening quote, contemporary Berbers like to trace their history back to the Massinissah and Jugurtha of Roman times,[6] thereby proving their historical legitimacy, their contribution to world history, their noble ancestry and their rebellious and democratic nature.

Yet, to find an unbiased account of the history of the 'Berbers' in the area that the French gradually took over from 1830 onwards is difficult, for the definition of the category itself is problematic. Although the number of invading Arabs during the successive 'openings' of the North African lands to Islam was minimal, the number of 'Arabs' in the converted areas increased exponentially after their arrival, as patrilineal genealogies proving Arab descent became extremely popular among influential Berbers in the centuries after the conquest (Norris 1982). With the creation of independent North African kingdoms and empires from the thirteenth and fourteenth centuries onwards, a certain notion of the intrinsic value of the category of the 'Berber' seems to have come into existence (Brett 1998),[7] although here once again the Berber appears as an oppositional category: the pagan who resisted Islamisation less than a decade ago now defined himself as a *mujâhid* fighting against Muslims who lacked religious zeal. Just as in the eastern Islamic lands the differences between Arabs and non-Arab Muslims (Persians, famously) were often a designation of social status rather than a reference to 'racial' identity (Lewis 1990), 'Berber' and 'Arab' appear in North Africa as flexible categories within a larger game of prestige and changing allegiances.[8]

[6] Both Massinissah (ca. 238–149 BC) and his grandson Jugurtha (who died in 104 BC) were Numidian kings mostly allied to the Romans. Sallust (86–34 BC, governor of Numidia) made the latter (a true Roman *évolué*) famous by violently accusing him of having rather successfully tried to corrupt the Roman Senate before attacking Roman military interests.
[7] A fourteenth-century book called *The Boasts of the Berbers* (*Kitâb Mafâkhir al-Barbar*, ca. 1313/4, re-edited by al-Halim 1996) described Berber heroism and noble genealogies and tales of a meeting of great 'nations' among which the Berbers counted (Norris 1982). At roughly the same time, the 'Berber' historian Ibn Khaldûn wrote his *History of the Berbers*, in which he mentioned the 'Berbers' as one among the various peoples that inhabit the civilised world (1847: 199).
[8] In practice, these categories seem very flexible and conceptually closer to ideas of large tribal groups as described and theorised by Dresch (1986). For a different, but equally pertinent, reading, see Berque (1974).

The category of the 'Kabyles', however, seems to have been more closely defined. In the sixteenth century, Haëdo, a Christian slave who spent several months in Algiers, identifies the Kabyles living in the city as a distinctive group composed of the only 'truly indigenous' population of North Africa, and originating from the mountainous regions east of Algiers. However, his distinction remains one of wealth and occupation: the Kabyles are poor workers who serve in the Turkish army or work for the rich families of Algiers as gardeners or handymen (Haëdo 1998 [1612]: 57). 'Kabyle' thus appears as shorthand for poor mountain dwellers, rather uncouth and barely civilised; it seems to be a social rather than a 'racial' category. It was not until the nineteenth century that the term 'Kabyle' became virtually synonymous with 'Berber'.

Alongside distinctions of occupation and wealth, the most important characteristic of the 'Kabyles' – as their name, derived from the Arabic *qabâ'il* meaning 'tribes', indicates – was that they did not recognise any government.[9] From the sixteenth century onwards, what is now Algeria was at least nominally under Ottoman rule, and presented a complicated mosaic of local political structures and forms, of areas and tribes controlled by the Turkish armies (where control meant taxation, often by proxy, rather than direct juridical influence), and vast independent lands, inhabited by a diverse population, where several influential families constituted more or less independent centres of power. Their influence was variously based on their religious legitimacy, their noble descent, or their wealth and military reputation, or all three (see, for example, Rinn 1891: 12; Nouschi 1961: 150). At the same time, Algeria was covered by a dense network of religious brotherhoods and *zawâyâ*.[10] It was at least notionally divided into tribes, and it appears that as a general rule most daily affairs were administered by the local village communities. In most cases, it was thus virtually impossible to distinguish neatly between political, religious, intellectual and economic institutions or sources of local influence (cf. Cornell 1998 for similar observations on Morocco).

Turkish garrisons had been established in the coastal regions and in more accessible places further inland, but they were mainly staffed with local tribesmen allied to the coastal towns that were under the direct

[9] The distinction between 'governed' and 'ungoverned' people and parts of the country seems to have been indigenous, but it also corresponded to contemporary European categories of thought, that drew a distinction between 'policed' and 'unpoliced' societies (Mollat de Jourdin 2005, see also Braudel 1975: 819 for the use of a similar concept in sixteenth-century Spanish North Africa). For the most famous and influential theorisation of this distinction in the Maghreb, see Montagne (1930).

[10] Sg. *zâwiya*, literally 'corner' (of a mosque). Throughout the Maghreb, the *zawâyâ* fulfilled a variety of functions in rural life: generally constructed around the tomb of a local saint, they served as teaching institutes of varying quality, where the teachers of the village Qur'ânic schools would be educated, and as sites of pilgrimages, institutes of charity, hostels, and meeting places for the religious brotherhoods. They often also managed considerable wealth, wielded military power, and were central to the local economy. Today, this term can refer to the site where a holy man is buried, to the residence of a *marabout*, to an Islamic higher teaching institute, the meeting, dancing and feasting of a group of pilgrims or Sufi adepts (which can take place anywhere), or any number of the above simultaneously.

influence of the *dey* of Algiers and the *beys* of the larger provincial towns, such as Constantine (Valensi 1969). Kabylia was nominally under Ottoman control, which was, however, only effective in the plains where military control was possible (Robin 1873); the village studied here overlooked a Turkish garrison, and it is probable that some taxes were paid in order to ensure access to low-lying lands. Overall, however, government control remained minimal, as noted by Hasan b. Muhammad al-Fâsî (Leo the African), who visited the area in the sixteenth century (al-Fâsî 1956 [1550]: 406). A similar observation was made two hundred years later by the French traveller Peysonnel:

> The Arabs of all these mountains, from Collo to the outskirts of Algiers, are different from the others. They have neither chiefs, nor nations, nor governors. Everybody is master and free to his will. They are, most of them, thieves, or rather, wild beasts living in these mountains. Neither the Turk, nor anybody else, has been able to subdue them; they live miserably as they please... As to their customs and ways of life, they are the same as those of the other Arabs, maybe a bit more savage; but the differences are very small. (1987 [1724-5]: 213 and 266)

Peysonnel further notes that Kabylia, due to its independence, is the refuge for everybody who had to flee the Algiers government or taxman (Peysonnel 1987: 266). His descriptions of Kabylia were frequently echoed by subsequent writers (for example, Dubois-Thainville 1927 [1809]: 132 ff.), who grew more admiring of the 'fierce independence' of the Kabyles as the eighteenth century drew to a close. Kabylia thus became the archetypical *balad al-sîba* ('country of freedom', i.e. outside the direct control of central government), without any political structures that were recognisable to local city-dwellers or European travellers; this, more than anything else, seems to have forged its reputation of difference, and provided the elements of what was later to become the 'Kabyle myth'.

France's 'new playground' and the invention of sociology

In 1830, Paris took a diplomatic incident between the French representative in Algiers and the Turkish *dey* as a pretext for occupation of the city, which had long been an important trading post for France.[11] What was intended as a brief military expedition gradually turned into the conquest of the coastal cities of the former Regency of Algiers and of their immediate

[11] Especially during the troubled decades during and after the French Revolution, France had relied heavily on wheat imports from Algeria, but did not find itself able – or willing – to honour the accumulated debts during the Restoration. This led to a heated exchange of words between the *dey* and the French representative in Algiers, at the end of which the former hit the latter in the face with a fan. A punitive expedition to Algiers to avenge this insult to France's honour seemed to resolve several problems, among which was the lack of popularity suffered by the last king of the Bourbons, Charles X. The *dey* signed his surrender to the French on 5 July 1830, twenty-two days before Charles lost his throne in the July Revolution. The true reasons for the conquest of Algiers are still hotly debated, and conspiracy theories as well as stories of hidden treasures abound (cf. Péan 2004).

hinterland, by an army that was largely left to its own devices because of persisting political trouble in France. As peace was restored in France itself, the French advance in Algeria was severely contested in Paris by the political forces of the opposition (cf. Tocqueville 1988 [1841]; Enfantin 1843). It therefore continued to proceed slowly without ever developing a coherent colonial strategy or policy (Ageron 1979). It was met with organised resistance, especially by an army rallied around the *amîr* 'Abd al-Qâdir, who resisted until 1847. After the latter's submission and subsequent departure for Damascus, indigenous resistance was mainly concentrated in the inaccessible mountains of the Tell and in the Sahara, while French raids into the north-eastern mountains – the area that was soon to be known to the world as Kabylia – and uprisings on its borders, led by various *mahdîs* and '*faux chérifs*' (i.e. *shurafâ'*, descendants of the Prophet), were frequent, and generally led to brutal suppression.[12]

In Paris, the prospect of military occupation of Kabylia, notorious for its resistance against the Turks, was particularly criticised. The opposition between the governed inhabitants of the coastal cities and the independent mountain dwellers, already present in earlier accounts, was again stressed. However, whereas, in the eighteenth century independence was tanta-mount to savagery, it was now, a hundred years later, invested with a new kind of revolutionary romanticism, and was interpreted as a sign of patriotism, attachment to the land, and hence materialism and rationalism. Tocqueville wrote in 1837 that 'with the Kabyles one has to deal with questions of civil and commercial equity, with the Arabs what matters are political and religious questions', hence 'the country of the Kabyles is closed, but the soul of the Kabyles is open to us, and it is not impossible for us to enter it' (1988: 47, 46). When the French military conquest of Kabylia was finally completed in 1857, the long debate about its legitimacy and usefulness had laid the foundations of the 'Kabyle myth'. They remained largely unchanged over the next century and were extra-ordinarily resistant to factual evidence (Ageron 1979; Lorcin 1995).

With the gradual military conquest of Algeria came its agricultural set-tlement. The first European settlers arrived in the fertile plains around Algiers in the 1830s. Subsequent revolutions, famines and wars in France and Western Europe increased their numbers steadily. In 1854–56, the European birth rate in Algeria for the first time exceeded its death toll; in 1855, 163,950 Europeans were permanently settled in the plains of northern Algeria (Ageron 1979). Conquest and agricultural settlement led to a severe restructuring of the local economy, and were followed by years of hardship in all of Algeria: between 1857 and 1871, between 200,000 and 500,000 people died of famine and epidemics, and the overall popula-tion in Algeria was reduced by 20% (Nouschi 1961). This, the French army command decided, was mainly due to confusion over property and usufruct rights in tribal lands, which was to be remedied by the application of a

---

[12] For the full horror of the conquest, see Bugeaud's – the leading General's – own account (Bugeaud 1948); for a complete list of these rebellions, see Mahé (2001).

unified code regulating private property and landholdings: the *sénatus-consulte*, decided by law in 1863, and gradually applied to all of Algeria. The *sénatus-consulte* institutionalised private property and provided a legal basis for the confiscation of all lands held in common and of all lands declared as *ahbâs* (sgl. *hubus*) or religious endowments. In other words, it led to the destruction of the material basis of all local tribal and religious institutions, with often catastrophic consequences (Nouschi 1961; Turin 1983). The land was redistributed among an ever growing population of settlers. By 1886, European settlement in the whole of Algeria had almost quadrupled, reaching a figure of 220,000 French and 203,000 other Europeans (Ageron 1979: 119–20). Kabylia, however, overpopulated, inhospitable and infertile as it was, remained largely free of European settlers.

In most of the newly conquered territory, the colonial army improvised an *ad hoc* administration based on the *Bureaux arabes*, a network of military offices and civil courts, whose officers would decide on all 'indigenous' matters arising within their district, with little or no control by the central administration (Frémaux 1993). The *Bureaux arabes* became relatively independent institutions, relying on the personal initiative of the officer in charge, on indigenous soldiers, pre-existing power structures and allied tribes. They were headed by officers of the colonial army, who were generally distinguished by their education (see Peyronnet 1930), their practical knowledge of the country, and often also their knowledge of Arabic. They were driven by a strong idealism and fervent romanticism, as promotion was rare and recruitment voluntary. This romanticism seems often to have served as an excuse for a type of rule closer to the European image of oriental princes than to any pre-existing form of local government,[13] but it also gave rise to serious scientific endeavours, as the officers of the *Bureaux arabes* not only tried to establish a viable form of government, but also aimed at producing a detailed account of the situation they found. 'In Africa, the compass always follows the military banner', as the officer Carette wrote proudly in 1848.

During the forty years immediately following the conquest, these officers produced a large number of treatises on local geography, history and ethnography.[14] These were published either by the French government or by the various scientific associations and journals that sprang up in France and, later on, Algeria itself.[15] Kabylia, due to its notional 'remoteness' and

---

[13] Rinn (1891) noted that the Algerian colony allowed for 'aristocratic excesses' that since the French revolution had become impossible to indulge in in France itself (see also Frémaux 1993: 306).

[14] Most of these were published as part of the *Exploration sciéntifique de l'Algérie*, launched in 1838 by the French Ministry of War (under whose jurisdiction Algeria remained until 1858) with reference to the Napoleonic 'scientific expedition' to Egypt.

[15] The first and scientifically most reputable of these journals, the *Revue africaine*, although edited in Algiers, was widely subscribed to by academics, teachers and civil servants in France. It was sold by bookshops in Paris, London and Rome. On average 20% of its collaborators were or had been employed by the *Bureaux arabes* (Frémeaux 1993). Officers also wrote frequently for well-known journals published in the capital, such as the *Revue des deux mondes* (1835-1944). The latter regularly included notices of monographs produced by the officers of the

its non-Arab 'authenticity', was the favourite topic of the colonial ethnographers' writings, which even now constitute the bulk of anthropological, sociological and historical material on the area, and whose main tenets still figure prominently in contemporary Kabyle discourse.

The aim of most officers turned ethnographers was to produce an accurate picture of the country they set out to govern. Nevertheless, the conceptual tools available to them at the time were often wanting, as 'sociology' was just about to be invented: indeed, these officers were to have their share in developing it. The local administrative centres of the *Bureaux arabes* generally possessed well-stocked libraries, including classical works of Roman history thought to be relevant to the conquest (such as Tacitus' description of 'German tribalism' in *De Germania*), but also the latest in French science, philosophy and the nascent social sciences (Frémeaux 1993). Despite the distance between Algiers and Paris, and the relative isolation in which most officers lived, intellectual exchange with the 'mother-country' was vivid, and all writers remained closely attached to the intellectual, social and political preoccupations of their times.

These preoccupations were indeed manifold, as the nineteenth century in France was torn by a series of revolutions and counter-revolutions on different ideological grounds, claiming legitimacy in turn for constitutional monarchies, imperial republics and plebiscitary empires.[16] As a consequence, most novels, poetry, plays, and scientific and political pamphlets of the period bear witness to an all-pervading sentiment of historical uniqueness and transition, which would lead to the advent of a new world, built – or rescued – from what was left after the French revolution and the Napoleonic wars. In the novelist Alfred de Musset's words:

> The life offered to the young generation was divided into three elements: behind them a past forever destroyed, still fidgeting in its ruins, among the fossils of a century of absolutism; in front of them the dawn of an immense horizon, the first lights of the future; and between these two worlds... something similar to the ocean that separates the old continent from the young America;... in a word, the present century that separates the past from the future, that is neither one nor the other, and resembles both at the same time, and where one does not know, at every step one takes, whether one is treading on seeds or on debris... Napoleon dead, the divine and the human powers were in fact well re-established; but the belief in them had ceased to exist. There is a terrible danger in knowing what is possible, because the mind always goes further. There is a difference between saying: this could be, and saying: this has been; it is the first bite from the dog. (2002 [1834]: 20–2)

Within this atmosphere of uncertainty, but also of political and ideological diversity and innovation, modern political and economic terminology

---

[15] (cont.) *Bureaux arabes*, which in turn served as the basis of less highbrow publications such as those of the *Magazine pittoresque*.

[16] France was a constitutional kingdom from 1830 to 1848, a republic until 1851 and an empire based on popular plebiscite until 1870, when it came to an end with a disastrous war against Prussia and the uprising of the Paris Commune in 1871. It was only with the affirmation of the Third Republic after 1871 that some kind of political stability was achieved, although social and political conflicts still loomed large.

was forged: debates over the nature of society and the social bond, over the role of religion and the importance of science, dominated intellectual life. One question remained central to all of these debates: on what basis should the new France that was emerging from the ruins of despotism, ignorance and chaos, be organised? The answer, many intellectuals agreed, was to be found by the newly created 'social sciences'. This firm belief in the capacity of the social sciences which, like medicine, would 'cure' society, appears in Victor Hugo's prophecy for the new world to be created in the aftermath of the Terror:

> From now on, the diseases of society have to be treated, not with the scalpel, but through the slow and gradual purification of blood, through the extraction of excreted humours, through healthy nutrition, through the exercise of strength and capacities, through a good diet. (Hugo 1979 [1874]: 13)

The first French society of the social sciences had been founded in 1799. Although it was quickly closed down because of its potential for political subversion, it started a long series of learned societies and journals enquiring into the nature of man, likewise under close scrutiny by governments. From the 1830s onwards, taken up by popular figures such as Saint-Simon and Auguste Comte, the social sciences gained in popularity, and were often seen as the only way either to reform society or to prevent further revolutions. Public lectures and society meetings could turn into political and religious rallies, often replacing the idea of a scientist by that of a 'prophet of science' (Clark 1973). During these meetings, a whole range of new experimental models for society was invented (such as, for example, Fourier's *phalanges*), based on scientific theory, and organised according to measurable qualities, effort and labour rather than inherited privilege or 'religious superstition'.

New ideas developed by the ever-growing group of Parisian 'sociologists' were often tentatively put into practice in Algeria, where the intellectual trends of the metropolitan capital were highly influential, not least because undesirable political activists such as followers of Saint-Simon were often posted to the colony (Rey-Goldzeiguer 1977).[17] Saint-Simon's most famous disciple, Prosper Enfantin, wrote in 1843:

> If Algeria could be the place to test this new organisation [of society], if we could carry out this precious innovation in this country where *everything needs to be done*, carry it out far from all the obstacles that the outmoded laws of our old society or the exaggerated pretensions of our youth dreaming of the future would oppose to it in France, what grace would we not have to render God for this happy result of our short-sighted conquest! (Enfantin 1843: 117, emphasis in the original)

---

[17] The most important of these 'transportations' took place in 1851, 1852 and 1858 in order to 'eliminate socialists, republicans and other anarchists' (Rey-Goldzeiguer 1977: 122). Saint-Simon's followers were numerous in the French colonial army and elsewhere; the Suez Canal (opened in 1869) was constructed by the Saint-Simonian engineer Ferdinand de Lesseps, and in 1845, prominent Saint-Simonians had launched an 'industrial society' to further the exploitation of the forests of Constantine in Algeria. It was dissolved in 1855 without ever having undertaken any serious action (ibid.).

Thus, while in the Anglo-Saxon tradition, emerging social (and racial) theories found their practical and theoretical outlet in India, among North American Indians and Australian Aborigines (cf. Trautmann 1987; Kuper 1988), Algeria, alongside rural France itself, became the laboratory for French social theories, in turn influencing their main preoccupations. More than any other area in Algeria, Kabylia, increasingly seen as a model of primitive democracy, attracted sociologically minded authors, and became central to French debates about good government and the nature of 'race', nationhood, and the social bond.

'The ideal of an independent and inexpensive government ...'

The first regional monograph to be published as part of the *Exploration scientifique de l'Algérie* was Carette's *Etudes sur la Kabilie proprement dite* (1848, two volumes). It was intended as a practical guide for the establishment of a fruitful relationship with an independent Kabylia, as well as as a contribution to the advancement of science. For Carette, although the Kabyles are presented as a people different from the Arabs, this difference does not appear as based on physical or biological distinctions. It is a linguistic, historical and cultural concept, whose boundaries are variable and are represented by bilingual tribes and Kabyle peddlers. The idea of fluctuation pervades Carette's imagery: the Berbers as a whole are like islands in the sea of subsequent invaders, sometimes resisting them, sometimes temporarily 'flooded' (Carette 1848: 32). Their most important trait of racial distinctiveness is their language, which for Carette is a reflection of their moral standards: 'Of the differences that exist between the Arabs and the Kabyles, the most obvious one is that of their language. This is what mainly makes them two distinctive nations' (ibid.: 13).[18]

Consequently, almost the entire first volume of Carette's monograph is taken up with a painstaking analysis of Berber words and especially names. For Carette, the fact that the Berbers call themselves *imaziɣen* (men who are free and noble) shows their most salient feature, namely, their love of freedom, as manifested many times throughout history, during the Carthaginian, the Roman and the Arab conquests (ibid.: 31). Carette also notes that Berbers tend to name their villages and tribes after geographical features rather than after common ancestors. For him, this proves that they have developed beyond a concept of community that is uniquely based on kinship. Like French peasants and quite unlike the nomadic Arabs, they are rooted in the soil. As well as showing the fundamental cultural opposition

---

[18] As Trautman (1997) reminds us, this emphasis on language as an expression of morality and race was common at that time, as it allowed for a master narrative that linked all known peoples of the world on the basis of the Biblical narrative of the propagation of races after the Great Flood. It pervaded British orientalism and indophilia, and for decades existed alongside a more physiological conception of race. For a late application of these theories to Kabylia, see Darasse (1885: 492).

between Arabs and Berbers, this 'rootedness in the soil' translates for Carette into private landownership:

> Finding myself in this village, one of the inhabitants came to offer me a piece of land he owned... I mention this fact because it gives me the opportunity to ascertain how much, among the Kabyles, real estate is rigorously limited and clearly defined, and to what extent the individual transferability of land creates parallels and can facilitate a reconciliation between them and us. (Carette 1848 /II: 80 fn 1)

A detailed enumeration of every village's specialities, trade networks and production capacities – yet again proof of Kabyle materialism and industry – fills the second volume of Carette's monograph. His overall conclusion is that, because of their sedentary and thus materialistic nature, these 'Auvergnats indigènes' (ibid.: 397) should not be subdued by force – an expensive and thankless undertaking – but by economic co-operation. Carette pays relatively little attention to the political organisation of the Kabyles, although he notes that 'like the general tendency of their spirit, the constitution of the Kabyles is democratic' (ibid.: 470). Any other forms of political influence he detects, such as religious prestige and tendencies to aristocracy, appear to him as alien to the 'true Berber spirit', and he is confident that they will disappear with the French conquest. He also remarks upon the 'political maturity' of the Kabyle system: elections generally serve as a sanction for decisions already taken by the shuyûkh (village elders) and the 'ulamâ' (religious specialists), in order to avoid 'the confused vote of the crowd' (ibid.: 482).[19]

Five years later, Carette published his Recherches sur l'origine et les migrations des principales tribus de l'Afrique septentrionale et particulièrement de l'Algérie, in which he estimated the Arab and Berber populations of Algeria at one and two million respectively. In 1848 he still wrote about:

> A poor little people exposed to everybody's sight on the great highways of the ancient world, brav[ing] all peoples, and conserv[ing] in its mountains with its own traditional civilisation the spirit and the language of its fathers. (1848: 469)

But he now notes that in previous accounts, including his own, the number of Berbers was underestimated because the linguistic factor was over-emphasised. 'In reality', there are many tribes where 'the use of Arabic has been introduced, but that, from the ethnological point of view, have to be counted as Berbers; ... this is why I reduced the population of Arab origin to one million and elevated to two million the population of Berber origin' (1853: 443).

The hazardous principle of 'origin' was employed in the same year by the high-ranking officer Eugène Daumas in his Mœurs et coutumes de l'Algérie.

---

[19] An expression echoing the general malaise associated with the idea of popular democracy in the late 1840s (cf. Stendhal 1854), and frequently to be found in Saint-Simonian and later Renan's (1873) thought. In the year of the publication of Carette's monograph, Napoléon III was elected president of the Second Republic with an overwhelming majority, due mainly to his support by the Fourth Estate; three years later, he abolished the republican constitution and in the following year became emperor, in both cases approved by a vast majority of voters and sanctioned by a plebiscite.

Tell, Kabylie, Sahara, leading him to estimate the number of Arabs at 1,470,550 and that of Berbers at 959,450. A former student of medicine, Arabic-speaking and a prolific writer, Daumas was at the time of the publication of his monograph head of the *Affaires indigènes* at the French Ministry of War in Paris, but until his promotion in 1850 had served in the *Bureaux arabes* and had been largely responsible for their organisation. *Mœurs et coutumes* was re-edited in 1855, 1858 and 1864 – and in 1988 and 2001. Daumas agrees with Carette's earlier work that 'language is the true material (*pierre*) of all nationalities' (Daumas 1864: 190). However, whereas 'we others, peoples of the North, are in the habit of describing a nation with the name of the country where it abides, this is different for the Muslims, who do not know any other distinctions but that of race' (ibid.: 187). The Berbers or Kabyles – these terms indicated for him the 'aboriginal population' and were hence interchangeable – were now 'of an entirely distinct race from that of the Arabs' (ibid.:186). This was proved by their red hair and their lighter skin, both indications of possible Germanic origins.[20]

However, the 'racial' difference was still mainly demonstrated by the Berbers' morals and their social organisation, namely, their recognition of private property and their egalitarianism. They were 'republican to the point of being individualist ... politically speaking, Kabylia is a kind of savage Switzerland' (ibid.: 248, 232). Furthermore, Kabyle women were more independent than their Arab cousins, and prostitution was legal, which was an infallible sign of moral evolution (*sic*) away from the tyranny of the patriarchal family.[21] It was also further proof of the Kabyles' 'racial identity' and of supposedly Indo-European and Christian origins: 'In Kabylia, we discover that the holy law of work is followed, that women are more or less redeemed, and that many customs express Christian equality, fraternity and compassion' (ibid.: 265).[22] All these traits opposed them clearly to 'Arab fanaticism and debauchery', and to the 'aristocratic arrogance and laziness', which the agricultural settlers searching for cheap labour in the 'Arab' territory of the plains increasingly experienced. 'Race' and morality had thus become one.

In 1859, two years after the conquest of Kabylia had been completed, the army officer Hanoteau and the jurist Letourneux began their research for *La Kabylie et les coutumes kabyles*, which was finally published in 1872–3 in three volumes. Their aim was, on the one hand, to document Kabyle

[20] The hypothesis that the Kabyles are descendants of the Vandals and are therefore of 'Germanic' origin runs through much of the literature, and has proved extraordinarily resilient to refutation. Today, it is still frequently upheld by Kabyles.

[21] At the same time in Paris, the followers of Saint-Simon under Enfantin were lobbying for the legalisation of prostitution, which would be a step towards a higher moral evolutionary stage (Manuel 1962). Fourier advocated sexual liberation in his *phalanges*; and the early feminist Flora Tristan travelled through France to fight for the equality of men and women and the abolition of marriage and the patriarchal family (cf. Tristan 1980 [1844]).

[22] He thereby echoes theories about the original Christian faith of the Kabyles – or even all Berbers – that were common at the time (see e.g. Warnier 1865), and led to frequent attempts at conversion (as described by Philippe 1931), as well as contributing heavily to the popularisation of the 'Kabyle myth' (Direche-Slimani 2004).

society as it was before the conquest, just in time before it disappeared following its contact with world civilisation (France); and, on the other hand, to provide colonial administrators with a comprehensive compilation of Kabyle 'customary law' (*qânûns*). The largest part of *La Kabylie* (almost two volumes out of three) is thus constituted by a compilation and systematisation of local *qânûns* to be applied in civil courts.[23] Most of these were thereby fixed in writing for the first time. The compilation followed the categories consecrated by the *Code Napoléon*, and was commented on by a large apparatus of footnotes situating Kabyle law with reference to Islamic, Jewish, Vedic, ancient Roman, ancient Greek and old Germanic law. The compilation was intended to be scientific, that is to say, universalising. As Hanoteau's son noted several decades later, it was motivated by

> the idea of treating the Kabyle question scientifically in a comprehensive study... an erudite and exclusively technical work, reserved for the use of specialists, rather than a work for the enhancement of popular knowledge written for the general public. (Hanoteau 1923: 143)

This monograph was not the first to focus on 'tribal laws': Hanoteau himself had already published a *qânûn* translated into French in the *Revue africaine* (Hanoteau 1858), and was followed by Aucapitaine (1860 and 1863). Daumas (1864: 238) had even gone as far as claiming that the Berbers were 'the only Muslim nation' who had developed their own legislation.[24] But the systematic and global approach adopted in *La Kabylie* was new. Through this claim to exhaustiveness, 'Kabyle-ness' itself was turned into a legal category. It thence depended less on geography, 'race' or language, than on the collective capacity to conceive of civil law independent from religion. As such, it was liable to be changed beyond recognition by outside influence; in turn, different degrees of 'Kabyle-ness' could be established according to how far local customs had 'succumbed' to such outside influences:

> In Algeria, the name 'Kabyle' is given to the populations of Berber race who live in the mountains on the Mediterranean coast... Despite the common origin of these populations, their political and social state is far from identical... Some of them, who surrendered long ago to successive governments, have lost even the memory of their origin; they say and sincerely believe that they are Arabs, only speak Arabic, submissively obey the chiefs nominated by the rulers of the

---

[23] From 1860 onwards, a project was envisaged of institutionalising customary law in all Berber-speaking areas of Kabylia, but was never put into practice due to the change from military to civilian rule in 1871.

[24] The existence of customary law functioning alongside Qur'ânic law among a vast range of different Arab groups throughout the Middle East has been documented abundantly, and its practical importance is acknowledged among Islamic jurists themselves (Schacht 1966, see also Messick 1993). Daumas' and Hanoteau's conviction that everywhere else the Qur'ân constitutes the 'unique legislative source' (Hanoteau and Letourneux 1873: 135) is probably due to the literary and 'orientalist' nature of the information available at that time on the Muslim Middle East, which often followed local literate conceptions and which ignored the daily practice of most, and especially rural, Muslim populations. For most nineteenth-century observers who had preceded Hanoteau, the existence of customary law had mainly been of interest as proof of the Kabyles' 'secular resistance' to religious law.

country, and submit without second thoughts to the prescriptions of Muslim law. Others, although they accept the Muslim code and the authority of chiefs nominated without their assistance, have kept some of the democratic habits that are particular to their race. These habits temper in practice the excessive arbitrariness of the absolute power; but they are acted out without fixed rules and their efficacy always depends on the power of the government to enforce its decisions. Others, finally, have been able to conserve, thanks to a happy combination of circumstances, their independence until today, either totally, or at least without essential restrictions. They govern themselves through very democratic institutions, and regulate all the transactions of civil life according to ancient customs transmitted by tradition. (Hanoteau and Letourneux 1872: 1–2)

The hierarchy thus established between 'true Kabyles', inhabitants of the area where Hanoteau's research was based, and others, is still noticeable in contemporary Kabyle perceptions and discourse. In the same way, the notion that true 'Kabyle-ness' is a function of its capacity to protect itself against outside influence has survived until today.

In the remainder of his monograph, Hanoteau provides a detailed – and still largely the best available – description of the Kabyle political system.[25] All village affairs are settled at the *jamâ'a*, or village assembly, at whose weekly assemblies presence is obligatory and absence from which is punished by the payment of a fine. Through deliberations on individual cases, the *jamâ'a* establishes customary law; through its collective authority, it applies it. Everything, including religious matters, is under the *jamâ'a*'s jurisdiction. It is constituted by representatives (or rather 'guarantors') of the extended families or village quarters, who are 'co-opted' rather than elected. The *jamâ'a* is internally divided into usually two *sufûf*, or 'blocks'. These are associations of mutual assistance, which often extend beyond the limits of the village but do not correspond to our idea of political parties in that they never try to change the form of government, only to influence decisions taken within fixed parameters.

The next political unit above the village is the tribe (*'arsh*), also generally divided into two *sufûf*, and then the confederation of tribes, which is invoked only in cases of external aggression. Weekly markets are under the jurisdiction of the *'arsh*. Membership in the *sufûf* and to a certain extent in tribes is fluctuating, and several cases of villages changing tribes have been recorded in oral poetry (cf. Hanoteau 1867: 215). As any tribal structure is thus inherently fluid, and crystallises only in situations of need, the basic legal and moral authority remains the village. The village *jamâ'a* is vested with ultimate economic authority: it can expropriate by force in the name of the public good, and restrict the right to sell one's property. All considerable commercial transactions have to be made publicly in front of it. No

[25] It is difficult to tell how factual Hanoteau's description is, as there is no other document with which it can be compared. His description seems to be backed up by more recent analyses of still functioning *jamâ'as* (cf. Kinzi 1998). This, however, does not seem to be sufficient proof of its historic accuracy, as by now Hanoteau's description of the *jamâ'a* has become part of most Kabyles' self-representation and might even partly serve as a model for how a *jamâ'a* should be conducted or at least publicly represented (for a similar observation made as early as the 1950s, see Bousquet 1950: 492).

land may be sold to 'foreigners' (those who are not members of the village, thus the *jamâ'a*), and a foreigner's right to inherit is very limited. Family members always have the right of pre-emption (*shafa'a*) over their relatives' land. If they do not use it, it is the *jamâ'a*'s duty to buy the land in question, and thereby to act as the ultimate guarantor of the integrity of village property. The *jamâ'a* also controls the accumulation of excessive wealth through confiscation and the ordering of communal feasts or sacrifices.

Hanoteau's preoccupation with law and politics, however, was not merely practical. The opening remarks of the second volume of his monograph show his immediate concern with the nature of political organisation as such, which was being debated in France at the same time. Were political systems an evolutionary feature, the result of thought and science, or rather the 'natural' consequence and utmost expression of the inherent 'spirit' of a given society? Based on his experiences in Kabylia, Hanoteau argued the latter:

> The ideal of an independent and inexpensive government, whose secret our philosophers are still searching for through a thousand utopian projects, has for centuries been reality in the Kabyle mountains ... This state of affairs is not, as one can easily guess, the result of intellectual combinations ... It is the natural consequence of the associative and solidary spirit that instinctively animates these populations ... Are the human races, like the species among the animals, subject to mysterious laws, and is the political form chosen to rule each one of them thus the consequence and the result of individual instincts? (Hanoteau and Letourneux 1873: 1, 3)

Delayed in its publication by the war between France and Prussia, Hanoteau and Letourneux's work was widely acclaimed in Paris when it finally came out in 1872. Ernest Renan, who reviewed it in the *Revue des deux mondes* shortly after its publication, claimed that he

> did not know of any picture that would lead to a more profound meditation over the conditions of human societies and their inevitable compositions ... The Berber race has now not only incontestably gained acceptance in the world of anthropology; henceforth, it is the object of a science. (Renan 1873: 193, 140)

In his review, however, Renan turned Hanoteau's argument on its head. For him, the description of Berber society was proof of his theory of race and nationhood, which he formulated most famously less than ten years later (Renan 1882).[26] It showed that 'races are the moulds of moral education more than a matter of blood' (Renan 1873: 154), rather than vice versa, as claimed by Hanoteau himself. In either form, Hanoteau's main argument of the close relationship between 'race' and legal and political organisation became from then on commonplace in all writings on 'Berber society', despite – or because of – the increasingly efficient destruction of independent political institutions by the expanding colonial state.

---

[26] 'A nation is a soul, a spiritual principle' (Renan 1882: 26), echoing his earlier statement that 'the five things that constitute the essential attribute of a race, and allow us to speak of it as a distinctive unit within the human species, are language, literature, religion, history and legislation' (Renan 1873: 104).

Pulpits and primary schools

La Kabylie et les coutumes kabyles, co-authored by Hanoteau and Letourneux, a military officer and a civil servant, and reviewed by the eminent intellectual Ernest Renan, marked the shift of authorship away from the publications of the *Bureaux arabes*, and towards the university, as much as it marked the change from a military to a civil form of government. 1871 had not only been disastrous for metropolitan France, which had lost a war against Prussia and was still shaken by the Parisian Commune and its violent suppression, but it had also seen the most successful uprising against French occupation in Algeria. Based mainly in Kabylia, and supported by the local Sufi order, the Rahmaniyya, this uprising had rallied, according to Rinn (1891), up to 120,000 volunteer fighters, before it was violently suppressed by the French army. In retribution, the Kabyle tribes had to pay an amount close to ten times their annual taxes in 'war contribution' (Ageron 1968). Up to a fifth of their land was permanently confiscated. Due to the poverty of its soil, Kabylia had so far remained almost untouched by agricultural settlement. This was now to change, as a considerable part of the Kabyle expropriations were allocated to French refugees from Alsace and Lorraine.[27]

Henceforth, the Algerian territory was divided into two kinds of *communes* (districts). *Communes en pleine exercise*, where the majority of inhabitants were Europeans, were governed by French law and administered by an elected mayor. *Communes mixtes*, where the majority of inhabitants were *indigènes*,[28] were administered by an appointed administrator, ruling indirectly through a hierarchy of local *caïds* ('tribal chiefs') and *mezaours* ('village chiefs') they appointed. Most of the Kabyle mountains were divided into *communes mixtes*, whose limits often followed the former tribal boundaries, whereas in the fertile plains of the Kabyle valleys a growing number of small towns or colonial settlements became independent *communes en pleine exercise*.

The change from military to civil administration that came about in most of Algeria from the 1870s onwards is often held responsible for a deep shift in policy, from a more understanding and less destructive government by the *Bureaux arabes* to a clearly negative rule by land-hungry, racist settlers, who by then constituted almost 15% of the overall population, and their civilian representatives (see, for example, Ageron 1968).[29] This neat distinction has to be nuanced, as many officers of the *Bureaux arabes* lacked the

[27] A high percentage of the confiscated land there was eventually bought back by its initial owners or by members of their family who, through work in the cities or for French farmers, were able to raise the money (Mahé 2001). This and the distribution of confiscated land to indigenous collaborators with the French reshuffled social hierarchies within tribes, villages and families. It also accelerated the process by which communal land passed into private ownership.

[28] Throughout the following, when referring to colonial times, I shall use the terms employed by the colonial administration for the indigenous population (*indigènes*) and the settlers (*algériens*). Any other terminology is equally controversial historically and politically, and might lead to confusion.

education and the will to understand that marked the best military authors, while many civilian administrators proved to be perspicacious, but remained unpublished. It is true, however, that the overall political tone and aims changed, due to increased settlement of the colony, but also to the deep historical changes of the time.

The Algeria of the 1880s was not the same place it had been in the 1850s and 1860s; but the France (and Europe) of the last quarter of the nineteenth century was also no longer that of Saint-Simon and Comte. Successful settlers' colonies had become an indispensable appendage to all self-respecting European nations, and outlets for international rivalry and economic expansion rather than for political utopias. In France, over the preceding decades, royalty had died a long and painful death, and had finally given way to a highly administered meritocracy, the Third Republic. The fear of a second Commune persisted, relegating fundamental questions about 'primitive democracies' to the background. The idealistic belief in science and progress was gradually permeated with biological determinism and the resulting fatalism, and gave way to increasing pessimism and neo-romantic longings for 'tradition' and 'original communities'. The Dreyfus affair in the early 1890s succeeded in rallying a large number of intellectuals in Dreyfus' support; it also gave ample expression to an essentially racial notion of France and the French nation as endorsed by Dreyfus' opponents (cf. Barrès 1897).

As the belief in Comtian positivism and Saint-Simonian idealism faded, sociology had to reinvent itself. It became an academic discipline in its own right, with its own institutions and restrictions, thanks to the efforts of its most famous late-nineteenth-century representative Emile Durkheim. North Africa was never to play a prominent part within this new school, and became increasingly marginal in metropolitan sociological thought (Valensi 1984).[30] Rather than the subject of learned monographs, Algeria became the inspiration for orientalist novels, paintings, and fantasies of unlimited eroticism, exoticism and freedom, often projected onto the nomadic South, which was still only partly under French control.[31] At the same time, the first tourist guides to Algeria were produced (Salinas 1989). As a general

[29] Echoing Lyautey's (the commissary-general of Morocco and ex-minister of war) famous statement made in the 1920s that 'the agricultural French settlers have a pure *Boche* mentality, with the same theories about inferior races destined to be exploited without mercy. Among them neither kindness nor intelligence can be found' (quoted by Ageron 1968: 1208). Between 1876 and 1886, the European population of Algeria increased by 36%, and between 1891 and 1901, by another 20%. By the turn of the century, almost 600,000 Europeans were living in Algeria alongside 5 million Algerian Muslims (Ageron 1968: 550).

[30] For a unique attempt to study Kabylia from a Durkheimian perspective, see Maunier (1927).

[31] In 1863, Flaubert had published his (during his lifetime) most successful novel, *Salammbô*, set in Numidian North Africa, but whose protagonists bore a striking resemblance to Flaubert's North African contemporaries as imagined in Paris. Its first edition of 4,000 copies was sold out within two months. Flaubert's success was mirrored by that of Fromentin's paintings and travel description (1857, 1858), by Maupassant's travel journals (1884, 1890) and by Daudet's *Tartarin de Tarascon* (1872), all of which were at least partly set in Algeria, and most of which saw a new edition virtually every year until the first decades of the twentieth century (for a full bibliography of literary works on Algeria, see Tailliart 1925).

rule, this literature left little room for the sober and by now thoroughly 'pacified' mountain dwellers of Kabylia.

Thus, from the 1870s onwards, publications on Kabylia became relatively rare, their readership was more restrained, and the geographically specific 'Kabyle' was increasingly supplanted by the more general term 'Berber'. The few works that did appear had changed in purpose and nature. On the one hand, there was a series of works on religious phenomena in Algeria, which were still based on direct field-observations and on the politically strategic necessity to understand, such as Trumelet (1881), Rinn (1884, 1891) and Depont and Coppolani (1897). On the other hand, with the creation of a chair of African History and Antiquities at the university of Algiers in 1880, research became more abstract and was rather motivated by the search for 'deep structures' than by direct observation and military strategy. For a short time, this university chair provided the institutional framework for works of high quality, as exemplified by the series of articles published by the historian Emile Masqueray and his students. It also imposed, however, a more rigid definition of the 'field' of Berber Studies (Colonna and Haïm Brahimi 1976).

Emile Masqueray was a prolific writer and traveller. Between 1882 and 1886, he published more than twenty articles in the journal he had himself founded, the *Bulletin de correspondance africaine*, on topics as varied as sociology, history, archaeology and linguistics (cf. Bernard 1894). These articles were often the result of his extensive travels across Algeria (cf. Masqueray 1893). Masqueray intended the impact of Berber, or, as he preferred to call it, African studies, to be more than merely regional; he wanted them to lead to deep insight into the nature of human society as such. His doctoral thesis, the *Formation des cités chez les populations sédentaires de l'Algérie*, published in 1886, was therefore an attempt to apply the evolutionary scheme developed in Fustel de Coulange's *Cité antique* (1864) to Berber society.

'History', for Masqueray – as for Fustel and Maine (cf. 1861) – was the progress of man from small social units based on 'natural' ties and exploitation towards more complex forms, where the individual could emerge and realise his potential, freed from the chains of kinship, irrational tradition and religious superstition. This progress was brought about by the coalition of several kinship groups in a larger social unit or *cité*, loyalty to which would over time outweigh the original bonds of kinship. Eventually, as had happened in Ancient Greece and Rome, the *cité* would be composed of free and equal individuals linked by their common goals and their free will, rather than by 'nature' or 'instinct'. For Masqueray, the only possible motivation for such a formation of non-kin groups was fear of attacks by other such alliances. Evolution was thus the result of confrontation, and proceeded through the establishment of power-balances among increasingly larger groups: 'all the *cités* of one territory would thus be the result of a series of opposition' (Masqueray 1983 [1886]: 29). According to Masqueray, North Africa provided an ideal experimental ground for these theories, as among its population all the stages of social evolution were present at once, ranging from semi-nomadic settlement in the Aurès via the Kabyle village to the Mzabi town. From a political model and a geographically specific administrative urgency, Kabylia had been demoted to a passing evolutionary stage; more generally, the focus had shifted from society to the individual, although the underlying questions about the nature of the social bond remained the same.

Although Fustel's influence appears clearly in Masqueray's model of historical progress, Masqueray disagreed with Fustel on one major point, namely the role of religion. Whereas Fustel described religion as a necessary evolutionary concept, vital to all human association and development, Masqueray saw it as harmful to the 'natural' development of societies. Masqueray fully acknowledged the importance of the *marabouts* (hereditary religious specialists) in Berber society, but saw them as inherently obstructive to historical evolution. As the *marabouts* were the representatives of a universal system, they were independent from the series of oppositions that was constitutive of local communities. They therefore had 'a thousand occasions to surpass the limits of jurisprudence and to play a considerable political role' (Masqueray 1983: 125). Fearful of losing their central position if the local societies developed to a higher stage, *marabouts* had thus a vested interest in maintaining the lack of 'national' unity that guaranteed them their central social position. In Masqueray's view, it was the role of France, and the rational knowledge that it could transmit, to liberate North Africa from the religious ties that bound it and hindered its evolutionary progress. Such a reasoning, which also owes much to the anti-clericalism of earlier writers, is still an integral part of contemporary Kabyle discourse.

Unlike Hanoteau and Letourneux's work, Masqueray's thesis was hardly mentioned in Parisian intellectual circles (Colonna 1983), apart from in a footnote alongside Hanoteau and Letourneux in Durkheim's *Division sociale du travail* (1893). Masqueray himself remained rather marginal to the Parisian intellectual establishment of the late nineteenth century. But he became associated with another, increasingly influential institution: the French Ministry of Primary Education. In 1882, a law had been passed in France to make primary education compulsory for everybody, and in 1883, free and obligatory schooling was extended to Algeria.[32] Due to financial difficulties, protest by the European settlers, and the general resistance of the indigenous population to sending their children to French schools (Ageron 1979: 153–7), the 1883 decree was put into practice in only a few selected areas.[33] In order to decide

---

[32] Schooling in Algeria had long been an issue for colonial administrations (for a summary of the debates surrounding it, see Turin 1983). Several projects had been initiated since the conquest, often less to assure the good education of the *indigènes* than to control the already existing institutions, feared for their power of social and military resistance to the colonial government. These attempts had all failed, and soon after the conquest and the subsequent confiscation of religious endowments that had assured the financial survival of numerous urban and rural teaching institutes (*madâris* and *zawâyâ*), the educational situation of Algeria was disastrous, to the point where it became virtually impossible to find enough recruits for the judicial and civil administration (Turin 1983).

[33] In 1887, in the whole of Algeria, there were 54 primary schools for the indigenous population, as compared to 718 (in 1882) and 1200 (in 1892) primary schools for the European population (Ageron 1979: 155). The overall level of schooling (4.26% for the whole of Algeria in 1906, Ageron 1979: 161) remained inferior to that estimated for before the French conquest

upon these areas, the then minister of education, Jules Ferry, turned to Masqueray, who suggested certain villages and tribes in Kabylia as especially suited for French schooling. His decisions were based on several factors: a continuing municipal tradition, a low density of European settlement, and a pre-existing educational or mercantile tradition (Masqueray 1880). Masqueray's choices were well made, and by 1885, 800 Kabyle students were enrolled in eight primary schools. At least in certain areas of Kabylia – incidentally those where most of the military monographs had been written – the '*instituteur du bled*' (rural primary school teacher) became a stock figure, and primary schools, often constructed at a certain distance from the village itself, became part of the landscape. Wherever they were built and accepted by the local population, these schools transformed local and regional power relationships, and profoundly changed local conceptions of knowledge. Thus, throughout Algeria, the impact of Masqueray's nineteenth-century choices can still be felt today.

With Masqueray's death in 1894, the academic interest in 'Berber studies' waned. Masqueray's successors mainly produced linguistic works or studies of 'folk' religious practices; world-historical and 'political' questions almost totally disappeared (Lucas and Vatin 1975).[34] Berber language, civilisation and history were no longer taught at the university but at the *Ecole Normale d'Alger* (teacher training institute, founded in 1883), which trained both French and indigenous primary school teachers. Thus, as the 'Kabyle myth' gradually lost ground in the French ethnographic imagination, it started to find its place in the expanding primary education of Kabylia. The 'Kabyle', as constructed by the French, were part of the curriculum taught in these schools (for example, Gallouedec and Maurette 1922), and soon re-appropriated by the first generation of Kabyle students themselves. The careful selection of regions where schools were first constructed enhanced already existing divisions between different parts of Kabylia, and between Kabylia and the rest of Algeria. Among the indigenous primary school teachers educated at the *Ecole Normale d'Alger*, the number of Kabyles, and especially the number of Kabyles from two or three particular tribes, was remarkably high (Colonna 1975). More generally, the number of French-educated Kabyles (or *évolués*, in the colonial jargon) employed in the colonial administration and increasingly also in those of the two new North African French Protectorates, Morocco and Tunisia, grew steadily. Kabyle lawyers and doctors made their first tentative appearances. The various ways in which these new elites came to adapt the central tenets of the French vision of Kabylia, as an essential part of, as well as in reaction to, various other intellectual developments, such as Islamic reformism and Algerian nationalism, are the subject of the following chapter.

---

[33] (cont.) (20% of boys, Emerit 1954). For a map of the geographic distribution of schools, see Colonna (1975).

[34] The best known linguistic works were published by Masqueray's student René Basset (1887, 1920). From the 1900s onwards, descriptions of 'folk Islam' abound, see, for example, Doutté (1908), Bel (1938) and Dermenghem (1982 [1954]).

2
The Republic of Martyrs

We were all naive. We came down from our mountains, our heads full of dreams
... We were dreaming about inscribing freedom in all our acts, democracy in all
hearts, justice and fraternity among all men ... But while the jubilant people were
celebrating their newly recovered freedom, other men, hidden in the shadows,
made plans about the future ... And one beautiful morning we woke up with a
bitter taste in our mouth ... The disaster was accomplished.
(Mimouni 1982: 196)

Early nationalism(s)

Primary schools were not long to remain the only institutions through
which Kabyles could get to know the intellectual and practical tools of their
French occupiers. In the First World War, 158,533 Algerian soldiers fought
in the French army, while 11,000 men emigrated to Syria to avoid conscription, and returned after the war (Mahé 2001). Some were taken to
France to replace factory workers busy at the front, and stayed. In 1914,
13,000 Algerian 'French Muslims' were registered in France, 10,000 of
whom were probably from Kabylia; in 1928 Louis Massignon counted
120,000 Kabyles in France:

> It is said that in certain *douars* [districts] of the Guergor 70% of men aged 20 to
> 60 years have come to work in France; they return home, profoundly changed
> – several naturalised – some communists... A large-scale assimilation, through
> the working forces, thus takes shape in certain Algerian *communes* – and this is
> a serious phenomenon; the colonial problem... occurs in Paris itself. (Massignon
> 1930: 169)

Since the beginning of the century, the population of Algeria had grown
exponentially, and more and more of the increasing number of landless
poor were flowing into the already overpopulated cities, where unemployment was soaring.[1] There they encountered an ever-rising number of poor
Europeans from all Mediterranean European countries, as most rural European settlements had been abandoned, while the overall numbers of

[1] According to Ageron (1979), the total population of Algeria increased by 64% (from
5,804,275 to 9,529,726) between 1921 and 1954. Between 1906 and 1954, the percentage
of the urban population doubled; the population of Algiers multiplied by two and a half. In
1955, out of a total indigenous workforce of 2,300,000 wage labourers, 850,000 (37%) were
officially un- or under-employed (Stora 1993: 15).

European settlers had continued to rise (Lefeuvre 2004). In 1936, there were 1 million European settlers living alongside an indigenous population of over 6 million (Ageron 1968: 550).[2]

Among the indigenous elites, new forms of solidarity such as Islamic reformist or *progressiste* discussion circles, *associations*, Muslim sports clubs, local branches of French trade unions and political parties, and local chapters of the newly created Algerian federation of Boy Scouts became common (Carlier 1995). Between 1905 and 1940, roughly a hundred cultural associations were created in the district of Tizi-Ouzou alone (Salhi 1999a). Following the example of the Young Turks, the Young Algerians (later re-organised in the *Union des amis du manifeste algérien*) and the *Fédération des élus musulmans* (1927) strove for political and educational reforms in Algeria, but within the framework of a French protectorate. In 1926, the first radical nationalist party was founded by Algerian emigrants in France under the leadership of Messali Hadj. In 1937, the party was reconstituted as the *Parti du peuple algérien* (PPA), and its headquarters were, at least notionally, moved from Paris to Algiers. In the meantime, the Islamic reformist *Association des oulémas*,[3] founded in 1931 by the *shaykh* Ben Badis in Constantine, had started to open primary schools where classical Arabic was taught using French educational methods. These schools tended to be restricted to urban centres in most of Algeria; the Soummam valley was, with the Berber-speaking area of the Aurès, the only rural area where reformist schools had any clear success. Although the *ouléma* rallied to the open nationalist struggle only relatively late (1956), the links between reformist and nationalist thought and organisation were manifold, and both movements were to be central to the development of Algerian nationalism and the independent Algerian nation-state.[4]

The first decades of the twentieth century saw a wave of intellectual activities by indigenous intellectuals, in both French and Arabic. As colonial injustice was increasingly understood in terms of democracy, socialism, Islamic reform, or all three at once, first attempts were made to rewrite

[2] The proportion of 'foreigners' within the (exclusively European) *peuple algérien* rose to the extent that worries over their lack of 'French-ness' became frequent, although some writers started to dream about the creation of a new, superior Mediterranean race (see, for example, Bertrand 1921 and Llamo 1956) – a dream (and for many a worry) that led to an increasing divide between the *algériens* and the *français de France* (a sentiment also expressed in Albert Camus' (1994) fragmentary autobiographical novel).

[3] The main tenet of the *ouléma* was that reform or restoration (*islâh*) of Islam according to its original sources was the prerequisite for the restoration of moral integrity in the Muslim world. For this, 'deviant' local practices such as 'maraboutism' and local saint cults defined as a form of idolatry (*shirk*), had to be 'eradicated'; and resistance to French 'acculturation' and education were vital (cf. Association des ouléma 1937). All in all, the *ouléma* succeeded in opening 70 primary schools with 3,000 pupils in 1934–5, and 153 schools with 13,100 pupils in the departments of Algiers and Constantine alone in 1938 (Ageron 1979: 338). However, these figures never exceeded 3% of the total number of pupils in primary schools.

[4] The list of historical, political and sociological research, of biographies and first-hand accounts of Algerian nationalism is long, although in Algeria itself – and even in France – the notion that 'true history' still needs to be written is widespread. The most complete and most cited, but not necessarily most objective, works are Harbi (1975, 1980), Meynier (1981), Stora (1985, 1986) and Carlier (1995).

Algerian history according to nationalist standards (see Touati 1997). As in French historiography (cf. especially Gautier 1927), Algerian history was presented as a long series of foreign invasions, alternately from the 'East' or the 'West'; however, it was now the Eastern invaders who were seen as 'civilising', against the Europeans who had come merely to occupy and destroy (McDougall 2006; cf. al-Hafnawi 1907; al-Mili 1963 [1929]). This new historiography emerged from the same tradition as the Kabyle myth itself, and projected many of the traits that had traditionally been ascribed to the Kabyles, such as their love of the land and of independence, onto the Algerian nation as a whole. Yet it also aimed to redefine and cement Algerian unity, by focusing, as its French precedent had done in France (Weber 1976), on religious and linguistic homogeneity, and therefore tended to reject implicitly any claims to a separate Berber identity, qualifying it as a colonial invention. The underlying rationale of this new national history, and its emphasis on historic precedence, however, also left ample room for the expression of Kabyle identity, as part of a project that was more often than not perceived by its authors to be inherently nationalist, inasmuch as it was questioning French supremacy and readings of history.[5]

In 1904, the Kabyle *instituteur indigène* Sidi Saïd ben Amar Boulifa published a collection of Kabyle poems as a direct reaction to Hanoteau's (1867) compilation. His aim was to prove the complexity of Kabyle literature and thus the Kabyles' high state of civilisation and their 'essentially democratic, egalitarian and liberal character' (Boulifa 1904: xxv). In 1925, he published his monumental *Le Djurdjura à travers l'histoire*, which claimed a direct continuity between the Massinissah and the Jugurtha of Roman times and today's population of Kabylia. Boulifa's work was followed by a series of publications or unpublished writings by Kabyle primary school teachers, including novels, memoirs, historical works and poems. These were closely inspired by the French Republican creed and the works of their French military and academic predecessors (cf. Aït Ali 1962; Ibazizen 1979), and are frequently cited by today's Berber movement as their intellectual 'ancestors' (see, for example, Guenoun 1999 and Chaker 1999).

The Second World War involved an even higher rate of conscription in the French army than had the First World War. It led to the immediate experience that the French army could be beaten; and it involved broken promises of reform, a disastrous famine, and the gradual popularisation of political and cultural ideas of the time. As described by the Kabyle author Mouloud Mammeri in his wartime novel *La colline oubliée*:

> In a world where the changing luck of war made all certainties disappear, and that had thoroughly been shaken by a universal blow, everybody searched for the path that would lead to new salvation: there were those who were vaguely

---

[5] Another group of Kabyle intellectuals were educated by Christian missionaries (*Pères Blancs*). The most famous of these are the Amrouche family, Jean, author of *L'étérnel Jugurtha* (1985) and Taos, singer, poet and author of a collection of poems (1976), whose father had converted to Christianity and who had been brought up by the *Pères Blancs*; and their mother, Fadhma, whose autobiography (1982) became famous. The status of these and other converts remains ambiguous even today (Direche-Slimani 2004).

haunted by the memory of the ancient greatness of Islam and who hoped to return to it using new means, those who, having worked in a factory with French workers, thought of the union of all proletarians across all borders, those who did not think of anything, those who made money. (Mammeri 1992 [1957]: 72)

At the end of the Second World War, in May 1945, the PPA instigated a demonstration in eastern Algeria. Its violent suppression caused several thousand deaths, increasing fear and hostility on both sides (cf. Yacine 1956), and the formal interdiction of the PPA. The party was reconstituted in 1947 as the *Mouvement pour le triomphe des libertés démocratiques* (MTLD), in order to participate in the 1947 elections. It gained an impressive majority among the indigenous voters in the few areas where the election results were not tampered with (Bouaziz and Mahé 2004).[6] In the years following the elections, the MTLD lived through several crises. These were caused by internal divisions and coalitions and by diverging opinions about how the party should be led, how the struggle for independence should be conducted, and what kind of independent Algeria should be fought for.[7] In 1947, the more radical fraction of MTLD militants founded the *Organisation Spéciale* (OS), maintaining that independence could only be achieved by violent means. It was dismantled by the French police in 1950, but its members remained active, and were largely represented among the leaders of the organisation that was to launch the war of independence four years later.

The war of independence

On 1 November 1954, several bombs exploded simultaneously in various places in Algeria, launching a war of independence that was to last eight years. Although most observers attributed these attacks to the MTLD, the organisation that assumed responsibility for them acted under a different name: the *Front de libération nationale* (FLN). It represented itself as the union of all 'truly nationalist' forces in Algeria, and aimed at dissolving the party-political differences that had so far 'paralysed' the Algerian nationalist movement.[8] In France, the 'events' (as the Algerian war of independence

[6] The Algerian electoral system was divided into two *collèges* or electoral bodies, one composed of all French passport holders (French and European settlers, Algerian Jews, and naturalised Algerian Muslims, i.e. roughly 15% of the population), the other composed of the remaining 85% of non-naturalised Algerian Muslims. The collective vote of the first *collège* accounted for two-thirds of the overall representatives at the Algerian departmental assemblies (the *Délegations Financières*); the second *collège* for the rest (Stora and Daoud 1995).
[7] One expression of these conflicts was the elimination of a large number of leading members in 1949, which is now generally referred to as the 'Crise Berbériste', as many of those expelled were Kabyles, see Carlier (1984) and Hadjeres (1998) for more detail.
[8] According to the political scientist Hugh Roberts (2003: 41), 'the FLN was neither a political party nor an ordinary army... It was a political movement fighting a revolutionary war for a nationalist purpose, and from the outset was at odds with all pre-existing political organisations in Algeria and determined to outflank and eliminate them. It eliminated them by absorbing them (except for the irredeemable disciples of Messali [Hadj, i.e. members of the

was officially referred to until recently), which had begun a mere six months after the disastrous defeat of the French army at Diên-Biên-Phu in Vietnam, had come as a surprise, and took several months to reach French public consciousness. In the meantime, the FLN had succeeded in taking control of the chronically 'under-administered' mountain areas of the Aurès and Kabylia, and of the inaccessible parts of Algerian cities, such as the Casbah (old city) in Algiers. In March 1955, the French government declared a state of emergency in its 'three Algerian departments'. In August 1956, the FLN organised its first congress in the Soummam valley, in order to co-ordinate the up to then largely improvised guerrilla attacks.

In the rural areas of Algeria, the FLN rapidly succeeded in implanting a military hierarchy and a parallel justice system based on pre-existing local institutions and Islamic principles. By November 1955, most of the Soummam valley was administered by the FLN.[9] They consecrated marriages, judged cases of civil law, land claims and adultery, and punished any co-operation with the French administration and the consumption of alcohol and in some cases even tobacco.[10] Meanwhile, the French army launched an extensive anti-guerrilla campaign. Large parts of the Algerian countryside were declared *zones interdites*, all villages in these areas were destroyed, and their inhabitants had to move to rudimentary *centres de regroupement* in the valleys. The French army established 'special administration units' (*Sections d'administration spéciales*, SAS) in all larger villages, and enrolled – often by force – a large number of auxiliary forces or *harkis* from among the indigenous population. The SAS organised and paid armed 'self-defence groups', offered basic medical services and schooling, constructed roads with the help of local labour, and supervised or spied on the population and denounced 'terrorists' (see Barret 1997). By the end of 1959, more than twenty SAS centres had been constructed in the immediate neighbourhood of the village where my research was conducted. As agriculture had become impossible, local income depended almost entirely on remittances sent back from France and on the local French payroll, and every man who was not away in France or fighting with the FLN had been drafted into the French army.[11] The borders with Tunisia and Morocco, main purveyors of arms to the FLN, were blocked with an electric fence. Torture was generalised.[12]

[8] (cont.) PPA/MTLD], whom it set about eliminating physically) and it absorbed them by dissolving them inside itself, by atomising their membership and by reconstructing this human materiel in a new way.' For similar observations, see Meynier (2002).

[9] AOM 93/4332. All archives consulted and the abbreviations used to refer to them are listed in the bibliography.

[10] Relatively harmless crimes included listening to the colonial radio and registering births, deaths and marriages with the French; but also fighting, smoking and neglecting domestic and public hygiene. More important transgressions included lying, stealing, gambling, rape, homosexuality, drunkenness and adultery (Benabdallah 1982).

[11] AAF 1H1684 D2.

[12] For a graphic description of the torture employed, see *La question* by Henri Alleg (1958), one of the roughly 500 (Liauzu 2004) Europeans who had rallied to the FLN during the war. 66,000 copies of his book were sold in France before it was censored shortly after its publication, and it continued to circulate illegally on a large scale (Stora 1993: 67). That the French

The need for secrecy among the guerrillas, the fear of French infiltrations and internal conflict within the FLN and between the FLN and the MNA (former MTLD) caused constant suspicions of internal enemies. This in turn led to a series of so-called purges within the nationalist camp. Of these, the massacres of Mélouza and Oued Amizour (both in the Soummam valley) of 1956 and the internal 'purge' conducted in 1958 by Colonel Amirouche, commander of the *wilâya 3* (military command of Kabylia), are the most famous.[13] This suspicion of alleged traitors and the nagging uncertainty as to who really was a guerrilla fighter and who just pretended to be one increased as, with the growing number of war dead, the number of locally known and trusted *mujâhidîn* (nationalist fighters)[14] shrank to almost nothing. The suspicion of traitors became essential to nationalist rhetoric, both during the war and after independence was gained. Even now, the shadowy figure of the 'fake *mujâhid*' or traitor is one of the most central mythical ideas around which political argument – for or against the government – is constructed.

By 1957, four successive French governments had been toppled over issues related to Algeria. In 1958, the war led to the dissolution of the Fourth Republic. Under the Fifth Republic, the war continued despite de Gaulle's tentative declarations of his intention to grant Algeria independence. In Kabylia, a third of all rural settlements had been bombed to the ground by 1959, and most agriculture had been abandoned (Bourdieu and Sayad 1964). The vast majority of FLN fighters stationed inside Algeria had been killed, captured or at least disarmed. Some had managed to flee to either Tunisia or Morocco, but most had died. In the village where my field-work was conducted, a quarter to a third of all adult men had been killed. Estimates of the total number of war dead on the Algerian side vary from 243,378, claimed by the French army, to a million, or more recently even one and a half million, claimed by the FLN.[15] In any case, this meant that the leadership of the FLN that emerged after the war to negotiate independence had spent little time in Algeria itself during the fighting – a fact which came to be bitterly resented by the local population after independence, and

[12] (cont.) army had systematically employed torture as a means of warfare was widely known in France during and after the war (cf. Vidal-Naquet 1972). It has, however, hardly ever become part of official knowledge or remembering, so that all new 'revelations' about torture (such as those made by General Aussaresses 2001 recently) are publicly treated as sensational before rapidly being forgotten.

[13] In France, these violent struggles were no less present. They remained largely unpunished by the French authorities, which did not see any inconvenience in their immediate results. Benjamin Stora (1993: 36) estimates the death toll of the struggle between the MNA and the FLN alone at 4,000 victims in France, and 6,000 in Algeria.

[14] Literally 'those who fight the *jihâd*', or 'holy war'. The exact meaning of *jihâd*, however, has been hotly debated by Islamic thinkers. In Algeria, the term *mujâhid* generally refers to fighters in the war of independence against France, although it is also increasingly used by groups which are hostile to the present Algerian government, whether they are 'Islamist' or not. In many cases, it has lost most of its religious significance.

[15] Most historians agree that both sets of figures are unlikely to be correct, and that the real number of war deaths must lie somewhere in between. For a further discussion of these figures, see Perville (2004).

further increased the suspicion of 'fake *mujâhidîn*' who supposedly appropriated a revolution they had never fought for (cf. Bessaoud 1991).

When independence was agreed in 1961, the Algerian regiments of the French army launched a *coup d'état* in Algiers (see Vaïsse 1983). After its failure, French settlers, claiming to have been abandoned by their own government, organised themselves in the *Organisation d'action spéciale* (OAS) and took up arms, causing altogether 1,700 violent deaths (Kauffer 2002). Although the *Accords d'Evian* (signed in 1962), which clarified the terms and conditions of Algerian independence, guaranteed the safety of 'Algeria's European population', most settlers left precipitately in summer 1962. They were scared by the violence triggered by the OAS, and by frequent kidnappings and disappearances of French settlers and Muslim 'collaborators' – who accounted for a large part of the Muslim population – throughout Algeria.[16] Independence was proclaimed in July 1962.

The years of war and those immediately preceding them are the years when many of the foundations of the recent sociology and anthropology of Algeria were laid. Overtly non-political and 'time-less' ethnological descriptions of Kabyle rituals and legends were produced, as if trying to capture a world of coherence that was, at least superficially, rapidly disappearing.[17] At the same time, the theory of their inevitable demise was launched. In France, the Algerian war had allowed left-wing solidarities, shaken by internal debates about Stalinism, to re-form in opposition to the French state (Eisenhans 1995); and it had provided a revolutionary outlet for a handful of French intellectuals supporting the Algerian side during the war. After independence was gained, Algeria, the 'motor of the Third World' (Etienne 1995), became a symbol of successful development, humanitarian enthusiasm, third-world solidarity and non-Stalinist socialism, in France and elsewhere (Malley 1996; Le Sueur 2001). This left little room for enthusiastic descriptions of 'traditional' peasant societies, but rather encouraged descriptions of French war crimes and their victims' passage to 'modernity'. Thus, Pierre Bourdieu, who started his research in Algeria during the war, turned the very 'disenchantment of the world' into the subject of two of his first three publications: the analytical essay in *Travail et travailleurs en Algérie* (1963) and *Le Déracinement*, co-authored with Abdelmalek Sayad in 1964.

Both publications analyse the process by which colonial occupation led to a profound restructuring of the value-system underlying 'traditional' Algerian society. This happened as the growing importance of wage labour introduced a new way of looking at work as a measurable quantity with a fixed price, rather than as a way of life. This increasingly devalued tradi-

[16] Roughly a million European settlers left the country immediately after the war, followed by a quarter of a million *harkis*, indigenous French soldiers, or other 'traitors'. These figures mean that more than a third of the Algerian population of the 1950s was either dead or had left the country at independence. They constituted for many among them the third that had been the wealthiest, but also the most educated and qualified: more than 90% of teachers did not present themselves at the beginning of the academic year 1962-3 (Benghabrit-Remaoun 1998).

[17] See, for example, the works of Morizot (1962) and Servier (1962). Both authors were colonial administrators; Servier became the Algerian governor general during the first years of the war of independence.

tional occupations such as agriculture, in a colonial situation where any other jobs were scarce. It thus 'de-peasantised' the peasant without offering him any other opportunities. It changed the way social relations, time and morality were construed by peasants; and it ultimately led to the irreversible destruction of the peasant way of life:

> The logic of the colonial situation has produced a new kind of men, who can be defined negatively, by what they have ceased to be and by what they have not yet become, de-peasantised peasants, self-destructive beings who bear in themselves all contradictions. (Bourdieu and Sayad 1964: 161)

For Bourdieu and Sayad, the 'uprooting' undertaken by the French army during the war of independence was thus the logical conclusion of a process that had started with the French conquest of Algeria more than a century earlier. As it had created a 'new kind of man' – the negative reflection, but also the precondition of Frantz Fanon's revolutionary 'new man' (Majumbar 2005; cf. Fanon 1959, 1961) – it was irreversible and definitive.

A year later, Bourdieu published his first 'anthropological' article on Kabylia (Bourdieu 1965), in which he described the coherent peasant society whose demise he had deplored a year earlier.[18] This article was followed by several similar studies of 'traditional' Kabyle society, inspired by Lévi-Strauss rather than Weber (Bourdieu 1972, 1980), and bearing strong resemblance to their nineteenth-century predecessors. Comparing these to Bourdieu's earlier writings, 'Kabyle society' appears as torn between an imported and brutal 'modernity', which had led to irreversible social changes (the subject matter of 'sociology'), and a past of 'true Kabyle-ness', of social and moral coherence, complexity and stability, the domain of 'anthropology' (Addi 2002). These two 'Kabylias' appear as incompatible, and Bourdieu tells us little about how they co-exist on a daily basis. They are clearly both ideal social models that owe as much to European and Algerian preoccupations with 'modernity' and 'tradition' as they do to purely local realities. This does not make them any less important for the comprehension of contemporary Kabylia, however, as they inform local self-perceptions, government policies and much of the recent academic literature on Kabylia. According to Fanny Colonna (1995: 31):

> The Algerian agrarian policy of the 1970s, that could not fail to weigh heavy on all research in a peasant environment, was thereby legitimised by a learned knowledge produced directly during one of the biggest crises that the Algerian peasantry had ever experienced. It used the notion of an 'uprooted' peasantry to represent time as divided between a golden age of perfect rural life and the present, characterised by archaisms, delays, and, indeed, regressions.

The consolidation of the Algerian nation-state

The immediate post-war period was marked by unclear local and national power relationships, and by a series of factional struggles between the

---

[18] This essay owes much to Maunier's (1927) work on Kabylia within the *Année sociologique* tradition.

various groups within the FLN. These eventually led, several weeks after independence had been granted, to the declaration of Ahmed Ben Bellah as President, with the backing of the FLN troops stationed in Tunisia and Morocco, and against the will of the military commanders of two of the key *wilâyât*, Algiers and Kabylia. In 1963, Hocine Aït Ahmed, one of the most senior members of the war-time FLN, and his newly constituted party, the *Front des forces socialistes* (FFS), led an armed uprising against the central government. This uprising embraced a large part of Kabylia. It seems to have been the first sign of an increasingly widespread feeling that the region had been 'cheated' of the painfully earned fruits of the revolution (Favret 1972).[19] The rebellion was suppressed rapidly and violently, and its leaders fled to exile in Europe.[20]

In 1965, Colonel Houari Boumediène, commander of the army, who had brought Ben Bellah to power, overthrew the latter in a *coup d'état*, and then remained President of Algeria until his death in 1978. During his reign many of the basic features that now characterise the Algerian political system became prominent: the supremacy of the FLN, which had become synonymous with the state; the overwhelming importance of the war of independence, of those who fought it (the *mujâhidîn* or *maquisards*)[21] and of those who died in it (the *shuhadâ* or 'martyrs'); and an ideological eclecticism or rather the absence of any clear ideology, despite publicly proclaimed 'state-socialism' and a half-hearted agrarian revolution from the 1970s onwards. What all these characteristics have in common is the all-pervasive dominance of the state. As described by Mohammed Harbi:

> The role of the state was decisive in the formation of society. It created, from scratch, a new bourgeoisie and a new working class, and it turned the intelligentsia into civil servants ... The new bourgeoisie, of humble extraction, is thus composed of upstarts who owe everything to their participation in the war of independence. (Harbi 1980: 381)

This led to the establishment of a peculiar system of interconnected patron-client relationships, in content modern, in form often reminiscent of local precedents (Harbi 1980; Bentaleb 1984; Henni 1990a). Access or 'closeness' to the state, which was increasingly wealthy due to the exploitation of the vast resources of oil and natural gas in the Sahara, became the precondition of all individual economic and social success. Everyday con-

[19] More generally, Favret sees the rebellion as expressing the fundamental ambiguity of the relationship between Kabylia and the central government: on the one hand, individual Kabyles try to gain access to state resources; on the other hand, they maintain a potentially rebellious stance, in order to be able to exert pressure collectively on the national government should it refuse to comply with their demands.

[20] In retrospect, this often came to be seen as the first in a long series of 'Berber uprisings' against a culturally monolithic central government (cf. Aït Ahmed 1983; for a critical appraisal of the political trajectory of the FFS, see Monbeig 1991).

[21] *Maquisard* (guerrilla fighter) and *maquis* (scrub, bush, used to mean guerrilla camp) both echo the terminology employed by the French Resistance during the Second World War, as if to claim the moral high ground up to then monopolised by the French (many members of the French army fought by the FLN had been *résistants*). Both terms are still widely used in Algeria, not only when speaking about the war of independence, but also when describing more recent guerrilla fighters and camps, such as those set up by the 'Islamists' in the 1990s.

sumer goods, cars, building materials and imported electrical goods had to be obtained through 'connections' with one of the representatives of the state, which preserved the monopoly over trade. Corruption, or rather, 'connections' (*piston*), was not only rampant, but a form of life – the only possible form of life. Individual or collective strategies aimed at getting 'closer' to the state, by multiplying possible paths of access to state resources (Bentaleb 1984, Henni 1990b, cf. also Bayart 1990).

The relationship with France remained tense. Public rhetoric abounded in the condemnation of French attempts to maintain a pseudo-colonial influence over the Algerian economy. These tensions escalated in 1971, when Boumediène decided to nationalise oil and gas wells in the Sahara, which had *de facto* remained under French economic control (Blin 1990). In 1973, he officially suspended Algerian emigration to France,[22] and quarrels over the legal status of the almost 200,000 French-born Algerian second-generation emigrants became frequent. Despite these public tensions, actual co-operation and economic ties between France and Algeria remained strong; during the 1970s, France sent several thousand *coopérants* to Algeria, many of whom are still remembered in the village where I lived. Both governments also actively collaborated in the surveillance of Algerian nationals in France, who long remained under the direct jurisdiction of the FLN's branch in France (Stora 1994).

Among the key demands of the nationalist movement had been equal access to education for all, and, to a lesser degree, the use of Arabic as the one and only Algerian national language. This meant that to offer free education for everybody, and to Arabise the national education system, were two central promises the government had to keep in order to maintain, or rather obtain, political legitimacy (Benghabrit-Remaoun 1998). In the first decade after independence, the number of children in primary schools tripled, and that of pupils in secondary schools increased tenfold. Although the few qualified teachers who remained in the country at independence had been educated in French, primary school education was conducted in Arabic as soon as possible with the help of underqualified local teachers and 'imports' from Egypt and Syria.[23] Secondary and higher education also switched gradually to Arabic.

During the 1970s, linguistic issues, used as shorthand for 'cultural' conflicts and the need to decolonise Algeria fully by abolishing the privileges of the French-speaking elite, were politicised to a point where open debate became impossible (Grandguillaume 1983). Rapid Arabisation, often pursued by violent means, was met with scepticism by French-speaking intellectuals and by a large part of the state apparatus itself, which was mainly composed of French-educated former colonial officials. Despite official policies, most of the national administration, the government and

---

[22] This, however, did not greatly affect the number of Algerians in France. According to French figures, their number doubled between 1968 and 1988, to be close to a million by the 1990s, not counting the growing number of French-born second-generation emigrants in France (Lacoste-Dujardin and Lacoste 1991).
[23] See Chachoua (2001) for a vivid description of the impression left by the latter.

state-run companies continued to function in French. Higher education also remained bilingual: the more prestigious natural sciences were taught in French, whereas the less prestigious humanities and social sciences were taught in Arabic. This meant that, on the one hand, the French-speaking elite continued to reproduce itself through its privileged access to private or foreign schools, while, on the other hand, a large number of Arabic-speaking degree-holders were pushed onto a job market that did not have room for them. Algeria was thus 'Arabised' by a French-speaking elite who themselves tended to educate their children in French. 'Arabophone' and 'Francophone' became shorthand for a 'cultural', social and political divide (Haddab 1979; Kadri 1999).

This divide, which echoed the educational divide between French- and Arabic-educated intellectuals that had started to crystallise in the decades leading up to the war of independence, was quickly assimilated to the distinction between Kabylia and the rest of Algeria. Due to their long history of French schooling and of emigration to France, Kabyles were indeed more 'Francophone' than most other Algerians – or at least they seemed to be from an 'Arab' point of view. They were accused of usurping too many administrative posts (of which they indeed occupied a fair share, see Quandt 1972), and of constituting an ominous *hizb fransa* (the party of France) within the government, whose aim it allegedly was to lead Algeria into ruin for their own personal gain and that of their 'French friends'. Meanwhile, the Kabyles themselves claimed to suffer from their 'exclusion' from national politics, which they increasingly ascribed to the 'Arabo-Islamic' stance publicly defended by the government.

Revolutions

From the late 1970s onwards, the voices of the dissatisfied grew louder. In France, several marginal militant Berber groups who denounced the 'Arabo-Islamism' of the Algerian government had existed since independence.[24] Now, they started to attract a large number of second-generation Kabyle emigrants, who in turn organised themselves in local cultural associations (Direche-Slimani 1997). The 'new Kabyle song' that aimed to bring Berber musical tradition in a modern form to a large audience, both Kabyle and French, thrived, and concerts started to draw large crowds in France (Goodman 2005). For second-generation emigrants in France, to be French-Kabyle rather than French-Arab became a publicly acknowledged and valued identity. In Algeria, Mouloud Mammeri, a friend and colleague of Pierre Bourdieu, and himself educated in the French classical tradition, re-invigorated the *Centre des recherches en anthropologie, pré-histoire et ethnologie*

[24] They were represented mainly by the *Académie Berbère*, the *Groupe d'Etudes Berbères* at Paris VIII (Nanterre), the *Bulletin d'Etudes Berbères* and the *Union du Peuple Amazigh* (Direche-Slimani 1997). Some of their increased popularity was due to the fact that they had found their place among the students' movement of May 1968.

(CRAPE, founded by the French in 1950).[25] His evening classes soon became a focal point for many dissatisfied young Kabyles in the capital, who then returned to their villages with their newly acquired knowledge. It was there that they first learnt to think about 'Berber-ness' as a valid part of Algerian culture, and to express their dissatisfaction in terms of cultural exclusion; and it was there that they first came in contact with nineteenth-century literature on Kabylia and with the ideas developed by the Berber movement in France. At the same time, the first 'Islamist' meetings were held in the mosques of the capital and provincial towns (Burgat 1988: 163).[26]

In the late 1970s, the two Kabyle regional capitals, Tizi-Ouzou and Béjaïa, were endowed with their own universities, as part of a more general decentralisation of higher education. Career prospects and life-plans thereby became more regional, and ideas that had initially been developed by the Berber movement in France and Algiers were popularised throughout Kabylia. At the same time, Algeria went through a general political, economic and social crisis. President Boumediène had died in 1978, and his death had laid open tensions among the leading members of the FLN and the army. His successor Chadli never commanded the same popular respect as Boumediène had done (Stora 1994). By then, the first generation of children who had no direct experience of the war of independence had grown up. They were the most highly educated generation of Algerians so far. A large number among them had just entered university, where they increasingly started to question, either in the name of 'Berber identity' or in the name of Islam, the legacy of the war as the unique source of national political legitimacy.

In 1980, after a lecture at the University of Tizi-Ouzou on Kabyle poetry by Moulod Mammeri was banned, the 'Berber Spring' exploded: a sequence of revolts and strikes centred on the claim for the official recognition of Berber as a national language, and its introduction into the national curriculum. For both the protesters and the government forces, this rebellion was more than just a matter of language, however. The linguistic issues raised were seen as symbolic of a larger political and social struggle for a more democratic and less exclusive form of government, and for a

---

[25] Much of Fanny Colonna's research was undertaken while she was associated with the CRAPE. Mouloud Mammeri himself was a prolific and very popular writer, and contributed strongly to the recognition and collection of oral poetry and culture in the Berber-speaking areas of Algeria, thereby (re-)creating a Berber 'domain' that was often inspired by his nineteenth-century predecessors (see, for example, his work on 'oral literature' in the Gourara in the Algerian south (1985) and in Kabylia (1989); for a collection of his articles, see Mammeri 1991).

[26] To the growing disquiet of European and North American observers, Islamist currents had developed throughout the Muslim world since the 1970s. They generally shared the basic ideological themes developed by the Islamic reformers of the early days of nationalism, and agreed with them on the need for moral reform of the political sphere of society. Throughout the following, I shall use the term 'Islamist' to mean such groupings and ideas, for want of a better term (for a discussion of uses and abuses of this or other terms, see Burgat 1995). The literature on political Islam is by now abundant, see for example Kepel (1993), Roy (1994) and Burgat (1995). On the development of Algerian Islamism, see Burgat (1988) and Martinez (1998); for a collection of Algerian Islamist writings, see al-Ahnaf et al. (1991).

more open and 'modern' cultural and social policy.[27] Although the revolt was rapidly suppressed by the national government, ideas about 'Berber culture' as integral to the identity of Algeria and as a source of national and regional pride persisted and still survive in a continuing 'Berber movement' in both Algeria and France.

One year after the Berber Spring, the first Islamist incident in Algeria took place in El Oued, south of the capital, where a known *mujâhid* from the war of independence established a guerrilla camp in the mountains, in order to fight against the Algerian government, in the name of Islam, after his brother had been killed by the police (Charef 1994; Merah 1998). He and his supporters were captured, killed or condemned to prison. His trial became the occasion for large demonstrations of solidarity with his beliefs. In 1982, 'Islamists' and 'secularists' confronted each other at the university of Algiers; one of the latter was killed and the university mosque shut down. A week later, 5,000 'Islamists' listened to the first public manifesto proclaimed by Abassi Madani, the future leader of the most successful Algerian Islamist party, the FIS. He and many of his followers were put in prison (Aggoun and Rivoire 2004). Many of the Islamist tenets he and his movement had put forward, however, were absorbed into government programmes. Throughout Algeria, Islamist clothing started to appear. In 1987, the prominent Egyptian Muslim Brother al-Qaradâwî was named head of the Islamic University of Constantine. At the same time, the then President Chadli was canvassing support from Islamist opinion makers for his economic reforms (Roberts 2003).

In 1988, after a not very unusual speech by President Chadli, accusing the emerging middle classes of lacking zeal for the ongoing revolution, several days of rioting broke out in Algiers and elsewhere. These rapidly turned into a general strike. The rioters were almost exclusively young men or boys, who attacked public buildings, supermarkets selling and stocking luxury goods, FLN party offices and state-run shops. Protest against the *hogra* (disrespect) was the central point of all claims, and every problem appeared as ultimately reducible to a lack of morals in public life. Mock trials were held in the streets, with police officers forced to accuse themselves of corruption and to walk the streets naked. The rioters described themselves as *shuhadâ* (martyrs), hence appropriating one of the key items of official rhetoric and legitimisation of power, and placing themselves within a long tradition of rebellion against unjust and *kâfir* (unbelieving) governments (Benkheira 1990; Khadda and Gadant 1990).

Although the riots of 1988 were brutally suppressed (Chitour 1990; Aggoun and Rivoire 2004), they led to a relative opening up of the political

[27] For more detail, see the proceedings of the *Séminaire de Yakouren*, published in 1981 in Paris, which formalised the protesters' claims. The Berber Spring was widely commented upon, especially abroad, by emigrant Berber activists and sociologists alike. Their interpretations of the 'events' range from economic causality (Roberts 1981) via the notion of inevitable historical continuity (Guenoun 1999) to the idea of a profound expression of the Berber people and its democratic aspirations (Chaker 1999) or to the accusation of a mere resuscitation of colonial categories (Lazreg 1983). For a detailed chronology of the events, see Chaker (1982).

system.[28] Associations and parties sprang up everywhere in the country to prepare for the 1990/1 elections. Between 1988 and 1994, 5,839 associations were registered in the *wilâya* of Tizi-Ouzou alone (Salhi 1999a). Nationwide, more than 50 political parties were created (Martinez 1998). The most popular of these parties was the main Islamist party, the *Front Islamique du Salut* (FIS), for whose electoral success, if not for its constitution, the 'mob' of 1988 and the general frustration the riots had expressed seemed largely responsible. After the landslide FIS victory in the local elections of 1990 and in the first round of the parliamentary elections in 1991,[29] the electoral process was interrupted by the government and military, who accused the FIS of plotting the establishment of an 'Islamic State'.[30] The FIS was dissolved. Its leaders had already been put in prison before the elections had even started, and its suspected followers were sent in thousands to prison camps in the Sahara, prepared several months beforehand. Finally released after often extremely brutal treatment, they frequently had no choice but to join one of the many armed groups that formed to fight the national government and army throughout the 1990s.

This was followed by a decade of prolonged and extremely bloody and gruesome violence, which partly reshuffled social hierarchies and created its own economic structures (Martinez 1998). The current estimate is of 150,000, mostly civilian, deaths (Aggoun and Rivoire 2004). That a large number of attacks on civilians were committed by the military rather than by Islamists seems by now beyond doubt (cf. Yous 2000; Souaïdia 2001; Samraoui 2003), although the extent of the army's involvement is still hotly disputed, mainly because, due to mutual infiltration, boundaries between the military and the armed groups remain obscure. Nobody, even locally, seems to know what really happened during the 1990s, and how such a degree of violence could have been possible. This is true to an extent where the lack of any clear information appears almost as the defining characteristic of the 'events' and of the Algerian political system as such. It seems to be this very lack of clarity that leads to the presupposition of a hidden coherence between apparently random events that is so often main-

---

[28] Although, as Roberts (2003) points out, this 'opening' did not necessarily make Algerian politics any more democratic or transparent, as it often remained superficial, with different parties now reflecting what before had been different factions within the FLN.

[29] Winning 55% of the *communes* in 1990, and 47.27% of total votes in the first round of general elections in 1991 (Martinez 1998). The participation in the elections was very low, however, and all in all only roughly a quarter of Algerians voted for the FIS.

[30] The success of the FIS has often been portrayed by international observers as much as by representatives of the FIS itself, as a rupture with FLN rule and practices. However, in terms of its constitution, its internal functioning and even its ideology and policy, this rupture seems far from total. According to Hugh Roberts' analysis, 'the FLN was not the product of a secular or a socialist vision, still less a Marxist one, but of a vigorous nationalism in which populist, Islamic and pan-Arab elements have co-existed without difficulty. In this perspective, the success of the FIS can be seen to be a development of a central aspect of the FLN's ideology, the Islamic aspect, not a repudiation of this ideology overall... Far from adopting a revolutionary and correspondingly uncompromising practice of refusing to have anything to do with the actual state, the FIS persistently operated an unacknowledged alliance with some of the most powerful elements of the state.' (2003: 35-65, 86)

tained both by Algerians and by outside observers (cf. for example, Aggoun and Rivoire 2004).

The French press and academic establishment reacted very badly to the Algerian Islamists' political success. It was implicitly seen as a final and irreversible rejection of core French values, in the development of which the French vision of 'Algeria' and its 'civilising mission' in the former colony had played an important part. It was therefore almost seen as a 'betrayal' of the long established Franco-Algerian relationship. In the words of political scientist Bruno Etienne:

> Of course, the worst of disillusions is caused by Algeria because Algeria (is?) was France, because the Mediterranean runs across Eurafrica like the Seine across Paris, and because, as the leading force of the Third World, Algeria carried all our illusions. (Etienne 1995: 33)

The 'Islamist threat' seemed to turn into a more tangible reality in France when, in 1994, an Air France airbus was hijacked, and when, in 1995, a bomb blew up in the Parisian metro, killing eight people. Both attacks were allegedly carried out by an Algerian radical Islamist group, although certain authors blame the Algerian secret services. In any case, this attack, followed by several less deadly ones, warranted the material and political support of the French state to the Algerian government's politics of eradication, which continued to contribute to the violence that depopulated parts of the Algerian countryside throughout the 1990s.

Kabylia, still recovering from the Berber Spring of 1980, had stayed surprisingly quiet during the riots of October 1988. The tentative installation of a multi-party system that followed the riots permitted the reconstitution of the FFS and the creation of a second Kabyle party, the *Rassemblement pour la culture et la démocratie* (RCD). It also permitted the constitution of the *Mouvement culturel berbère*, which represented the almost 6,000 cultural and village associations that had been created in the years after 1988 alongside the still functioning village assemblies. The number of Kabyle votes for the FIS was very low; in many constituencies, the FIS had not even bothered to present a candidate.[31] Although a large number of the guerrilla camps were based in the mountainous area of Kabylia, the area was seen by Kabyles, other Algerians and outside observers as the safest and least disturbed in the whole of Algeria. Kabyles tend to blame the rise of political Islam and the violent events of the 1990s on outside intruders, variously defined as 'Afghans',[32] 'Arabs' or '*les services*' (secret services), which, in Kabyle rhetoric, all amount to roughly the same thing. Political Islam and the

---

[31] As a general rule, the FIS was far more successful in the cities than in the countryside (Martinez 1998). The low number of FIS votes in Kabylia is nevertheless striking. It seems to be due to the existence of credible regional oppositional parties other than the FIS, to a strong 'modernist' and radically secular current in the region, and to the general sentiment that the FIS was hostile to Kabylia. This does not mean that it did not have any Kabyles among its membership.

[32] This term generally refers to Algerian fighters who participated in the war in Afghanistan in the late 1970s on the Afghan side, but it can also mean Muslim foreigners who have come to Algeria to fight.

violence of the 1990s are thus often seen as yet another step in a long series of attempts to undermine the region, which started with the 'confiscated revolution' of the war of independence. Seen from France, meanwhile, the Kabyles' reassuring 'immunity' to political Islam was additional proof of their lack of religious fanaticism, their democratic spirit and their openness to 'modernity' (cf. Lacoste-Dujardin 1992) – in short, as confirming the nineteenth-century colonial analysis.

In 1994–5, the Berber movement organised a year-long general boycott of schools, to push the claims already voiced in 1980. This led to the creation of the government-run *Haut commissariat à l'amazighité* (HCA), which was in charge of introducing Berber to schools, but proved to be of little immediate effect. Conflicts over when and how to end the strike caused an open split within the regional coordination of the Berber movement. The resulting two parts aligned themselves with the two regional parties, and thereby lost much of their former political legitimacy. In 1998, after the killing of the Kabyle singer Matoub Lounes, who had been publicly condemned to death by the Islamists, thousands took to the streets in Kabylia. The government was openly accused of collaboration with the Islamists, and held responsible for Matoub's death. By the late 1990s, for most Kabyles, the Islamists and the government forces had become virtually synonymous; all popular trust in public institutions or even the efficacy of institutional political action had disappeared.

The 'Black Spring'

In 2001, riots broke out in Kabylia, but did not spread to the rest of Algeria. The issues at stake were familiar: as in 1988 in the rest of the country, the protest was mainly directed against the *hogra*. Following the death of a student in an office of the *gendarmerie*, attacks were launched on police and *gendarmerie* posts, on government institutions and party headquarters throughout the region. Both regional parties, the FFS as well as the RCD, were rejected as corrupted by 'political politicking' (*la politique politicienne*), and attacks were directed against party offices. The *gendarmes* were accused of alcoholism and immoral behaviour:

> The *gendarmes* attack the honour of our girls and our women ... what is the point of living in a country where honour is scoffed at, where corruption has become a moral asset (*érigée en valeur*)? ... [*gendarmes*], go home, this is not your country (Protesters, quoted by Alilat and Hadid 2002: 39, 40, 75).

The *gendarmes*, who referred to the protesters as 'sons of France, Mitterrand's children' (ibid.: 75), repeatedly opened fire on crowds. By the time the worst three months had passed, more than 80 protesters had died.

Despite similarities with 1988, differences were also apparent. For most Kabyles, and also for most outside observers and the international (i.e. French) press, these riots and their violent suppression were seen as yet another episode in the long struggle of 'Berbers' against a central government that could not and would not take into account their inherently democratic aspirations. The most striking feature of the riots, however, was not their reference to 'Berber culture', which initially remained largely absent from the protesters' claims, but their *post facto* mode of organisation in citizens' committees or *aârouch* ('tribal committees'), joining several 'village assemblies' in a nominally apolitical political institution (*Le Matin*, 3 May 2001). Despite the unified terminology used in the media (where the term '*aârouch*' appears to have been coined),[33] the organisational structure of the rebellion was far from homogeneous, and it appropriated a large variety of 'modern' and 'traditional' models and competing sources of legitimacy. These involved labour unions and local associations alongside village, tribal and a majority of spontaneously created committees. Similarly, the structure and the mode of representation adopted varied from one locality to another and from one occasion to another. On the communal and regional level, the local representations were organised by a committee; the true basis of political legitimacy, however, remained local.

The main aims of these local representations were initially to contain the riots and to avoid more deaths. Gradually, their demands became more formalised, and included the withdrawal from Kabylia of all security forces perceived as 'foreign', the acknowledgement of Berber as one of the national languages and cultures, the granting of the title 'martyr' to all those killed in previous riots, the granting of 'democratic rights' and unemployment benefit to the Algerian people, fighting against the *hogra*, and the legal prosecution of police officers guilty of violence in Kabylia according to international law (Coordination des Aarch, Daïras et Communes 2001a, see Text Appendix 2A, p. 157). Much as in the FIS rhetoric of ten years earlier, the *aârouch* contested the FLN's monopoly of historical legitimacy: dates and places that were highly significant for the nationalist struggle were re-appropriated by Kabyle demonstrations (Coordination des Aarch, Daïras et Communes 2001b), demands were made for re-writing history (Alilat and Hadid 2002: 75) and the title of *shuhadâ* given to those killed and wounded in the riots (*Liberté*, 21 May 2001). In 2002, the *aârouch* called for a boycott of the 'electoral comedy' of the municipal elections. This call was followed throughout the region, although one of the regional parties, the FFS, had openly opposed it.

At the time of my fieldwork, the *aârouch* or citizens' committees, three years after coming into existence, had lost most of their prestige and popular legitimacy, although virtually none of their demands had been heeded. They were frequently accused of having 'sold out to', or even of having been initiated by, the government, or of quite simply wanting to cause trouble without any results. The overall security situation in Algeria had calmed down. In April 2004, Abdelaziz Bouteflika was re-elected

---

[33] According to a verbal communication by Salma Boukir and Alain Mahé. This is obviously a difficult point to prove, but their opinion fully corresponds to my own findings. None of the early documents produced by the various local committees used the term *aârouch*, in any case.

President. Kabylia, once more, half-heartedly boycotted the elections; less out of conviction, it seemed, than out of a deeply felt political, social and often also economic frustration, as if the disenchantment of the world predicted by Bourdieu in the 1960s had taken place to a degree that nobody could then have imagined. I was often told that the greatest danger now came from the Kabyle autonomists (the *Mouvement pour l'autonomie de la Kabylie*, founded by the Kabyle singer Ferhat), who were the only ones capable of benefiting from the current political frustration. Even more frequently, I was told that it was time to retire, to look after one's family, to find, if possible, some claim on which to justify the demand for a French visa, or even better, a passport, and if this failed to rebuild the house with a solid steel door, rather than try to change the world. But then, the government was withholding all construction permits, and if you had not been 'active' with this or that person in charge... And after all, Algeria is the most beautiful country in the world, if only 'they' would let it go...

The recent 'events' in Kabylia appear as a combination of several elements. More than anything else, they reflect the disastrous social and political situation of contemporary Algeria, and the growing distrust in institutional politics; but they also clearly draw on ideas and terms derived from the historical construction of Berber identity, and thereby mirror the long and confrontational relationship between Algeria and France. At the same time, they are inscribed into global discourses of irreducible 'identities' conceived in essentially racial terms, but expressed 'culturally'; and they feed into political propaganda that reduces social conflicts to a Manichaean opposition between 'freedom' and 'fundamentalism'. Yet they remain deeply inscribed in their national and historical context, and need to be understood as such. The following chapters will outline how the various historical, intellectual and social movements discussed so far have come to produce a certain, lived, but often controversial, notion of identity and community within a particular Kabyle village, and how this notion has come into play at various moments of its recent and not so recent history, finally leading up to the 'events' of 2001.

3
Shifting Centres

> This village has developed slowly. Years and generations, suns and rains, war and peace, tears, the returns of spring, laughter, secret pain, crazy ambition, mad happiness, hidden dreams, calloused hands, the sweat of one's brow and feet scraping naked over stones have shaped this village that resembles no other. What the centuries have made, a wind ffff (he blew on his fingers) of one dark night can destroy, be it the darkness of the sun or the darkness of your minds. (Mammeri 1965: 340)

The following four chapters aim to describe Ighil Oumsed, an 'ordinary' village (if any village can be ordinary) in Kabylia, where I carried out most of my fieldwork. The present chapter deals with the aspect of the village that strikes any visitor to the area before anything else might come to his or her mind: its spatial organisation. Special attention will be paid to the various ways in which this spatial organisation is perceived, used, and thereby constantly reinterpreted by villagers, and to the impact such practices have on the self-perception of the village community. Although at first sight the village presents a very clear spatial organisation, which can be related to notions of social order and to internal divisions within village society, and which tends to be cited as a proof of historical continuity, it is argued that this clarity disappears at further analysis, and gives way to flexible spatial practices that tacitly allow for and express social change.

How to draw a map

The first time I came to the village was by night on the day of my arrival in Algeria, after a long flight and a day-long car journey. I could thus not remember any of it the next morning. Through the following days, although I had been taken around the village, I found it very difficult to find my way. For this reason – and because it seemed like a sensible thing to do for an anthropologist – I asked for a map. The first suggestion was that I should go to the town hall in Chellata, an hour's drive away; the second that I should ask a young architect originally from the village, but who had since moved away. It seemed that maps were for people from the outside, or perhaps that the authority to establish a map had to be external. I asked the family with whom I was staying for help. The girls just laughed: the village was too big, they only knew their village quarter – and their cousins' houses in the nearby villages and towns, which, through frequent visits and communications, were much less 'far away' or 'exterior' than those of their immediate neighbours.

I finally managed to persuade my host Arezqi's youngest brother, Karim, to draw a map of the village. He set himself to work right away, while Arezqi himself – a well known 'Berberist',[1] trade-unionist and 'village intellectual' in the area – feigned lack of interest. As Karim started with the mosque as the centre of the village, however, he was straightaway interrupted by his elder brother: obviously, the centre of a Kabyle village had to be *tajmaɛt*, the public square, where the men of the village meet (the nineteenth-century ethnographers' *jamâ'a*, see Chapter 1). But where was *tajmaɛt*? The former central village square that was still pointed out to me as such had long become marginal to everyday encounters and had in practice been replaced by another square called *aslad* ('the flat stone'). This place had 'in the old times' marked the outside of the village, where strangers to the village would wait to be announced before entering the village proper. The village meeting hall, which was also sometimes referred to as *tajmaɛt*, and which for more formal meetings had replaced the former open-air meeting place, offered through its now similarly marginal location only a very impracticable 'centre'. This was even more the case, as access to the meeting hall now required a key, which was kept by the president of the social association (the former village assembly), who is also the director of the local primary school.

After some reflection, Karim decided to stick to the mosque as the village centre. He gave up very quickly, however: on his drawing, the roads just would not meet where they had to (Map 3.1). He left to see his friends, and presented me with a beautifully drawn map the next morning (Map 3.2) – apparently, they had spent all night working on it. The mosque had been replaced by the square (*aslad*) in the centre of the drawing. The old *tajmaɛt* had thereby become marginal. The village itself was represented as a network of roads and paths, forming an almost perfect circle around *aslad*, and dotted with places or buildings of public interest. The house I was staying in was the only one marked on the map, to help me find my way from there to the 'important' places in the village: the school, the mosque, the coffee houses and the cemetery. Although it only vaguely resembled the maps that were later given to me by the local council, it was perfectly functional in that it would always indicate the right turn or path to take to get to a well-defined place. To me, it seemed largely self-explanatory.

Arezqi had not been sleeping either, and over breakfast handed me his version of the village (Map 3.3). Although he had drawn the village as a schematic circle centred on the mosque, he did not mention the mosque as a building. The village therefore did not appear as clustered around the mosque, but the mosque as having been placed in (or as usurping) the

---

[1] Throughout the following, I shall use the term 'Berberist' to indicate people, ideas and organisations that endorse some or all of the ideas of the Berber movement of the 1980s and 1990s in Algeria, and tend to be locally identified as part of it.

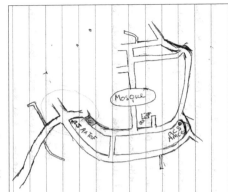

Map 3.1 Karim's first drawing of
Ighil Oumsed
Map 3.2 Karim's second drawing
of Ighil Oumsed

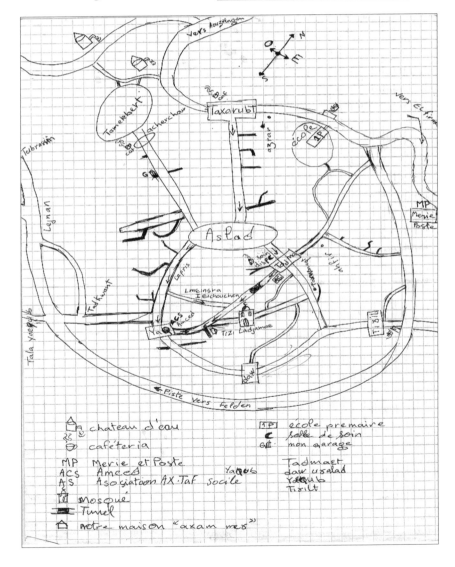

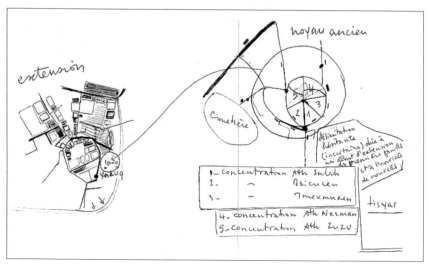

Map 3.3 Arezqi's drawing of Ighil Oumsed

Map 3.4 The 'official' map of Ighil Oumsed (different *iderma*, family groups, marked in different shades of grey)

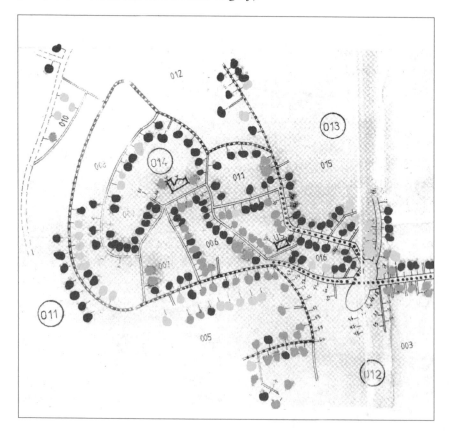

natural centre of the village. Arezqi's drawing did not define the village by its roads and public buildings as Karim and his friends – all from different families – did on their version, but divided it into quarters which appear as homogeneous blocs, set apart by different colours, according to the 'family group' (*adrum*, pl. *iderma*) who live there. As a map, it was as useless practically as it was incorrect geographically. It nevertheless very neatly represented a way of constructing and describing community space, a conception of space without which the village in its social representation cannot be understood.

In a 'confusion' that pervades all geographical statements, places in the village and in its surroundings tend to be defined via the people supposed to live or to have lived there. At the same time, people tend to be ordered into categories through spatial representations.[2] When talking about the 'family groups' or *iderma* that are supposedly identical with the quarters, Arezqi thus refers to a category that, although difficult to delimit, certainly exists in village discourse. This category is still functional in that it creates groups of belonging or rather defines who is one of 'ours' and who is with 'them'. In everyday use, however, it is not always applied, and it co-exists with a broad range of other such categories appealed to according to the immediate context and the personal circumstances and disposition of the informant.

The category of *adrum* or 'clan' also refers to the classic model of Kabyle social organisation as outlined by Hanoteau and Letourneux (1873: 6) and virtually all later writers on Kabylia – a fact of which Arezqi was certainly aware. In this model, the Kabyle village appears as part of a larger segmentary system. The smallest unit in this system would be *axxam*, the house, followed by *taxerubt* (a term which I did not encounter in Ighil Oumsed), which is also called *taɛrift* or *adrum*, or the 'extended family'. Several of these would constitute *taddart*, the village; several villages, in turn, would make *aɛrc*, the tribe, and *taqbaylit*, the 'tribal federation'.[3] As used within Ighil Oumsed, *adrum* does not always mean an 'extended family' with a single ancestor. Some of the *iderma* are seen as mere associations of families from various backgrounds and origins. It is, however, widely claimed that, 'in former times' villagers would generally marry within their *adrum*. This

---

[2] The debate over the prevalence of spatial or social representations goes back to the 1950s and 1960s, see, for example, Leach (1961) and Barth (1953), who favour the spatial solution, and Lancaster (1981), who opts for the social. More recent anthropological writings (see, for example, the collection of essays in Hirsch and O'Hanlon 1995), often inspired by social geography (e.g. by Harvey 1996), have shown the absurdity of such an opposition: although not identical, the spatial and the social are interdependent, and one has little meaning without the other.

[3] Following Hanoteau and Letourneux (1873). Of the 'levels' they mention, *axxam* (house) and *taddart* (village) are most frequently used in contemporary everyday conversations and identifications in Ighil Oumsed. The *iderma* tend to be treated as 'secret knowledge' (see below). The *aɛrc* has been absorbed by the recent political use of the term and is now only ever used to refer to the *comités des citoyens* that sprang up in 2001 in the area (see Chapter 2). *Taqbaylit* is virtually never referred to, unless it is used to mean the Kabyle language or 'Kabyle-ness' as a whole.

fact is hardly corroborated by the available lists of marriages over the years.[4] It nevertheless strongly informs the village imagination of what an *adrum* should be or used to be. Although the members of *iderma* do not all claim to be descendants of the same ancestor, the names given to all three *iderma* are composed by *Aït* (the Kabyle equivalent of the Arabic *Beni*, or 'the sons of') and the name of a person nobody now remembers.

In practice, the attempt to determine group membership in terms of family-based *iderma* is further complicated by the fact that family relations can be interpreted in various ways, especially in a village where, despite local assurances to the contrary, every family has at some point married into every other.[5] When trying to establish an equivalence between the *iderma* and the village quarters, this difficulty is increased still further by the fact that female and male descriptions of spaces vary: women are much more likely to define houses and thus places and streets by the women living there than by the men or 'heads of the household'.

In Arezqi's sketch, the village nevertheless appears as made up of neat opposing blocs of people, whose divisions organise space. These abstract blocs are ordered by their putative time of arrival in the village, which is reflected by the location of their living quarters. Thus, Arezqi took care to mark the quarter where his family house is situated as the '*noyau ancien*' or the old centre of the village. It consequently appears in his drawing as the heart of the village, and is reproduced in a second sketch on a larger scale (Map 3.3). The other quarters, which by now constitute the largest part of the village, are portrayed as mere extensions, branching off in two different directions. For Arezqi, the centre (or *noyau*, literally 'kernel' or 'nucleus') of the village is thus firmly placed within his own quarter, encompassing in this definition the place as much as the people who are said to live there.[6]

The foundation story of the village, which, like many others in the area (cf. Masqueray 1983 [1886]: 25–30), can be summed up as a successive arrival of families from virtually all the surrounding regions, confirms his reading: although no family claims originally to be from the village itself, arrivals can be ranked according to who came first – and to who came last, and was thus likely to have been accepted into the village as a client family. The supposedly clear distribution of space within the village serves as the main proof for this ranking, and villagers from the 'old families' were very

---

[4] *Registre des mariages de la commune mixte d'Akbou*, ACA, see Table 1. The local town halls in Chellata and Akbou preserve much of the registers and administrative papers of colonial times. The registers that I shall refer to most frequently are the *Registre des mariages* (RM) and the *Tableau de recensement* (TR), which listed all young men under the obligation to serve in the French Army.

[5] Although 'officially', Kabyle kinship is reckoned according to patrilineage, in practice villagers tend to refer to maternal as much as to paternal kin, depending on the situation, the age and the sex of the speaker, and the personality and influence of the maternal and paternal kin respectively. For a theoretical discussion of these practices among Kabyles, see Bourdieu (1972) who makes a distinction between 'official', i.e. patrilineal, and 'practical' kinship. Realities, however, are even more confusing than his explanations.

[6] As far as I know, there is no Kabyle equivalent to Arezqi's '*noyau*'. In Kabyle, the old centre is generally referred to as *ɣaɛkuv*, a term which does not imply the same hierarchy as *noyau* does.

keen that, as additional proof of their family's precedence, I should see the ruins of their 'ancestors' settlements' which dot the landscape around the village.

Arezqi's map came with an explanation three times its size. In this explanation, he divided the *noyau ancien* into five symmetrical parts. Three of these were described as almost exclusively inhabited by families who are part of the group of the 'old families' generally referred to as the *adrum* Aït Boudjmaa (composed of the Yennat, the Ihamlalen, the Imessaouden and other families). One part is given to the 'second' group of families, the Aït Sliman, which Arezqi described as follows:

> Aït Hamidouche (Ben Hamidouche), first nucleus of the party 'Aït Sliman'... Aït Mansour (Oumansour, Benimansour), clan from a village from [the neighbouring tribe] Ouzellaguen, who rallied to Ighil and have remained until now in conflict with their [own] village and *douar* of origin, to whom an old tradition of vengeance linked them still until before the war. They subscribe to the party of the Aït Sliman... The Aït Hamidouche have also strengthened their party through families who came later.

The fifth and remaining part is allotted to the 'third' *adrum*, the Aït Hamimi:

> Other families came to the village at various times and in various circumstances: inheritance, marriages [*alliances*] with families, refugees (exiles?) after their involvement in conflicts that pitted Ighil against the [neighbouring tribes] Ouzellaguen and Aït Waghlis... It is probable that of these scattered families was born the third party: Aït Hamimi.

Arezqi thus established a clear hierarchy between the different *iderma*, in terms of their historical precedence, mirrored by the lay-out of the village and the ruins of surrounding settlements. This hierarchy is also reflected in the internal links that unite them as a group: whereas the Aït Boudjmaa are said to be 'cousins', the other groups comprise 'scattered families' who have entered the village as refugees, and who are linked among themselves only by their inferior status. Similarly, their origin is not always known. Arezqi added a list of their origins where he knew it, but omitted the fact that the 'old families' are by general consensus said to have come from the Medjana, the 'Arab lands' east of the Soummam valley, which are seen as a former stronghold of Ottoman rule in the area.[7]

Arezqi's preoccupation with legitimacy as derived from local origin or at least from first arrival seems surprising in an area where nobody claims to be 'indigenous' (see the founding story of the village outlined above, and Masqueray 1983 [1886]: 28), and where the very idea of being from the land seems often to indicate a lack of culture and refinement.[8] It points towards two co-existing hierarchies of values, which simultaneously praise

---

[7] The tribes from the Medjana are generally described as the *makhzan* tribes (military auxiliaries) of the Turkish *bey* in Constantine, and the local *juwâd* (noble, warrior) family Moqrani who had, for most of the Ottoman period in Algeria, sworn allegiance to him (cf. Rinn 1891).
[8] Cf. Abdelfettah-Lahri (2000: 243) for a similar observation made in the nearby harbour town Béjaïa. Similarly, descendants from the nearby tribe Aït Waghlis, seen as the 'intellectuals' of the region, are proud to maintain that they were originally of urban extraction, and had to flee to the mountains during the Spanish occupation of Béjaïa in the sixteenth century.

outside origin and village ancestry, depending on context, with the latter being favoured both by French and Berberist theories about 'Berber identity'. Thus, in the same conversation, villagers might explain their position within the village community both in terms of their families' early arrival in the village, and in terms of their foreign, ideally urban, origin, their ostentatious self-distancing from 'village ways', and their present 'connections' with the outside. This allows for a constant re-negotiation of position and status within the village community.

Arezqi's scheme made another basic distinction: that between 'marabouts' and 'Kabyles'. Maraboutic families can be found all over Kabylia. Legend maintains that they originate from Morocco and came to Kabylia during the sixteenth century to teach religion and act as imams in the Berber-speaking areas of North Africa (Rinn 1884). For several centuries, they acted as village teachers, preachers, healers, scribes and holy men, distinguished from the 'Kabyles' where they could afford this by their function and status. During the first half of the twentieth century, they came under harsh criticism, by the reformist movement for their 'superstitious' practices, and by the nationalist movement for their involvement with the French administration and for their 'feudal' exploitation of the peasant population. More recently, they have come under fire from Berberists who see them as 'alienating' and 'Arabising' the 'simple Kabyles'. The status of maraboutic families in Kabyle villages is now as diverse as their family histories and the social balance of their villages. Many succeeded in entering new high-status careers such as medicine and law; others became farmers or workers as their poorer ancestors had done for centuries.

In Arezqi's schema, maraboutic families were listed separately, but almost as a mere historical reminder. On his map, they do not have their own space in the village, and mainly figure as 'maraboutic [families] dissolved in the peasantry'. Thus, Arezqi did not mention the most important maraboutic family, who up until the 1970s furnished the village imam: the Ouhaddar or, as they are locally referred to, *axxam* (the house of) Shaykh Tahar. This family, although most of them have left the village, is still present in village geography; their family house serves for many of the village women as a landmark, a meeting place and a dispensary of the ancestor's *baraka*;[9] it also contains a collection of old manuscripts and village archives. For Arezqi, however, it does not quite belong to the village itself. In a concoction of all possible criticisms ever voiced against maraboutic (or more generally religious) institutions and practices, he often described them to me as the representatives of an 'alienating' outside force or as a 'left-over' of 'feudal' times, and he vehemently denied the 'Kabyleness' of Shaykh Tahar's descendants. The house of Shaykh Tahar therefore did not have its space on the map, nor rightfully in the village itself.

After the mayor of the local council in Chellata finally gave me the official government-issued map of the village (Map 3.4), it was unfortunately

[9] Lit. blessing, benediction; in North African Islam, spiritual power or life-giving force held by saints, their descendants, and places and objects associated with them.

impossible to ask for more maps drawn by villagers, as I already had the 'real' one. Ironically, the mayor himself had warned me before he gave me the map that it would probably be totally inaccurate. People never like to state all their property rights and wealth to officials, as they fear taxation; they might also overstate their ownership in order to advance their side in a conflict about the ownership of a certain building, of parts of it or of a piece of land. This did not stop villagers from considering the official map as valuable. If it did not truly describe all that mattered, at least it fixed space in writing, and thereby created a standard that could then be considered as 'reality'.

The government map was similar to those drawn by Karim and his friends: no hierarchy was established, and the houses were numbered starting from the outside rather than the 'centre' of the village. The village did not appear as a juxtaposition of solid blocs, but as an agglomeration of undifferentiated buildings. The only distinction permitted was that between private and public buildings, and an arbitrary segmentation by roads and numbers. However, everybody whom I asked to find his or her own house on the official map failed to do so. This did not discourage in the slightest the large number of people who asked me for a photocopy of the map and especially of the list that states the ownership of all the houses marked on it. Due to this sudden and secretive interest, the 'real' (and probably publicly accessible) map and the list stating everybody's holdings in fixed and non-negotiable figures seemed almost like something indecent to possess.

The ambiguity of space

As the difficulty of drawing a map that truly represents the village and the exaggerated interest in the 'real' but unintelligible map show, spatial and social positions in the village are invariably interlinked, and are invariably controversial. No space in the village is neutral, and the relative status of any given group or individual can be read by the variety and kind of spaces they might occupy.[10] On closer scrutiny, the 'official' map indicates that the overall pattern of house owning and residence is far more complex than it appears on Arezqi's drawing (see Map 3.4). People move, and although it is usually declared impossible, they also sell and buy houses, or live with their affines. Furthermore, although people sleep and eat in certain houses and are associated with them, men, whose place is still defined as the outside,[11] tend to spend most of their time elsewhere. Where exactly they do this forms a complex spatial distribution, varying according to age,

[10] For a strikingly similar observation in the rather different political context of northern Lebanon, see Gilsenan (1996: 45–7).

[11] Men are supposed to enter even their own houses only to eat and sleep. For a fuller account of this, see Bourdieu's (1965) classic article on the sense of honour in Kabyle society, whose underlying tenets are still true, although some of its surrounding practices might have disappeared or been replaced by others.

family group, political opinions and occupation, not to mention the time of the day and the season.

The office of one of the five associations in the village, the *association culturelle*, for instance, is located in the former *tajmaɛt* of one of the village quarters of the Aït Boudjmaa and is still strongly identified with the people who live in this quarter. It is generally referred to by the name of the quarter (*yaɛkuv*), rather than by the name of the association (*amsed*). However, it also tends to attract and be identified with a certain age group, with a group of a certain educational level and economic position within the village, and with those adhering to a well-defined body of ideas and values, associated with 'Berberism' and generally expressed in French rather than in Arabic or Kabyle. Similarly, the main village square tends to be reserved for older people, and the few young people who occupy it at times tend to be unusually quiet. The 'secondary' village squares situated inside the village quarters tend to be reserved for the inhabitants of the quarter, although they also frequently attract people of similar age and interests. The 'regulars' of the two *cafés* in the village are known as two separate groups (cf. Du Boulay 1974; Herzfeld 1985). The *tajmaɛt* and the office of the *association culturelle* are locked and access is consequently reserved to their presidents and colleagues.

Women are supposed to stay in the house, which is still the main space associated with them, although re-negotiations of the boundaries between 'male' and 'female' spaces are constant. Women also maintain control over the gardens, which are situated inside the village, but are set apart from its streets and houses. Women have also increasingly taken control of the agricultural lands outside the village: since the war of independence, men have largely refused to do agricultural labour, which is seen as a low-status and a low-profit occupation. Women similarly tend to describe the village space as defined by socially determined, invisible boundaries, which vary with the circumstances, and rarely correspond to those drawn up by men. Although these boundaries are hardly ever expressed verbally, they become manifest through visiting practices, especially on occasions such as the celebration of the *'îds*, the days of reconciliation.[12] Although I had been told that during the *'îd*, 'everybody visits everybody else. We go into all houses, you'll see, you'll know everybody!' (Linda Yennat), we did not visit every house, far from it, nor did I manage at first to make much sense of why certain houses absolutely had to be visited, whereas others did not seem even to exist in the eyes of my guide, although they stood in the same village quarter, and were inhabited by 'cousins' belonging, according to Arezqi's schema, to the same *adrum*. 'Everybody' clearly was a relative category that excluded as many villagers, cousins and neighbours as it included.

---

[12] The *'îds* (lit. 'feasts') are the most important festivals of the Islamic year, one marking the end of fasting after Ramadan, the other commemorating Abraham's sacrifice, and celebrated with the slaughter of a sheep. Visiting practices during feast-days and throughout the year are crucial to female social life throughout the Middle East and North Africa, see, for example, Altorki's (1986) account of Saudi Arabia, and Menely (1996) on Yemen.

The annual ritual of the distribution of the *zakât*, the religious 'tax' notionally given to 'all the village poor' after the month of fasting,[13] similarly maps out the village in its own particular way, according to largely female perceptions of spatial and social boundaries. It is in itself a negotiation that temporarily defines the 'village poor', a group which might change from charitable act to charitable act. As the 'village poor' in practice turn out to be mainly one's cousins, and individual itineraries are largely confined to a single village quarter, the distribution of the *zakât* physically traces and makes 'connections'. It establishes and strengthens certain family and friendship links, but not all. These then serve as the limit of the group and the physical space generally referred to as 'ours' (*nney*). These rituals and the visiting practices associated with them are repeated every year and on special occasions, such as weddings, births and deaths, while less prestigious but nonetheless 'political' visiting is an everyday occurrence. Any kind of visiting practice constantly undergoes almost imperceptible changes due to changed relationships between families and friends whose causes often escaped my initial lack of Kabyle sensitivity. They forged links more solid than any spatial or even kin-based proximity could (cf. Bourdieu 1972: 89).

Thus, social and spatial boundaries in the village are constantly redefined through changing spatial practices, as the boundaries between 'us' and 'them', 'our space' and 'their space', and even the 'village' and the 'outside' are never fixed, but are nonetheless essential to village life, thereby maintaining the functional ambiguity of a situation that is rigid and flexible at the same time. Any attempt at permanently fixing the boundaries, especially for the benefit of a foreign researcher who was going to write them down, was either used to impose a certain reading of reality as represented by the different possible ways of drawing maps outlined above; or it was drowned in precision until everything became vague; or else it was met with suspicion.

Thus, several weeks after my arrival in the village, I expressed the wish to be shown around the village graveyard (Photo 3.1). I had been told that it was similarly organised according to *iderma* divisions: the families who had come first occupy the top half and those who had come later are found towards the bottom, close to the entrance gate. As the dead cannot move, nor resist 'order', the graveyard seemed to be the place where conceptual and practical spatial arrangements might correspond to each other. This impression was confirmed as the school director and president of the *associaion sociale* of the village tried to discourage me from my visit: 'That's to see the *iderma*, isn't it? I see, you know how these things work. We'll talk about this later; it's of no importance' (Mohand Ramdani). Yet, when I

---

[13] Paying the *zakât* is one of the 'five pillars' of Islam, and, like the month of fasting, central to village religious life. It is thereby a constant cause of conflict in families, especially between men and women, who are overall more careful of religious prescriptions. To pay the *zakât*, every village household gives a certain amount of money or four measures of semolina for every person in the house who has accomplished the thirty days of fasting, and two each for the dead who used to live there and are still remembered.

Photo 3.1 Village graveyard

visited the graveyard despite – or rather because of – his warning, Mohand's worry turned out to be groundless: until they started to be gradually replaced by permanent graves made out of concrete, Kabyle graves used to be rough stone heaps. Roughly half of the graves in the village cemetery do not bear names. Every thirty years or so, graves would be re-used. Older burial places would be forgotten, and desperately searched for during the annual visit to the cemetery during the *'id*. Even those who rest eternally are thereby mobile, and my visit to the cemetery could not produce the 'true' map of the village, but just a rough sketch based on the increasing number of named concrete graves (Map 3.5).

Shifting centres

One common feature of all of the maps described above is that they tell the story of a movement away from the 'original' village centre towards a variety of new possible centres. The *noyau ancien*, mainly inhabited by the 'old families', was centred on the village mosque. It had first been enlarged by the construction of French army barracks just outside the village on the road leading up to it in 1956. As part of the 'pacification' programme put into practice during the war of independence (1954–62, see Chapter 2), the

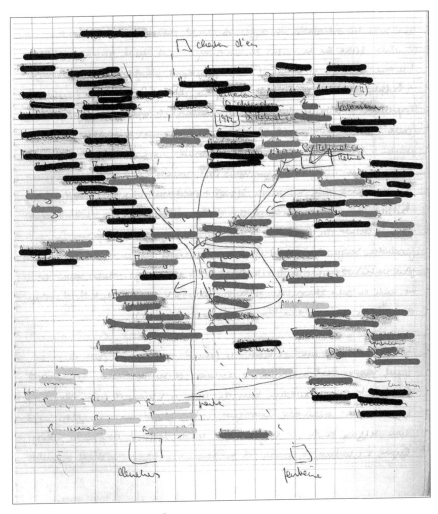

Map 3.5 Village graveyard
(different *iderma* marked in different shades of grey)

French army fenced the village in and established a checkpoint at *aslad*. Alongside the path that led from *taxerubt* ('the Carob-tree', now a public square at the entry of the village, see Map 3.2) outside the village, to *aslad*, they constructed a swimming pool, a cinema, a rural health centre and a prison. Before their arrival, only a few houses and some agricultural buildings, mainly belonging to the 'new families', had stood in what was then *laxla*, or the 'wilderness' outside the village. The French army also opened a school further down the valley on the road they had paved on their arrival. Today's school, although several times reconstructed since then, is still in the same place. Traces of the French installations can still be seen when walking from *taxerubt* to *aslad*, but most of the barracks were taken over straight after the war by those who had previously owned the land and some of buildings on it, or simply by those who were powerful enough to occupy them.

Up to now, the population of this village quarter has remained mixed, but members of the 'new' families predominate. Around the former French army barracks, especially along the only paved road that leads down to the valley, more and more people have constructed their houses. On the side facing the mountains and a large part of the fields, little construction has been undertaken, as these areas are not accessible by road and are generally too steep for modern building. The new houses vary in style and material from those that dominate in the *noyau ancien*: they tend to be built out of concrete rather than stones and clay, they do not have an inner courtyard but several windows facing the road and the garden, and they are usually set apart from their neighbours.[14]

Taxerubt is now where the recently legalised private transport arrives and departs. The concentration of new buildings around *taxerubt*, the new focus of village activity, means that the ancient centre has become marginal to village activities, and that buildings that were formerly situated outside village limits are now within them. These newly integrated buildings include the two coffee houses that have now become part of the village, the primary school that is on the verge of doing so, and even the local *mairie* (town hall)[15] and post office that look as though they will soon be within village limits. This means that all representations of state power, formerly situated outside the village space and thus clearly set apart, are now, at least geographically, part of it. They have also become more central to village life in practice. This, however, does not mean only that the state has increased its direct hold over the village community, but also that the village – or some villagers – have increased their hold over and access to state institutions.

All administrative positions in the school, the town hall and the post office are by now held by villagers, and appreciated as positions of relative influence. The school, since being 'taken over' by the village in this way, often serves as a meeting place for villagers, and as a setting for village activities, thereby partly replacing the *tajmaɛt* – to which, as mentioned above, the school director or his cousin hold the keys. The town hall is still seen as very much 'outside' the village, but it has similarly been 'taken over' and has started to become central in its own right: the post office and the new village monuments to the war dead and those who died in 2001 (constructed by the state authorities) are situated next to it, and the village's *association sportive* used to hold its popular karate school on its grounds. It remains, however, the space most closely associated with the government.

This spatial development reflects the historical development of the village,

---

[14] This change in architectural style is common throughout the Middle East and North Africa. See Bourdieu (1977) for a classic analysis of the social repercussions of this change.
[15] The village *mairie* is an office that offers some of the most basic administrative services to those who do not wish to undertake the hour-long journey to Chellata, the administrative centre of the *commune* of which the village is part. The village *mairie* does not have any decision–making powers. It employs two permanent members of staff.

the region and the country as a whole. As the village centre moved gradually away from the mosque and towards the school, the balance of families within the village changed accordingly, as new sources of influence and legitimacy developed and were appropriated, by some families more quickly than by others. The shift of the geographical centre of the village was thereby accompanied by a shift of influence and authority away from those who lived around the mosque and towards those who lived in the new village quarters near the school. Although, as will be seen in Chapter 4, many of the changes that led up to this reshuffling of influence had begun in earlier stages of the colonial period, it is the war of independence and the immediate restructuring of society it caused that now appear as the moment these changes were most dramatically brought about, the moment, let us say, when the cards were re-dealt (although, as some say, the rules have stayed the same), and when the new 'ruling class', composed of former resistance fighters and freshly educated administrators, started to assert itself.

Even in small village communities of minor importance, such as Ighil Oumsed, the new state and the war that created it became the main purveyors of power, economic resources and legitimacy, and the influence of those who had either participated in the war or managed to become part of the national administration remained for several decades overwhelming. Access to these new administrative structures or privileged access to the centralised system of economic distribution became essential for survival, or at least for success and a position of influence within the village community. These factors (and a steady income through relatives who emigrated) were also all that would allow construction of one of the costly new villas characteristic of the new quarters. Therefore, to live close to the school has become in itself a sign of successful integration in the new system, whereas the obligation to remain in one of the old houses, constructed out of locally available stones, tiles and clay, was a sign of a relative failure to establish the necessary 'connections'. Hence, it was no coincidence that the *association culturelle*, the local reflection of the Berber movement that was very critical of the 'privileges' accorded to the 'revolutionary family', set up its office in one of the old quarters and was at its beginnings mainly composed of people from 'old' families (at least notionally, if not in reality).

Arezqi's schema was thus in a certain sense very close to the social and economic reality of the village. It reflected the sentiment of a shift of influence away from the old to the new quarters, and therefore also – at least symbolically – from the old families to the '*arrivistes*'. Yet, although this difference might be locally associated with divisions between families, this assumption does not appear to be grounded in actual patterns of ownership and residence. A close look at the government map shows that the predominance of groups of (patrilineal) families in certain village quarters has been maintained (supposing it existed previously), but that the further one moves away from the *noyau ancien*, the less distinctive the quarters become in terms of 'clans' determined by what Bourdieu (1972) would call 'official' (i.e. patrilineal) kinship (Map 3.4). Many of the 'old' families have indeed known how to preserve their former influence, and have been able to build a second house next to the school. The difference between the inhabitants of the old and the new quarters is thus mainly a difference between those who succeeded and those who did not in gaining access to the resources of the independent Algerian nation-state, although this might be, in village discourse, glossed over as a distinction between family groups.

The projection of identity onto land

The divisions of the living quarters in the village are reflected in the distribution of the village's agricultural land and grazing grounds. The foundation story of the village explains how these divisions came about:

> At the beginning there was nobody where the village is now. Then the first families came from the Medjana. They were cousins: the Aït Yennat, the Ihamlalen, the Imessaouden. They each constructed their own hamlet, next to their own spring, down below. One day, a shepherd took his flock to the mountains. One of his goats went into a bush, and came out with a wet beard. That's how the shepherd discovered the spring. The people from below then moved up here to defend themselves more easily, but each family kept the land where they had lived first. Other families from all over the country first settled above the village, in four hamlets, and then came to join it too. They too kept their lands where they had lived first. Later on, the spring was filled with stones to build the mosque that's still there. That was a long time ago. (Akli Benhamidouche)

Thus seven now abandoned villages are commonly pointed out as being the original homes of the families who came together to make up the core of Ighil Oumsed: three below the village, which are collectively identified as the original hamlets of the Aït Boudjmaa; four above the village, 'belonging' to the Aït Sliman. The exact locations of these seven villages are known. They often show traces of former, or even more recent, settlement.[16]

The ruins of these villages, and the patterns of landownership they imply, are frequently cited as an explanation for the ideal social and spatial organisation of the village:

> It is easy to distinguish between the *iderma*: those who own land below the village belong to the Aït Boudjmaa; those who own land above the village belong to the Aït Sliman. The others have bought land wherever they could, where we let them do so. (Fodil Ihamlalen)

Such a division of landholdings would not only reflect an ideal of historical

---

[16] Two of the former settlements situated above the village are mentioned as burial sites for villagers from Ighil Oumsed by the first available administrative document on tribal and village boundaries, the French *sénatus-consulte* (1893: 99, CDC). Kabyle villages frequently have different graveyards for each *iderma*, but this is not the case in Ighil Oumsed. The above document suggests, however, that there still were several graveyards in Ighil Oumsed in the late nineteenth century. This might point to a relatively late incorporation of some of the 'seven villages', and to the historical importance of the divisions into *iderma*.

precedence, but would also describe an unequal power relationship between the various family groups in the village: due to the constitution of the soil, the further one climbs, the less profit there is to be had from the land. Cereals can only be grown on the lands below, and families from 'above' are reduced to owning some olive trees and grazing grounds. Their property is further limited by the extension of the 'forest' that covers the highest part of the mountain slope and is considered communal grazing.[17]

At the same time, such a distribution of land points to a certain reading of colonial history. Originally, it is said, village lands stretched from the top of the mountains to the river down in the valley, and from the limit with the Ouzellaguen in the East to the lands of the neighbouring village, Felden, in the West. In 1871, a regional insurrection against the French colonial army broke out, and was defeated (see Chapter 1). As a collective punishment for the leaders of the insurrection and for all the tribes that had been involved, roughly one-fifth of all tribal lands were confiscated and given to newly arrived French settlers in the valley. Another quarter of all lands were temporarily confiscated as a guarantee for payment of the fine. The Illoula Ousammeur, of which Ighil Oumsed is part, were among the first in the Akbou region to pay off their considerable debt, which amounted to about ten times their annual taxes. They thus could rapidly make use again of the agricultural land. The fifth that had been given to the settlers, however, had been lost forever.

The confiscated land comprised virtually all the village landholdings below a certain altitude. This did not only mean that the most valuable arable lands were taken away from the village, but also that, according to the notional pattern of landownership described above, the 'old' families and those that had managed to accumulate a maximum of rich agricultural lands were the most affected by the expropriations, and had thus most reason to compromise with the colonial administration. Through the decades following the 1893 *sénatus-consulte*, and up until the outbreak of the war of independence, some of these families managed to buy back a large part of their own land and land owned by other, less fortunate or less adaptable, expropriated families or family members (see Chapter 4). Land ownership was thus, in a long and gradual process, re-shuffled according to the new balance of power and wealth within the village; village society was reorganised accordingly, as 'proofs' of historic precedence could now be acquired on the market.

In any case, patterns of landholding never seemed to have been as neatly determined as village discourse would like to make out. Kabyle property

---

[17] The distinction between families from 'above' and families from 'below' can be found throughout Kabylia (cf. e.g. Carette 1848, Hanoteau and Letourneux 1873). Indeed, Ighil Oumsed belongs to the tribe Illoula Ousammeur, or the 'Illoula from below', as opposed to the Illoula Amalou, the 'Illoula from above'. Although the nature of this division has not attracted much attention throughout the more recent literature, it might indicate a socio-economic distinction, as it does here, but also a varying degree of involvement with the Ottoman – or other – government mainly in control of low-lying lands.

rights, as described in detail by Hanoteau (1873: 250 ff.),[18] are complicated. Kabylia is chronically short of good agricultural land, and inheritance is supposed to be equally split between all sons of the family, who might be numerous. Furthermore, most of the considerable number of former religious endowments (*ahbâs*, sgl. *hubus*) in the area passed, at least nominally, into private hands, to avoid their expropriation during the implementation of the *sénatus-consulte*, when all *hubus* lands were confiscated as state property (see Chapter 1). The exact status of some of these properties remains vague, thus further complicating the determination of patterns of land ownership. This and the intricacies of Kabyle property rights and a long history of selling, buying and inheriting make it practically impossible to trace the clear general partition of land invoked by villagers as physical proof of their origins and the time of their arrival in the village. This does not, however, alter the villagers' claims that the land, like the village itself, neatly represents the social and historical order of the community of its owners.

Despite constant changes in the pattern of land ownership, the boundaries of village land as a whole seem to have been maintained over time. This was often achieved only by the village's capacity to act as a communal body in defending its lands against outside encroachments, one of the rare occasions, it seems, when villagers agree on common tactics. The *tajmaεt* or village council still has a say in all large land transactions, and acts as the ultimate authority on land ownership, although many quarrels among villagers have also been brought before the tribunal in the nearest town, Akbou. In the rare cases where village land is sold to 'strangers', the plots thus sold are still ultimately considered as under the authority of the village council. The same logic applies to villagers who have acquired land outside the village borders: these properties are considered as privately owned, but of no concern to the village as a whole. The sum-total of land owned by villagers as individuals thus does not equal the amount of land over which the village as a body retains a certain control, on whose protection it prides itself, and within which transgressions from generally accepted behaviour are seen as an offence against the village community as a whole.[19] This situation inevitably leads to tensions with neighbouring villages.

One example of these tensions is given by the age-old conflict surrounding the sites associated with two of the four upper original hamlets mentioned above: Aït Moussa ou Ahmed and Moussa ou Ali. Aït Moussa ou Ahmed is located next to the spring that provides almost all the water used in Ighil Oumsed, but that partly flows through land that has been bought by members of the neighbouring tribe, Ouzellaguen. The application

---

[18] Bousquet (1950) notes that Hanoteau's detailed descriptions need to be taken with a pinch of salt: most actual arrangements between heirs are based on mutual compromise (cf. also Bernard and Milliot 1933). For similarly complicated property rights in a society of small independent landholders, see Behar (1986) on northern Spain, and Mundy (1995) on Yemen.

[19] This practice can be found among peasant societies throughout the Middle East, and has been documented especially for Yemen (Dresch 1989). For a more detailed discussion of the emphasis on protected moral spaces belonging to and defining social groups, see Dresch (1986, 2007).

of the *sénatus-consulte* offered an occasion for this conflict to re-emerge. The *sénatus-consulte* took note of a claim that was put forward by the representatives of the Ouzellaguen to register Aït Moussa ou Ahmed as belonging to their lands, as most of the fields surrounding these two sites had been bought by individual members of the Ouzellaguen. The *jamâ'a* or tribal council of the Illoula reacted to the claim as follows: [20]

> The *jamâ'a* of the tribe Illoula declares: that the contested area has always belonged to its territory; that everybody knows that this fact is beyond doubt; and that the acquisitions mentioned by the people from Ouzellaguen cannot lead to the annexation to the Ouzellaguen of this area, where many people from the Illoula still own land that they will never sell. That the mosque Moussa ou Ali mentioned in the claim put forward by the *jamâ'a* of the Ouzellaguen is used as a place of burial for the section Aït Moussa ou Ahmed, Illoula; that this mosque, which is in perfect condition, is kept in this condition only by people from this section; finally, that, although the water of the spring Tala Ibaoulène provides for the daily needs of the section Tizi Merlas, Ouzellaguen, the rest of the water of the Ighzer Aït Moussa ou Ahmed is used by the section Ighil Oumsed, Illoula.[21]

Village territory is thus established through reference simultaneously to long-term private ownership, to 'generally admitted' facts, to the effort a group of villagers had spent in the maintenance of the site, to the sacredness of graveyards, and to established patterns of water rights.

Although the French on this occasion decided in favour of the Illoula, the conflict had not been resolved. It still lingers today, as became clear to me when Arezqi accompanied me on my first visit to Aït Moussa ou Ahmed (in ruins) and Moussa ou Ali (where an empty hut still serves as a pilgrimage site, mainly for women of the village). During this visit, we came across a man from the Ouzellaguen who was constructing a house, on his privately owned land, as he took care to emphasise, out of stones found in the ruins of the former village. He told us about the cemetery he had discovered. Arezqi did not say anything, but frowned – what *was* that man doing there? The water of the spring similarly is a permanent cause of tension:

> There is always trouble – can you see the hotel over there? That's somebody from the Ouzellaguen, who built a big luxury hotel, in the mountains.[22] It's on land belonging to the Ouzellaguen, but he always tries to take our water – with the help of his friends in Ighil Oumsed, obviously. (Arezqi Yennat)[23]

---

[20] The tribe's 'elders' were organised as a *jamâ'a* or tribal council in order to help the French officers to determine and ratify the tribal and village boundaries. It seems unlikely that this *jamâ'a* corresponded to any pre-existing institution, as villagers – and the ethnographic literature – only ever mention the constitution of tribal committees as an *ad hoc* emergency measure.

[21] *Sénatus-consulte de la tribu Illoula Asammeur*, 1893: 28, CDC.

[22] Hotels often serve alcohol, and are generally seen as places of ill repute. They should be situated in the towns in the valley rather than near villages in the mountains. The offence is thus not only material, but also moral.

[23] Arezqi's distrust of the 'friends' of the Ouzellaguen is telling. Many villagers are said to have come from the Ouzellaguen or at least to have transited their lands. These families often still have land holdings and allegedly links of solidarity with their place and tribe of origin. Although tribal boundaries as such are not open to negotiation, people easily move across them, and intermarriage with certain villages of the Ouzellaguen is and always has been frequent (see Appendix 1A, p. 151).

This underlying tension periodically bursts out into minor conflicts between the two groups, which are quietened, but never resolved, by communal action and a public display of village solidarity and strength:

> The last time we all got together to do something, it was to protect the spring – its water had changed its course, and we had to put it right again before it caused trouble with the Ouzellaguen. There had to be a lot of us, so that they would not come to bother us. I organised all this: for three days, I went up and down and up and down with my donkey – everybody from the village was there.
> (Yahia Bouallaoua, former village *amyar* or 'president' of the village council)

The land confiscated under colonial rule and that had not been bought back by villagers similarly prompts village wrath and, to a lesser degree, collective action. With independence, most villagers had hoped that this land would be restored to its former owners, but it was kept as a state domain (*domaine autogéré*) under the direct control of the army, and later the FLN administration and its local representatives.[24] In 1998, the land was, by official decree, restored to the family of the former *bach-agha*, Ben Aly Chérif, who had owned it as the war of independence broke out (Oulebsir 2004).[25] The opposition of some villagers, mainly from the 'old' families, to this restitution has been intense, but so far to no avail. Similarly, Ben Aly Chérif's former agricultural labourers have claimed rights to the land, thereby developing a conflicting notion of ownership as achieved through labour rather than historic precedent, which is potentially undermining village claims. Passions, in any case, run high on both sides, to the point where some of the claimants' lives have been threatened.

Although agriculture alone has never accounted for the economic survival of the village, and although a large part of the village lands have not been worked since the war of independence, notions that the village and its combined land-holdings constitute a 'moral space' (cf. Dresch 1986, 2007) whose protection is of concern to the village community as a whole thus remain fundamental to village identity. Property in land has always been and still is more significant than its mere economic yield, and the control of village lands by the village, much as the distribution of land among villagers, still has a strong symbolic significance.

Rhetorics of spatial disorder

In recent years, 'village politics' are said to have become increasingly complicated (although it might just be that the memories of former complications

---

[24] In 1963, all colonial properties were restructured as the *secteur autogéré* ('self-managed sector'), which by 1965 comprised 2,312,280 ha of arable land, accounting for 60% of national agricultural production. Legally, all domains and industries incorporated into the *secteur autogéré* were run by committees elected by the farm or factory workers (Stora 1994: 19). Locally, this period of 'self-management' is mainly remembered as the first establishment of the 'new elites' who had emerged during the war.

[25] *Bach-agha* was the highest rank in the French colonial administration given to an indigenous administrator.

have faded). These complications are frequently expressed in terms of spatial disorder and of the transgression of boundaries in any sense of the word. That is to say, they are expressed in terms of the re-negotiation of the dividing lines between 'ours' and 'theirs', the inside and the outside, the private and the public. A recurrent theme of conversation is the 'ugliness' of the village, and the lack of respect people show by building too high or too big and wherever it pleases them; the lack of water and the disappearance of the gardens due to excessive construction; and the lack of unity and security in the village, which should theoretically be a safe place:

> They burgled a house, a couple of days ago, they stole two large barrels of olive oil, all there was in the house, and the TV, and they took it all out over the roof, in broad daylight. That was in one of the houses on the outskirts of the village, but still, the neighbours should have seen what was happening. It never used to be like this, we never had thieves in the village. Today, nobody cares, everybody just thinks of himself. (Farid Yennat)

Fleeing the 'disorder' and the 'ugliness' of small spaces, people choose more and more to 'retire' from the village as far as they can. As was often pointed out to me by people from elsewhere, Ighil Oumsed is in fact remarkable for having preserved much of its original – at least spatial – coherence. Other villages in the valley, such as the neighbouring Ighil Nacer, have totally dissolved into independent settlements set up by individual families, and scattered all over their lands, leaving the old village behind, empty and in ruins. Nevertheless, I often heard comments in Ighil Oumsed about how nice it would be to live where it was easier to 'breathe', where you did not have to look at your neighbour's house, but where you could have a 'nice view'. This generally referred to a view of the forest, the mountains or the fields, and most certainly not the other houses of the village. The most recent constructions have followed this general mood: more and more houses are now built in areas consciously set apart from the village, which is described as dirty, smelly, disorganised and a source of constant annoyance:

> Actually, I don't really like the new house in *tibhert* [in the garden area] – if I could, I would like to live in *mender* [in the fields], far away from the village, in peace. That's where I like to be; the village is just full of nosy people who bother you and cause you trouble. (Fadila Yennat)

Although villagers describe the dispersion of village houses as a new development, some of the preserved ruins around the village and older villagers' memories of a more dispersed settlement bear witness to earlier moves away from the centre.[26] Some of these moves seem to have been seasonal, some definitive, as if the village population had always been torn between a centrifugal and a centralising tendency. This, however, does not stop villagers from worrying about the current trend, described as

---

[26] According to older villagers, it used to be common practice to have a secondary residence on one's fields, which could easily become a primary residence, if the owner felt like it. Ruins of such recent settlements can be found alongside older traces of settlement on village land, and several older villagers recall being born or having been brought up 'in the fields', before moving back to the village proper.

unprecedented and as symptomatic of – or conducive to – a profound change in the village community itself. This worry, justified or not, seems to indicate to villagers a general social malaise, reflected in what is generally perceived to be the increased difficulty of defining spatial boundaries.

This malaise becomes apparent in the conflict surrounding the establishment of the new village graveyard (cf. Scheele 2006a). The village graveyard is at the heart of village life: funerals are one of the rare occasions when all village men meet, and are obliged to meet. One of the principal functions of the *association sociale*, which has by now replaced the *tajmaɛt* or village council, is to punish absence at funerals with fines.[27] To be buried in the village graveyard is the ultimate sign of village-ness that emigrant or urbanised villagers conserve. Thus, the Parisian village committee, composed of emigrants from the village whose families have lived in Paris for up to three generations, has as its main purpose collecting funds to repatriate the bodies of those who die abroad. Villagers who have moved to more comfortable lodgings in the valley still bury their dead in the village, although recent attempts have been made to set up a graveyard near their houses. These attempts were heavily criticised by the social association in Ighil Oumsed: as the village faces dispersion on all levels, the village cemetery has come to seem its last bastion of unity.

Although in former times, as outlined above, Kabyle graves were marked by relatively short-lived heaps of stones brought along to the funeral one each by each villager, since independence, many graves have been constructed in concrete, copying a form that until then was the prerogative of saints (see Photo 3.1). As an immediate consequence of the changed mode of burial, graves now last much longer, and graveyards tend to become too small. In Ighil Oumsed, this state of affairs had become intolerable by the mid-1990s, and the only solution to the problem seemed to be to open a new graveyard. The village council duly decided on this, identified a suitable piece of land, acquired it from its owner in exchange for communal labour on her house, and went about planning the lay-out. It then stumbled over a series of less soluble problems: in which order would the dead be buried in a village that everybody agreed had changed so much? Might those relegated to the lower half of the old cemetery claim another, more privileged space? Who could decide on such matters, and how? The project of an additional cemetery was abandoned, and the local council decided to replace it by a football stadium, much against the will of some of the older villagers, and especially of the village representatives in Paris.[28]

In terms of the occupation of space, the dead have one major rival: the sons yet to be born. Fathers, or potential fathers, pride themselves on the construction of large villas, which, as everybody seems to agree, litter the

[27] For a similar emphasis on the participation of all villagers at funerals as a necessary means to maintain the village as a community in northern Spain, see Behar (1986).
[28] The choice of a football stadium was not as random as might appear at first sight. The success of village football teams in inter-village tournaments – and the local facilities to host such tournaments – are of considerable importance for the regional reputation and the self-esteem of villages in the area.

countryside. The vast majority of these villas are virtually empty, as most children prefer to move away, or to emigrate. Even if they stay in the village, they prefer to construct their own house to live in, if they have any means to do so. Although some extended households still exist, they now tend to be seen by the younger generation as a temporary solution, and certainly not as desirable. Young girls dream of marrying somebody who owns at least a flat, and are likely to refuse a marriage proposal on these grounds. This changed attitude, which might mainly be an expression of changed means (the difficulty of sharing a house with your parents-in-law is legendary), does not, however, change the prevailing style of architecture. The very sons who left their father's house as soon as they could mostly construct very large houses in their turn, reserving the first, second or even third floor for their sons yet to be born, who will probably also try to leave the father's house as soon as possible. Meanwhile, the largest houses in the village are constructed by emigrants, and often wait in vain for their occupants to arrive or to 'come back'.

At the same time, those of the younger generation who actually reside in the village and who do not have the means either to leave it or to set up their own house do not quite know where to put themselves. 'Public' space is still the monopoly of the older generation, and to appear in or dominate village space is a sign of importance and 'strength'. The spaces open to young people are thus very limited. This is so despite the fact that the '*jeunes*' by now largely outnumber the '*vieux*', as, due to restrictions on labour emigration to France, exponential population growth and increased unemployment over the last decades, there probably never have been and never will be again so many young people in the village.[29] In Ighil Oumsed, young men tend to spend their free time, which often amounts to most of the day, in places away from the central square: at the entries to the village when going towards the fields, on the small squares marking the entry to the different village quarters, or at *taxerubt*, the place of arrival and departure of the privately run mini-buses, whose drivers are usually younger brothers or cousins of their owners. One of the workshops on one side of *aslad* has been turned into a hall full of football-tables, and, especially in the evenings, is packed with young men. The same is true of a garage on *taxerubt* that, during Ramadan, was turned into a cinema with the help of a video projector borrowed from a cousin in Akbou. Apart from these few places, which are nowhere near large enough to accommodate everybody in the village, the places where young men can meet and do what they want are all outside the village, mainly in the various coffee houses or on the public squares in Akbou.

[29] Despite the large number of war dead and the exodus of almost a million settlers, the overall population of Algeria went up from 8.5 million in 1954 to 26.6 million in 1993 (Stora 1994: 49), at an annual rate of 3% during the 1970s, 2.12% during the 1980s, and 1.55% during the 1990s. In 2002, it had reached a total of 30.84 million (Economist Intelligence Unit 2002). The majority of Algerians (66% for the *wilâya* or department of Béjaïa where Ighil Oumsed is situated, Wilaya de Béjaïa 2000) are thus under thirty years of age. Nationwide, 27% of the active population are unemployed; in the *wilâya*, this percentage is as high as 37%.

The very definition of the category *'jeune'* (the French word is generally used even when speaking Kabyle) is relatively new, and variable, and owes much to the increased importance of schooling and university education. However, it is not restricted to students, and depends on the position the *jeune* has achieved in life rather than on his actual age. Due to the economic situation, the achievements that mark adulthood socially, such as financial independence, marriage and children, are increasingly difficult to attain; standards tend to rise and are more and more questioned by those who choose to opt out of a system they, on all levels, cannot and probably never will be able to afford. The group of *jeunes* thus grows even further, and can stretch to include men almost forty years old, who are still unmarried and maybe also unemployed. As unmarried men cannot set up or own a house, and cannot truly find their place among the male villagers who occupy most 'public' spaces, a feeling of not having one's own space in life – either in the village or in society as a whole – prevails among the younger generation, and is often used as a short-hand for their general, all-pervading frustration. From this point of view, the events of 2001 can partly be understood as an attempt by the *jeunes* to claim public space as their own.

Girls do not have their own space in the village. They are supposed to stay at home unless obliged to do otherwise, which usually means until they can get married and eventually run their own household. The fact that it is considered increasingly difficult for a woman to get married, because so many young men leave the village or cannot afford marriage, reduces this hope, or at least postpones it in many cases. The situation of girls in the village has changed dramatically over the last decades, however, leading to a changed appreciation of the boundaries between male and female spaces. Most girls now continue schooling after primary school. Several girls in the village now work until they get married, and leave the house by themselves to do so. Villagers' attitudes towards working women are ambivalent: on the one hand, they are seen as more educated and in a sense more valuable because they are working and because they know how to get by in the outside world; on the other hand, employment remains morally dubious, as it involves unmonitored contact with unrelated men, and girls who work are thus doubly careful not to challenge village norms. For the girls themselves, however, access to and knowledge of the outside world are clearly positive things to be proud of. The main differences they note among themselves tend to be expressed in terms of their possible movements: 'There are those who stay (*qqiment*: sit) at home, and those who go to school, and they have nothing in common – me, I stay at home' (Sonia Alilat).

Clothes are used to underline these differences: most girls in the village agree that the traditional, free-flowing Kabyle dress should be strictly reserved for inside the house and maybe the village, but should never be worn outside; proper outside garments should reproduce French fashion. This has had an impact on ideas about female beauty: while the 'traditional' beautiful woman tried to be round and would be compared to a partridge or a pear-shaped calabash, modern girls wear trousers and try to be as slim as the French stars seen on television. Girls who exclusively live 'inside' are thus associated with obesity and a lack of style; while 'modern' girls, dressed in tight jeans, slowly conquer village space, as they walk to the village public phone, and wait in large groups for minibuses to turn up in the public square on their way to work or school. The girls' changed attitude to 'public' space bears witness to the gradual changes that village space has undergone. It shows the various ways in which, through daily practices that imperceptibly challenge or erode village norms, it is redefined by villagers, and thereby becomes in itself an idiom for social change.

Space, within the limits of the village and beyond, is thus never neutral. In everyday conversation and practice, spatial representations and space itself are used as expressions of social order and historical continuity, but also as tools for profound social conflicts and changes, as if the notional rigidity of the categories employed verbally is a necessary precondition for their practical flexibility. Conflicts about the definition of space often become conflicts about larger issues: about the balance of power between various groups within the village, with or without reference to oppositions and allegiances that are at play in Algerian society at large; about the boundaries between the village and the outside world; about the legitimacy of certain villagers to establish and transgress these boundaries; about the capacity of the village as a community to establish and regulate its own moral space; and about the extension of this moral space in physical space and time. In the following chapter, I shall look at how this moral space was affected through the rapidly changing century of French colonial rule, and how villagers now relate to these changes.

4

The Theft of History

> A secret is a social relation, dividing those who know its content from those who do not, to whom it is imperceptible... People can only be let in on a secret; it does not by that token become common knowledge, even if, in the extreme case, everybody knows it: the secret is quite a different sort of knowledge to common knowledge or common sense. (Jenkins 1999: 225–6)

After my informants had decided that I had received sufficient geographical material about the village, there was a general consensus that I should now look into its history. However, opinions about what this 'history' might be, and more importantly, who would know it and have the right to speak about it, varied from villager to villager. Arezqi, for example, suggested trips to various neighbouring villages and towns, where he had fixed appointments with a large number of 'experts' on 'Berber history', most of whom had been to university, if possible in France. In the village itself, he maintained, nothing was to be found: 'We don't have any history, everything is oral, and most of it has already been lost, because our old people die.' Similarly, when I wanted to interview one of the village elders who, as many villagers had told me, had always 'pulled the strings' in the village, his brother tried to discourage me vehemently: 'Why would you want to speak to him? He is just a little shepherd, he has never been outside the village, he doesn't read or write, he can't even speak French: he doesn't know anything' (Méziane Ramdani).

This does not mean that villagers are not interested in history. On the contrary, history is seen as among the principal sources of all political, social and cultural legitimacy. Access to or even ownership of historical sources, always described in terms of the written word (the ominous and omnipresent 'papers'), necessitates and generates social and political influence. History is fundamental to many a villager's commitment to political or cultural causes, and any criticism of social hierarchies tends to be expressed in terms of the 'theft' or the 'falsification' of history (cf. Shryock 1997). History, however, is produced in the 'centres' of the world, and it is known to outsiders who generally keep it 'secret' or 'hidden' from villagers. Consequently, history is conspicuously absent locally: past local events do not constitute 'history', as they are known to insiders and should be hidden from outsiders (cf. Herzfeld 1987: 41–6; Dresch 2000).[1] My

---

[1] For more general works on the production of history in the Middle East and North Africa and the relationship between 'oral' traditions, the written word and the literary tradition of Islam, see Peters (1977); Davis (1989); Dresch (1989); Dakhlia (1990) and Anderson (1991).

search for local history thus became a contradiction in terms, as it was always said to be found where I was not. Many villagers clearly perceived this absence of history as the direct result of an unequal power relationship between the village and the history-producing world, or, on a lower level, between various groups of villagers themselves.

In actual fact the village has not only lived through its own history, but has also produced throughout the years its own historical sources, and its own category of village intellectuals who write, describe, re-arrange and memorise this history. These sources, French archival records and oral accounts allow us to reconstruct local history and its obvious gaps. They also allow us to analyse the role of local intellectuals and the changes and continuities in their position. To retrace village history therefore not only gives us an insight into the history of Algeria from a local point of view, but also helps us find an answer to the apparent paradox outlined above, namely, the general consensus among villagers that history is all-important at the same time as totally absent from the village itself.

The marabouts

Alongside the often repeated statement that local written sources do not exist, and that the area has thus in some way been deprived of its own past, another suspicion bordering on a conviction is frequently raised:

> It's the marabouts. They write, and then they keep it all to themselves. That's the difference between them and us. That's why they are more powerful than us. People say that there is a book about the history of the valley, a rare manuscript, that explains everything, and that used to be in Ben Aly Chérif's *zâwiya* – we could never get it, that's why we know so little about ourselves, they don't want to share their power – they are the ones who hide our history. (Arezqi Yennat)

Although the archives of the regional maraboutic families do indeed contain information on local social and economic history over the last two centuries, the above statement does not seem proportionate to the historical value of the actual content of the archives. Rather, it expresses the ambiguity that characterises the position of today's maraboutic families.[2]

In Ighil Oumsed, five of the fifty 'French' family names[3] correspond to

---

[2] The position of the marabouts as mediators between opposed segmentary groups in North Africa has famously been theorised by Gellner (1969). Although his theories are still widely used by North African writers themselves, the actual position of marabouts seems to have always been far more complex than Gellner indicated (see e.g. Hammoudi 1974). Much of their influence seems to have depended on their capacity to mediate between the village and the 'world' as represented by the scriptural tradition of Islam rather than on their neutral position within a segmentary system of which they were often an active part (cf. Eickelman 1977; Touati 1990; Filali 2002).

[3] In the village, all families have a 'Kabyle' name, used among villagers themselves, and a 'French', i.e. official, family name which dates from the first *état-civil* drawn up for rural Algeria from 1882 onwards, and completed for the *douar* Chellata in 1892 (held at the ACC). The French name is often based on a slight deformation of the Kabyle name, but not always; and families that are treated as separate by the *état-civil* might be seen as one family and be referred to by the same name in Kabyle.

maraboutic families. However, three of these are said to belong to different *iderma*, and to have 'converted' to become 'Kabyle'. Of the other two, one is represented only by an old lady, not married, who seems to have little more significance than as a counsellor to women who meet in her house. In opposition to the 'converted' families, she marks her distinction by never leaving the house with her hair or face uncovered. The remaining family, the Ouhaddar or *axxam* (the house of) Shaykh Tahar are the ones usually referred to as the village marabouts:

> It's just like the *tijmaɛtin*: we have several, but they are usually small and belong to one family, and then there is one *tajmaɛt* for everybody, that's the village *tajmaɛt*. It's the same for the marabouts: there are small ones who belong to one family, and then there is *axxam* Shaykh Tahar who are like the village *tajmaɛt*, their house is open, they don't belong to anybody. (Louisa Yennat)

Although most members of this family have left the village to live in Algiers, Béjaïa and Akbou, leaving behind only one old aunt and her unmarried daughter, their house still constitutes an important centre in its own right. It is still seen by most old ladies as a source of *baraka* (blessing, see Chapter 3), and women of all ages and of all families tend to meet there frequently. It also holds an important library containing about 70 bound volumes of eighteenth- and nineteenth-century manuscripts comprising about 200 different documents and a collection of letters, contracts and notes dating from the beginning of the twentieth century (see Appendix 1B, p. 152).

Although villagers had warned me that it would be impossible to gain access to this library, the younger members of the family were very keen to help me in my research. One of them had himself conducted some research into family history, and seemed happy to be helped out by a 'professional'. I first met him in his office in Béjaïa, where he lives and works as an independent accountant. When I asked him for information about his family, he insisted that we met instead in the family house in the village, where he and his younger brother Djamil organised an interview with their aunt and were present to make things easier for me. However, by the end of it, they dominated most of the talk, and the old lady acted mainly as proof of the authenticity of the knowledge they already had.

Their family history starts with the arrival of their great-great-grandfather, Shaykh Tahar, in the village, coming from a neighbouring tribe renowned for its urban origin and Islamic scholarship. His descendants affirm that he has known personally all the great men of his time, Si Mohand ou Lhocine, the poet-saint (or veritable 'prophet' of Kabyle-ness, according to Mammeri 1989); Shaykh al-Haddâd, local head of the Sufi brotherhood Rahmaniyya and one of the instigators of the 1871 insurrection; and the Kabyle 'national' poet Si Mohand ou Mohand (see Boulifa 1904). Shaykh Tahar was accepted into the village as imam; he married a maraboutic girl from a neighbouring village and, over the years, succeeded in accumulating a considerable amount of land, bought from villagers or given to him by individual villagers or the village community in exchange for his religious functions. According to some villagers and the family themselves, Shaykh Tahar's land was mainly worked by one or several *khammâs* (sharecroppers); according to others, it was cultivated through an annual *corvée* – as introduced by the French – imposed on the village. In any case, he is described as the archetypical representative of the Arabo-Islamic *ancien régime* as imagined today. His death coincided with the 1871 insurrection, which was to change radically the political and social institutions of the Soummam valley:

> There are few areas where the moral consequences of the 1871 insurrection were felt as strongly as in the tribes of the Akbou *cercle* [military district], where it caused a complete upheaval. Before the insurrection, the entire country was under the influence of the great indigenous religious and political leaders; furthermore, it was one of the areas where, due to its distance from the centre, the actions of the military command were of least consequence. The collapse of the indigenous authorities... followed by the harsh repression of the insurrection has broken the traditional alliances and have shown the French authorities to the tribes in a new light.[4]

There is little known about the generation of Shaykh Tahar's children. Si Mohand Améziane, his grandson, however, left behind his private papers and letters, and a reputation as a shrewd businessman with a strong personality. His papers date from 1910, when he was only twenty-two years old, to 1937. They contain several contracts about land sales in the village, drawn up in Arabic and following Islamic legal prescriptions. They are mainly concluded between other parties, with Mohand Améziane legalising the transaction. Certain documents, also in Arabic, note the amount and conditions under which money was lent by him or others to villagers.[5] They also contain a collection of letters in Arabic and French sent by emigrants and soldiers, which were directed to him but very often conveyed messages to others, as shown by this letter which was originally written in French:

> My dear friend Si Mohammed Améziane ben Shaykh Tahar. I let you know that I am well and [I hope] that the present [letter] will find you the same. Send my regards to Si Mohand Saïd, to Si Mohand ou El-Arbi, to Mansouri Amar, and all the friends old and young. All regards from the writer. If you need anything you only have to write. Regards to Hammoudi Tahar. Regards to Khebbache Saïd, to Adjedjou Belkacem, many regards to Arezki Ihamlalen, to Si Mohand Saïd Aït-Oujehoud. Your devoted friend Mansouri Tahar ben Mohammed, 3ᵉ Tirailleurs Algériens, 9ᵉ Compagnie in Saint-Ahras, 4 January 1910.

Mohand Améziane's personal folder also contains a collection of receipts from firms and large shops in Akbou and Béjaïa. One series of these indicates that he was placing money with the local Singer company over at least two years, and that he was planning, once the amount was sufficient, to invest in sewing machines and other mechanical equipment. He also

---

[4] *Rapport sur la situation matérielle, morale et politique des tribus du Cercle d'Akbou*, 10/08/1875, AOM 62K8.
[5] Although lending money against a payment of interest is illegal according to Islamic law, it has apparently always been common in Kabylia, and has led to great misery in many cases (see Hanoteau 1873). That the local marabout, the representative of Islamic law in the village, should participate in it is thus not surprising.

acted as an agent for other families, who were perhaps less familiar with writing or the French economic system. He kept a series of papers that document his contact with the French: an evaluation of taxes his family had to pay, and a permit to travel to Algiers in 1918. His folder also contains a considerable number of amulets based on quotes from the Qur'ân that were probably written at the request of villagers.

Much as his grandfather had been a mediator between the village and the world of Islam, Si Mohand Améziane had thus become the indispensable middleman between the still largely illiterate village population and the administrative system, whose importance for the life of every villager gradually increased. His documents give a picture of the multitude of models in play at any one time that had to be mastered by anybody who sought to achieve or maintain economic and social prevalence in the village. Economically at least, Mohand Améziane's eclecticism paid off. According to the French tax registers of the 1930s,[6] only two families in the village were taxed more than the Ouhaddar. The average income of families which paid taxes (just over half of those listed, the others were probably too poor to be considered for taxation) represents roughly half that of the Ouhaddar. The Ouhaddar, although neither the richest family in the village nor the only one to be rich, thus certainly belonged to the upper economic stratum of the village, thereby adding to their already established religious prestige.

Yet, from the 1930s onwards, this religious prestige was gradually eroded, as the first ideas about Islamic reformism spread in the Soummam valley (see Chapter 2). By 1951, the reformist movement had established eighteen well-attended schools in the Akbou region.[7] Throughout the area, many of the local maraboutic families came under pressure from competing reformist teachers who accused the marabouts of collaboration with the French, and criticised not only their religious practices but also their mode of subsistence and the offerings they accepted from villagers and pilgrims (Salhi 1999b). As the local administrator noted in the early 1950s:

> In the religious life of the Kabyles the reformist *ouléma* have supplanted marabouts and religious brotherhoods... Through the construction of their *médersas* [reformist schools] they have established solid bases everywhere, and they threaten the marabouts in a dangerous way, either by provoking among their followers an almost total disaffection, or by winning over the best among them.[8]

Like many maraboutic families in the area, the Ouhaddar family started to sell their land and to leave the village where they could; at the same time, they partly adapted to the 'new creed'. The teaching of Si Rabah, Mohand Améziane's son, increasingly took a different turn, following the reformist model, and a distinctively political orientation, as one of his former pupils remembers:

I remember, when we started to be militants, we noticed that we had to know

[6] *Tableau de Recensement, Commune mixte d'Akbou* 1912-1953, ACA.
[7] *Monographie de la commune mixte d'Akbou*, n.d., AOM Sidi Aïch//5, see map 5.1.
[8] Ibid.

how to read and write in order to pass on messages. That was also the party's [PPA] directive. In the evenings, we thus went to the mosque, Si Djamil's father was teaching us Arabic, but also a bit of history and geography. When he left – during the war [of independence] the French accused him of being a *maquisard*, and he was tortured – his cousin replaced him. Apparently he also wanted to join the *maquis*, but the local leader of the party told him to teach proper Arabic and religion; he said that that was as important as fighting. (Yahia Ihamlalen)

During the war of independence, Si Rabah and his family moved to Akbou, leaving his cousin behind to act as imam and, so far as was still possible, as teacher. He stayed in the village and remained childless until his death in the 1980s. Si Rabah was appointed imam in the nearest city of Béjaïa, in a mosque known for its reformist connections.

Si Rabah's youngest son, Djamil, was brought up in Béjaïa, but has now moved back to Akbou and has opened a surgery just down the road from Ighil Oumsed. Although most villagers have adopted him as the 'village doctor', their attitude to him and his family remains ambivalent. As former large landowners, they were often described to me as representatives of 'feudalism'; as successful investors in capitalist enterprises, they are suspected of too much involvement with the French and their local representatives; as retainers of the traditional monopoly of the written word in the village, they are, as seen above, accused of having 'stolen' its history; as representatives of Islam, they are held responsible for village 'superstition' and ignorance, and for the suppression of its Berber culture. They were also often accused of connections with the Ben Aly Chérif family, the leading maraboutic family in the area which provided the local *bach-agha*, and which has locally come to represent French rule more than the French themselves.[9] By now, like many other maraboutic families in the valley – a relatively high percentage of doctors, lawyers and academics in the area are of maraboutic origin – the Ouhaddar have managed to 'convert' to more modern sources of influence. This further adds to the ambiguity of their status, and that of intellectuals as a group, who, despite being admired, tend to be seen as somehow forcibly 'corrupted' by their origin or even just by their 'privileged' position.

Aware of these criticisms, and of their difficult position within village society, the Ouhaddar take care to stress their involvement in Berber and nationalist history, by underlining Shaykh Tahar's personal acquaintance with various Berber heroes, as described above. At the same time, they emphasise the 'scientific' and 'Berber' aspect of their manuscript collection:

Shaykh Tahar was a great *'âlim*, everybody agrees: he knew a lot of things, not just religion, but also science, medicine, everything – you'll see that in the library. There is also a poem in Berber, I think. (Djamil Ouhaddar)

[9] Si Rabah – alongside several other villagers – had signed a document after the war of independence that confirmed Ben Aly Chérif's nationalist commitment during the war, and that allegedly helped the family to regain their land in 1998. This, however, does not account for all suspicions against the Ouhaddar family, which seem to stem rather from a wholesale rejection of maraboutic institutions.

The Ouhaddar are not alone in these attempts to revalorise the maraboutic heritage in the region by explicitly associating it with Berber history and sciences: similar efforts have been made by other maraboutic families and by a group of academics teaching at the university of Béjaïa (Scheele 2007a; cf. Aïssani and Mechehed 1998, Aïssani 2002; and see Chapter 5). However, so far, these attempts have had little impact on popular perception of local marabouts and of the intellectual tradition they represent. Thus, Arezqi was in a sense right in affirming that there is no local history in Kabylia, as 'maraboutic history', the only written history that exists outside French archival documents, is generally seen as either 'feudal' or 'alienating': in either case, as objectionable, external and inauthentic. Written history thereby tends to be perceived as an instrument of power rather than as a means of information, a power that hinges on the possession of or access to the written word. This perception, as I shall argue in the following sections, still tinges contemporary notions of history.

Local revolutions

One central tenet of the 'Kabyle myth', as outlined in Chapter 1, is the egalitarianism of Kabyle society. Yet, as every villager knows, there are important social and economic differences within the village. In many cases, these differences tend to be blamed on outside interference, as described in the preceding section. In other cases, history, read as a moral tale of 'right' and 'wrong' choices and their inevitable consequences, is used to explain contemporary inequalities, although direct historic causality is in actual fact often difficult to establish. Thus, several of the 'old' families are said to have been pre-eminent 'in former times' – zik, usually used to mean 'before the war (of independence)' – and to have lost their fortune during the war, having chosen the wrong camp during the colonial period; while others have succeeded in maintaining their position of influence, and yet others – from the 'new' families – have increased it through their support for the nationalist cause.

The most frequently quoted examples of these different historic destinies are the Imessaouden and the Ihamlalen families,[10] which are both part of the same adrum, the Aït Boudjmaa, but whose respective positions in the village vary widely: while most members of the Imessaouden family, tacitly accused of collaboration with the French, have by now left the village, the Ihamalalen seem to be its largest and most influential family, counting many members among the famille révolutionnaire. However, on closer inspection, neither of the two families ever seemed to have had what might be called a coherent 'strategy' during colonial times, and both maintained a

---

[10] 'Family' here means everybody with the same French or Kabyle surname, comprising anything between one and twenty households, and referred to in Kabyle by the French term famille, or, much more frequently, by the plural of the family name without any further specifications.

clearly ambivalent relationship with the French. Consequently, their differences seem to be rather of an economic nature. Whereas the Imessaouden concentrated on the accumulation of land, the Ihamlalen invested in small-scale industry and emigration to France. Despite contemporary attempts to transform local history into a moral tale of revolution, the history of the village is thus best presented as a series of more or less successful 'arrangements' with the colonial *status quo*.

The Imessaouden figure, in the French tax lists as much as in village memories, as the wealthiest of all the families.[11] They also provided the first *cheikh* (village leader under the military administration of the *Bureaux arabes*) that I could find a trace of in the archives. He was appointed in the early 1870s. To judge by the reports written by the *Bureaux arabes* and by the rarity of fines he collected, he seems to have kept a low profile:

> Marks of indigenous chiefs: (1874) Illoula... Mohamed Imessaouden, independent *cheikh*, fulfilled well his duties... nice man, to be handled carefully, serves well ... (1875) good *cheikh*, nice man, to be kept ... (1876) elderly man, renowned to be honest. Good *cheikh*. His administration does not cause any kind of complaint.[12]

Mohamed Imessaouden stayed in office until the end of military rule, in 1880, when the village passed under the direct administration of the local *caïd* and *bach-agha*, Ben Aly Chérif. From then on, the local representative in the village, now called the *mezaouar*, changed more often. The position remained largely within the 'old families', however, or with people from other villages placed there by the *caïd*.

By then, the economic situation in the Soummam valley was changing fast. The large fines imposed on tribes of the area after the 1871 insurrection had led to new dependencies, to the emergence or aggravation of social divisions, and to the general impoverishment of the area:

> Before the insurrection, the tribes of the [Akbou] *cercle* were among the rich tribes of Algeria. The insurrection and its effects have noticeably changed this situation of prosperity. The Akbou *cercle* has paid two and a half million [francs] of war contribution, and a considerable amount of land has been given up to colonisation... Usurers have speculated on the *indigènes'* obligation to settle immediately, and have made them sign costly agreements, which means that they paid in actual fact much more than the sums indicated above... Today, they still have to settle accounts, and bailiffs seized various properties of bankrupt debtors.[13]

Although within village society these differences never seemed to be totally fixed, and poverty always constituted a threat even to the wealthier families, the difference in taxes paid between the wealthier and the less

---

[11] *Tableau de Recensement, Commune mixte d'Akbou* 1912-1953, ACA.
[12] *Notes du personnel indigène. Cercle d'Akbou* 1874-76, AOM 62K2.
[13] *Rapport sur la situation matérielle, morale et politique des tribus du cercle d'Akbou*, 10/08/1875, AOM 62K8. 9,915 ha, i.e. two-thirds of the total tribal land of 14,872 ha were sequestered, of which 2,150 ha (almost 15%) were declared land reserved for colonisation. In order to regain their sequestered land, the tribe as a whole paid 400,000 francs (ca £950,000 in terms of buying power in 2004, INSEE 2005) (*Rapports annuels du cercle d'Akbou*, 1873-1879, AOM 62K8, 70K7).

wealthy families grew steadily,[14] and the Imessaouden succeeded in maintaining their leading position. Although sources of income were gradually diversified, surplus still tended to be invested in land; first of all, in order to buy back the land lost in the expropriations of the 1870s, but gradually also to include plots that had never belonged to the family, and indeed not even to the village.

Thus, in 1924, several villagers grouped together to buy an important piece of land from the local *bach-agha* Ben Aly Chérif:

> A property called Helouane or Allouane, located in the territory of the village Ighil ou M'ced... an area of about six hectares of which a part is agricultural, the other part scrub co-planted with some olive trees;... and a rural property located in the territory of Ighzer Amokrane... known as the farm of St Julien or Carldom, an area of about ninety-one hectares and eighteen *ares*... the constructions on this property consist of a simple ground-floor residential house and several indigenous shacks.[15]

Most of the land bought is thus clearly identified as colonial property, located in Ighzer Amokrane, which means that it originally belonged to the territory of the Ouzellaguen rather than the Illoula Ousammeur. Listed in the property document are 71 buyers, all from Ighil Oumsed. Five villagers, Ouhaddar Mohand (Améziane), Aissat Arab, Oumansour Tahar, Imessaouden Amar and Imessaouden Tahar, acted as their spokesmen. Despite the large number of buyers, the land was not shared out equally, and a clear division between the various families in the village becomes apparent: the largest buyers generally belonged to the 'old families', the Imessaouden in their lead (see Appendix 1C, p. 154). Yet, among the largest buyers can also be found families like the Ihamlalen who seem to have made their initial fortune through emigration (Appendix 1D, p. 155). The latter also seem to have been the first to invest in small-scale industries, mainly modern oil-presses and flourmills. Although families like the Imessaouden quickly followed their lead, the Ihamlalen maintained a leading position both in emigration and industry until the 1970s. Today, however, their mills have closed down and the only functioning oil-press in the village is run by the Khalil family, one of the 'new' families whose father is a renowned *mujâhid*.

By the time the first nationalist currents emerged in the Soummam valley, the economic situation in the village had thus already been transformed in response to the economic changes brought about by French rule. Furthermore, although the various political currents of the time now tend to be seen as opposed to each other and as mutually exclusive, the distinc-

[14] This tendency was not confined to Ighil Oumsed. In 1937, the administrator of the *commune mixte d'Akbou* estimates the distribution of the total annual income among the inhabitants of the *commune mixte* as follows: out of a total of 13,049 families, 456 (3.6%) are very rich, earning more than 6,000 F (roughly £2,000 in terms of buying power in 2004) per year; 807 (6.44%) are rich, earning between 5,000 F and 6,000 F per year; 2,295 (16.4%) are of 'middle condition', earning between 2,000 F and 4,000 F per year; 4,366 (35%) are poor, earning 1,000 F to 2,000 F per year; 4,951 (39%) are very poor, earning less than 1,000 F (ca £300) per year (*Enquête alimentaire*, 25/04/1937, AOM Akbou).
[15] *Contrat de vente*, 14/08/1924, CDC.

tions between the reformist movement, the various nationalist movements and local 'notables' were often blurred, and almost all village families seemed to have had their fair share in all currents (cf. Salhi 1999a: 24). In the village as on the regional level, competing national movements were often represented by the same person, or by members of the same family, and it seems that any one nationalist activity could be combined with any other, and often even with involvement in the French administration. As the administrator of the *commune mixte d'Akbou* observed in 1945, the first nationalist groups contained

> sometimes even members of the *grandes familles* who are traditionally friends of France..., a number of smaller dignitaries of maraboutic origin, whose families only play a reduced part in the Kabyle villages rally today to the [federalist] *Manifeste* movement as they are trying to gain influence. The young people of these families, especially if they have had some education ... tend to be the local leaders of the *Manifeste* party ... [Radically nationalist] Messalists [members of the PPA] and *ouléma* are active in the party of the *Manifeste* as the most determined leading agents.[16]

Thus, more than by carefully thought out strategies, villagers seem to have been motivated in their political and economic choices by practical considerations, and by an underlying perception of injustice. *Post facto* rationalisations appear mainly as comments on the contemporary situation, and thereby become a moral justification of the *status quo* and its obvious inequalities. This becomes especially clear when investigating the local history of the first Algerian nationalist party, the *Parti du peuple algérien* (PPA).

Traitors or heroes?

In April 1947, Messali Hadj, the leader of the PPA and the first Algerian nationalist icon, came to Akbou and the neighbouring town Tazmalt. His visit was a triumph:

> From this day onwards, it can be said that the larger part of the population, made receptive by these demonstrations, has been convinced by the propaganda of the PPA and supports it... Tazmalt has become the centre of nationalist activity in the area.[17]

News of his visit, alongside various nationalist ideas, made its way up the mountains, even to the more 'remote' villages of the mountains around Ighil Oumsed:

> The first time that I heard about Messali Hadj? That was in the village, I was still very young, when he came to Akbou. Some men in the village had seen him, they were laughing when they came back, and they said: 'there is a man who came. He said that the French will have to leave, but how will he make them leave? He thinks he can sweep them out with his beard, like this, as if there was anything that could just sweep out the French!' I went home and I told my father what I had heard, because I thought it was very funny and I wanted to know

[16] *Notes politiques sur la situation de la Kabylie*, 15/04/1945, AOM 93/20033.
[17] *Monographie de la Commune Mixte d'Akbou*, n.d., AOM Sidi Aïch//5.

who this man was. My father was afraid, and he told me never to mention that man again, that all this was very dangerous. Obviously, that made me even more curious. (Saïd Bensghir, now regional party leader of the PPA)

Even before then, nationalist ideas had not been totally unfamiliar to most villagers. Emigrants who had been active within the PPA or other political parties in France had been promoting them on their return to their village ever since the late 1930s:

> I started to work for the party in 1945, when I was still very young. There was somebody from the village, Belkacem Aït Ouali, who had come back from France. He told us about Messali and the PPA, and he said that the French have to leave. He set up groups in the village. We were maybe fourteen or fifteen militants at that time. Everybody was roughly my age, fifteen or sixteen… We would meet in the fields, never in the village, and we would discuss, and we would make weapons out of bits of old bombs left over from the Second World War that were lying around in the fields.[18] Arezqi's father was very good at that; we would meet in his shed in *mender*. We would also sing and learn how to read and write in Arabic. (Yahia Ihamlalen)

The influence of the PPA on the village grew over the following decades, as more and more activists – almost exclusively young and with no direct family responsibilities – joined. As in the valley, involvements of a single family with different nationally competing groups were common.

After the war of independence was declared by the FLN in 1954, all members of the PPA[19] were asked to join the FLN. Those who refused were declared by the FLN to be traitors to the national cause, and were violently persecuted (see Chapter 2). The monthly reports of the administrator of the *commune mixte d'Akbou* overflow with gruesome references to the 'settling of scores' between the two parties, especially in 1956.[20] In Ighil Oumsed, six out of the ten activists quoted by Yahia 'converted' to the FLN. The other four fled to France where they were to spend most of their lives. Although some members of the PPA returned to Algeria after the war, their position within their home villages had changed radically:

> After the war, we kept our heads down – for most people in the village, we were traitors. We did not go back to the village. I settled down in Akbou some time later, and once I got there, I kept quiet, out of fear. Now, since 1989, things are slowly, slowly changing. (Saïd Bensghir)

Of the four known PPA activists from Ighil Oumsed, two returned definitively to the village as late as the 1980s, twenty years after the end of the war. The third surviving PPA member still spends his life between his house in the village and Paris.

Soon after my arrival in the village, one of the young villagers, Ahsène Ramdani, son of a known PPA activist, showed me his collection of photos

---

[18] The Soummam valley was bombed first by the Germans and then by the allied forces during their landing in Algeria in September 1942.

[19] Although the PPA changed its name to the MNA (*Mouvement national algérien*) in 1955, villagers and former militants tend to refer to it as 'PPA', as if to bracket out its more recent history and its bad reputation of having collaborated with the French during the war. In what follows I shall do the same for the sake of simplicity.

[20] *Rapports mensuels de la commune mixte d'Akbou*, AOM 93/4332.

of *mujāhidīn* from the village. As I was discussing these photos with a group of young men from the village, questions quickly arose over whether the PPA activists depicted in some of the photos should be considered as *mujāhidīn* or not. These questions still play an important role in village society. Even now, official rhetoric defines former PPA militants as 'traitors', and former PPA members have no rights to claim pensions or any other kind of moral, political, financial or social benefits such as those enjoyed by their former comrades who joined the FLN. In the village, PPA families thus often express the feeling of having been cheated of the results of their struggle:

> Arezqi's father was making weapons, long before the war even started, and today: nothing, nobody ever says that he was a *mujāhid*; we are still poor; nobody ever gave me anything. Can you see now how there is no justice? At the same time, some people, who never did anything, who joined right at the end, they now live like kings! (Louisa Yennat)

I suddenly understood Arezqi's insistence, without ever mentioning his father's political activities, that I speak to the still surviving members of the PPA in the village: better to hear it from first-hand witnesses.

I also started to understand some of the new meaning the PPA was invested with in the village context. Not unlike Berberism, it stood for the recovery of a long-lost position through the recovery of a 'lost' or rather 'denied' part of local history. This history is now forcefully put forward by the returning exiles, who during their years abroad had been able to secure a material well-being impossible for anyone who stayed in the village. Backed by their material influence, but also by the tentative political liberalisation of the late 1980s and the relative freedom of speech it entailed (see Chapter 2), these former exiles now ask to be written back into national history.[21] They were very keen to speak to me, as they are aware of the importance of foreign researchers: it is only thanks to Benjamin Stora's (1986) book on Messali Hadj, which was often quoted to me as a reference, and lent to me on several occasions by villagers, that they have come to 'exist' within world history.[22]

The PPA's claims for recognition are well received by other villagers who feel they have in one way or another been 'cheated' by the 'system', and they are often identified as part of larger regional demands for justice and historical truth. They are also popular among the younger generation, who have lost trust in the 'official history' taught in school:

> They never teach us anything about our history. You can even compare the history books they give us in school: the dates and numbers they quote are never

---

[21] This is not only the case in the village, but throughout Algeria. Recently, the PPA has resumed a more public role in Algerian politics, and put forward claims that its role in Algerian history be formally acknowledged. As a first official sign of recognition, the new airport at Tlemcen has been named after the leader of the PPA, Messali Hadj.

[22] Immediately after my arrival in Algeria, the current president of the party, who was based in Lille (northern France), had been informed by local militants of my presence in the Soummam valley and of my interest in the PPA. He had even told them to 'look after me' and give me any food or money that I might need to conduct my research, and he agreed without much suspicion to talk to me and introduced me to several other militants, all resident in Lille.

the same. I always got into trouble, because I would disagree with my history teacher. At home, I would speak with my father about these things, so I knew a lot, and in school, I would just state the facts, only the facts. My teacher always told me to shut up. That's why we have so many problems now, because we don't know our own history... That doesn't mean that you should always believe what the PPA say – they are politicians just like the others. But we should have the right to know both sides, don't you think? (Yamina Khebbache, 23-year-old daughter of a PPA activist)

Similarly, one young and freshly recruited member of the PPA described his motivations for joining as follows:

Since school, I have been active in a lot of groups. For example, I was interested in Berber questions as soon as people started to talk about them. Since the beginning of the 1990s, when it became possible to found associations, I was always active. For example, I was a member of an association in Akbou. It's a shame it doesn't exist anymore, it could have helped you with your work: we organised an exhibition about the history of our region, because this history has always been hidden from us. We were talking about Berbers and Romans and so on. Then I discovered the PPA, I didn't think it still existed. I talked a lot with the old members, the first to fight for our country, and they convinced me: we had always been told lies about them, and they have some really important ideas. They did not change camps, despite everything, and they sacrificed themselves for their ideas – that means that they have a true political history, and that's what we need at the moment. (Saïd Lahdir, a young militant of the PPA)

When I asked him about family links with first-generation militants of the PPA, Lahdir laughed: 'No, actually, not at all: my father is one of the great *mujâhidîn* in the area, maybe you know him – everybody knows him'. Indeed, I did know him, having been quickly introduced to him at the ceremony organised to commemorate the anniversary of the beginning of the war of independence in Akbou. I remember a rather small man tripled in size by his burnous and his importance, who was visibly part of the 'select few', the very bastion of local FLN legitimacy. It was not surprising, I thought, that his son had chosen the only way to question the over-whelming presence of his father by questioning its very source of legitima-cy – while Lahdir added: 'But at the same time, my uncle has always been PPA, he was also one of the great men in the area, but on the other side – but I only learned that later on'.

For the younger generation, the PPA has thus, at least notionally, joined the ranks of the ancient Berbers as publicly declared 'victims' of the official history produced by the FLN, which has long denied them their recognition as the only true 'founding fathers' both of the contemporary Berber community and of the independent Algerian nation-state. In this reading, any potential change in contemporary Algeria is conditional on the prior public acknowledgement of 'historical truth and justice', and the moral flaws of the 'system' are blamed on this lack of historical truthfulness.[23] The 'historical truth' thus to be established, however, is pre-determined. Like the

---

[23] Similar claims have repeatedly been made by the Algerian Islamist parties (cf. al-Ahnaf et al. 1991).

'official' history of the FLN, it is a moral and political statement about the present, whose main aim is to legitimise or to question existing power-relationships. In other words, it is a history that creates new heroes, but that does not question the notion of heroism as such. The 'official heroes' thus attacked are slow to react, partly because, as the following section shows, they are strangely elusive.

The unknown *shuhadâ*

Despite the early commitment to nationalism in the area, the war itself, launched on 1 November 1954, took several months to declare itself properly in the Soummam valley. Judging by French reports, in March and April 1955, the situation was still 'calm'.[24] This was soon to change, and five months later, in September 1955, all indigenous administrators and other officials resigned their posts, for fear of being killed by the FLN. After some hesitation, the *bach-agha* Ben Aly Chérif and his family left the country one by one for Tunis, leaving everybody including the FLN and the French administration in doubt as to their true allegiances. By October 1955, the FLN had succeeded in supplanting the French administration outside the towns:

> The Algerian Muslims are now convinced ... that they will gain their independence ... and those whose private feelings still appear to make them tend towards our side are swept away in the wake of the rebellion by their instinct for self-preservation and the desire to protect their material interests ... While more and more of these people consciously avoid the influence of our institutions and the control of our administration, I have heard from a very reliable source that the local leader of the rebels [FLN], Mira Abderrahmane, makes people and notables who seek a meeting wait for more than a week ... All the *douars* located in the surroundings of Akbou are totally devoted to him. Through persuasion and terror, he has imposed himself on the rural masses who have always been very receptive to the prestige of strength. He rules like a despot.[25]

This is corroborated by villagers' memories of the way the village was administered at the time:

> During the war, we didn't have a *tajmaɛt* [village council], mainly because most village men had gone away. We were still sorting out our problems at village level, but the *amγar* [leading village elder] had been replaced by the FLN *chef*

---

[24] *Rapport mensuel de la commune mixte d'Akbou*, 20/03 to 20/04/1955, AOM 93/4332. In his journal, Mouloud Feraoun (1962: 22-3) described the beginning of the war of independence as seen from Kabylia as follows: 'December 4th, 1955. An insidious fear had crept in everywhere. Almost imperceptibly. People kept calm, but they knew that the threat of the *gendarme* was weighing down on them, that it was hanging over the villages and sometimes took shape ... The village filled with cries and mysterious sounds ... We did not manage to recognise these sounds. In the distance, they were the humming of engines: lorries, jeeps, motorbikes, planes? Nearby, the sound of steps, rustling noises, rolling stones. Somebody suddenly knocks on my door, somebody is turning the door-handle, somebody is whispering ... Somebody is taken away ... When I ask them ... who of our fellow countrymen had thus been taken away, they admit that it didn't exactly happen here, but in the neighbouring village.'

[25] *Rapport mensuel de la commune mixte d'Akbou*, 20/10 to 20/11/1955, AOM 93/4332.

nizâm,[26] the FLN were making the laws and judging village matters. Here in Ighil Oumsed, the *chef nizâm* was always somebody from the village, but he changed very often, because the French would catch him. (Larbi Mouhoubi)

As the FLN took over the area, the number of men from Ighil Oumsed who left the village to join the *maquis* (guerrilla camps) grew rapidly.[27] Taking into account the large number of emigrants to France, estimated at 40% of the adult male population in 1952, this meant that more than two-thirds of all the men were absent from the village for almost a decade. Adding also the considerable number enrolled in the French army, who were stationed in the towns in the valley or elsewhere in Algeria, suggests that the village was virtually emptied of its male population:

> You want to know where the men were? That's very simple: there weren't any! They were either away in France, or in the *maquis*, or in the [French] army, or old, or dead. During the whole war, only women and children stayed in the village, and as soon as one of the children was old enough, he tried to run away to the *maquis* before he was caught by the French and made a *harki* [French auxiliary], which was even worse than the *maquis*. (Mohand Akli Bouhamza)

The reasons for joining the FLN seem as diverse as those for joining the PPA, if not more so. They are now difficult to discern, as they are frequently absorbed by general reflections on patriotic duty, or seem morally so obligatory as to be obvious. The *maquis* often contained 'deserters' or people otherwise wanted by the police, as well as idealists, and in general those who had nothing to lose, whose number had been constantly on the increase, especially since the economic crises of the 1930s and 1940s. They were almost all very young, and the choice to join was not always theirs:

> This photo, that's the youngest brother, Ali. He went to the *maquis* in 1959, he had just turned sixteen, but as you can see in the photo, he was big and strong. His older brother, who was already in the *maquis*, came to fetch him to protect him against the French, who forced everybody else to enrol as a *harki*. Ali married quickly, and then he left. He died before his older brother did, in 1960. (Larbi Oumansour)

The French army responded to the military and social influence the FLN had achieved by the end of 1955 in the Soummam valley by declaring vast parts of it *'zones interdites'*, or 'forbidden areas' where anybody present could be shot without warning, in the hope that this would cut off the local supplies of the guerrillas. Most villages in the area were bombed to the

---

[26] According to a French army appraisal, the *chef nizâm* was one of the three FLN representatives at village level or else in the smallest administrative unit established by the FLN (the *douar*), alongside the *chef ravitailleur* in charge of food and arms supplies and the *chef terroriste* in charge of applying FLN directives to the village population (Grande Kabylie Est, *Zones d'implantation rebelles*, AAF 1H1684 D2). Apart from the last, these terms have found their way into everyday use, as they were based on terms used by the FLN themselves (Guentari 1990: 162).

[27] All in all, roughly 80 names figure as *shuhadâ'* or 'martyrs' on the official list of villagers who died while fighting during the war. Set against the whole village population of 1,243 three years earlier (*Monographie de la commune mixte d'Akbou*, 31/12/1952 AOM 93/20033), this amounts to a third or a quarter of all adult men in the village. Most victims died in often unknown circumstances outside the village or its immediate surroundings, and their remains – if they were found – were returned to the village after the war.

ground. As one of the larger villages, Ighil Oumsed escaped destruction, a military post was constructed next to it, and many refugees from the neighbouring village Ibouzidène (Ouzellaguen) – long linked to Ighil Oumsed through marriage alliances – waited the war out in the village. Reading through the French military reports of the time, the village appears in general as very safe, and images of *tricolore*-waving children seem more frequent than those of 'terrorist' threats.[28] The commander even mentions Ighil Oumsed as the only village that could still provide efficient social organisation in the area.[29] On anything but a superficial level, however, the overall situation remained ambiguous:

> In such-and-such a village which was recently still occupied by the rebels, the children greet the authorities with the rebel military salute, and the primary school teacher is proud to make his pupils sing an Arabic song for his visitors, which, once looked at more closely, turns out to be the song of the rebellion.... The population feels Kabyle and Muslim, which is apparently incompatible with France.[30]

Right from my first encounters in the village, I was introduced to uncles, aunts, grandparents and cousins who had been involved in the war, often, as I realised later, by people of lower status within the village, or whose families' commitment to the nationalist cause was doubtful. These visits frequently drew on family links that would otherwise not have been mentioned; they were without exception highly embarrassing. The relatives I was introduced to did not show any desire to talk about the war, or even to be reminded of it in any way. In reaction to our questions, they either just left the room with some mumbled excuse, or answered reluctantly. Thus, when an old lady was coaxed into talking to me by her favourite maternal grandson:

> - Tell us about your memories, Yaya [grandmother], about the war, how the French made you suffer...
> - I don't have time.
> - Please, Yaya, we will record you, like this everybody will know what has happened.
> - What's the use of that? I don't have time. (Djamel Benhamidouche and Nana Hadid)

Seeing that Djamel would not give up, his grandmother finally gave in, but still very unwillingly:

> I only remember the *maquisards* from when they came to our house, I was still very young, I saw them at night and I was told not to tell anybody. And the explosion of the cave where they all died, Ali, Larbi, everybody. I don't have anything to say. The French came and beat us and took everybody away.

With a total lack of sensitivity, Djamel interrupted keenly:

> They tortured you, didn't they? Tell us how they tortured you!

[28] ANA SAS Ighil Oumsed.
[29] AAF 1H1684 D2.
[30] *Rapport trimestriel de la commune mixte d'Akbou*, first quarter 1960, AOM 93/4332.

But his grandmother, for whom the war was not associated with heroism of any kind, but with personal suffering, carried on:

> They married me off, I ran away, they married me off again, my husband locked me up in this house for ten years, and when I came out, everybody said: 'where is your beauty gone?' I was very beautiful before the war. Afterwards, you wouldn't even recognize me... My youngest son died playing with a bomb that was left over from the war, he was twelve years old. That wasn't long ago. Nothing but the war.

Ahsène Ramdani, the photo-collector mentioned above, happily let me take a copy of his collection of photos of *mujâhidîn* from the village (see Photo 4.1 for an example). I wanted to show them to different families and people of different ages and orientations, to see who remembered whom, and in general what kind of reaction they would cause. Yet, nobody, whether old or young, and not even those who had lived through the war and voluntarily told very general stories about it, or those who defined themselves as belonging to the 'revolutionary family', could actually recognise any of the young men in the photos, apart from one or two that everybody knew. Those who were identified were usually recognised by their photo rather than by the person depicted in it, because the photo was displayed in somebody else's living room, as a constant reminder of the family's position in history.

The only general reaction I evoked was surprise that I had managed to get all these photos, and a warning that I might get into trouble at the border if I tried to take them out of the country:

> They don't like it, it's illegal, they are afraid of it. It's better to forget the young people like this who died in the war. If you keep the photos, they'll stop you at the border, for sure. (Karim Yennat)

This was the first time that anybody had ever warned me in this way, although I had often felt that I might get into trouble leaving the country with the interviews I had taped with old and new opponents to the government, and the photos I had taken of monuments, political events and the like. I did not get stopped at the border, despite the photos. Karim was right, however, in that nobody seemed to want to be reminded of the individual histories that lie beneath the general and continuing glorification of 'the war', which, despite the growing criticism of the FLN, remains the one and only unquestioned and unquestionable source of legitimacy, in the village as much as elsewhere. This lack of individual histories associated with the war also becomes obvious when looking at the graveyards of the *shuhadâ* or war dead, the most common form of war monument in the country: although these monuments are composed of individual and labelled tombs (in contravention of 'traditional' funerary practices, see above), their lay-out and shape are all the same, and the names on the tombs have often long been erased (Photo 4.2, see Scheele 2006a, 2007b).

If the heroes of the war of independence have forfeited all individual traits in favour of a morally predetermined history, their ugly twin-brothers,

Photo 4.1 *Mujâhidîn* from the village in the late 1950s (photographer unknown)

Photo 4.2 Graveyard of the *shuhadâ*, martyrs of the war of independence

the *harkis*, are even more elusive. Although, as an abstract category, the *harki*, the personification of treason and all things evil, is crucial to popular imagination, politics and moral judgements, any precise and personal information about individual and locally known *harkis* seems dangerous, if not impossible, to obtain. The only person who consented to giving me any concrete information about village *harkis* was a retired emigrant, living in Paris, who, despite constant assurance to the contrary, seemed certain never to move back to the village. In Algeria, only people from outside the village would mention village *harkis* to me, less to help me in my research than to accuse the village as a whole of moral failure. Thus, one employee in the town hall of Chellata, who was not from Ighil Oumsed, suggested with a big grin that I should consult the 1950s death register for the village: 'Then you will know who "died for France", you will know all the traitors in the village – you'll see, there are a lot of them, and they hide it well!' Similarly, when I interviewed Mohand Akli Bouhamza, who as a child came to Ighil Oumsed as a war refugee, in Arezqi's presence and with a running tape recorder, he could not resist spicing up his story with casual references to *harkis* from Arezqi's family. Listening to the two of them, I felt that I was watching a game with potentially dangerous side-effects rather than an attempt at historical reconstruction.

In today's village, both the ideal *shahîd* and the ideal *harki* still serve as explanatory models for contemporary political and social events. Individual histories of the war, however, have been forgotten, or standardised beyond recognition. Both the *shahîd* and the *harki* have thereby been turned into empty categories that can be filled in order to make sense of and explain the present with reference to a past that, although it is styled as immutable and almost mythical, is thus in actual fact very adaptable. Yet, these categories impose their own logic on those who use them: although criticism of post-war politics and even of FLN strategy during the war is constantly reiterated, the absolute moral value of these categories is seldom questioned, leaving little room for the ambiguity of lived history (cf. Scheele 2006b). In a sense, yet again, 'history', with all its grey areas, has thus clearly been 'stolen' from the local village community. As the mayor of Chellata, himself son of a *shahîd*, put it to my great surprise, after having called me up to his office:

> You know, this war, we should never have fought it: that's where all our problems come from. Everybody knows that in actual fact we gained independence through politics, not fighting, and that we would have become independent anyway. Because of this war, we are fifty years behind.

The aftermath of war

A ceasefire was proclaimed in 1961, and independence from France came one year later. The first months of independence were marked by political uncertainties, on the national as much as on the local level. As Mohand Akli Bouhamza, a child-refugee from Ibouzidène to Ighil Oumsed, recounts:

> Everybody was celebrating the end of the war, apart from us. My uncle had come back from the *maquis* as a hero. He went off somewhere to have his war injuries looked after, and he forgot about us. My father was still in France. The day of independence, we just stayed at home, and then we had to leave Ighil. We moved to Laɛzib [in the valley] to live with some relatives, and then to Akbou. We didn't know where to go. My mother went to speak with one of the local representatives of the FLN, to tell him that we were a family of *mujâhidîn*; he told us to just take any house left behind by the French. That's what we did... At that time, every Friday, the market day, there was a massacre. People were stoned to death, because they had worked for the French, but mainly I think because somebody who didn't like them had accused them of being a traitor. (Mohand Akli Bouhamza)

The last French sub-prefect of Akbou described these executions as follows:

> Suddenly, roughly from July 27th to September 15th, repression came crashing down without any particular reason... Seven hundred and fifty people were arrested and assembled in three 'interrogation centres'... In these centres, from where the screams of the tortured could be heard at a great distance, half of the detained were executed at a rate of five to ten every night... The local population did not take part in any of the tortures, apart from those of dozens of *harkis* who were paraded in the streets, dressed like women, naked, ears, noses and lips cut off, castrated, buried alive in chalk or even in cement, or burnt alive with petrol.[31]

---

[31] *Rapport du sous-préfet d'Akbou*, quoted by Hamoumou and Moumen (2004: 330-3).

No such atrocities seem to have happened in Ighil Oumsed, but the events of nearby Akbou most certainly did not go unnoticed in the village. Nobody ever mentioned to me who the authors of these atrocities might have been; the overall consensus seemed to be, however, that they were 'strangers' from the 'outside', people who had joined the FLN too late and now had to prove their allegiance through violence. These events marked the beginning of a new world that resembled in far too many ways the one that it had come to replace.

In Ighil Oumsed, 1962 is still seen as the date when the world changed, and time is usually divided into 'before' (the war) and 'after'. Despite – or because of – the generally endorsed notion of a radical social change brought about by the 'revolution' (as the war of independence is referred to in the official rhetoric), what exactly happened immediately after the war at the local level is difficult to tell. It seems clear that the profound social restructuring that had begun in the decades leading up to the war was consecrated in law, property and political and social influence. But how important had this restructuring actually been? In Ighil Oumsed, colonial domination had been experienced in its most direct form through the expropriations of land to the benefit of the Ben Aly Chérif family (as outlined in Chapter 3), which still provides the most common subject matter for any discussion of the times 'before'. Consequently, the first act that demonstrated at the village level that a 'revolution' had really taken place was the expropriation of the Ben Aly Chérif family's extensive land-holdings and their conversion into a public domain:

> During the war, after Ben Aly Chérif had left, his workers managed the land, all by themselves, as if he had never gone away. After the war, the army took over the land, and FLN officers were installed as administrators. They didn't stay for long; then Boumediène came, and the land was turned into state property. It was managed by people from the outside, administrators, but the people who were working on it all came from the village, just like before. (Larbi Mouhoubi)

Ben Aly Chérif's secondary house in the valley just below Ighil Oumsed was occupied by members of the three families which managed and worked the domain: the Ihamlalen and two other families. A small part of the land formerly owned by the Ben Aly Chérif family, but which had not been incorporated into the public domain, was taken over by various villagers immediately after the war, or even during the troubled period before the ceasefire. They were rarely those who claimed former ownership. The division of Ben Aly Chérif's property and the constitution of the public domain, where villagers had hoped for a restitution of their family lands, clearly symbolised the new power structures that were to dominate post-independence Algerian society: power was passed on to those who had 'made' the new country-to-be, rather than the others who might have been the former owners of the land, but who during the war had become guilty by omission.

The *mujâhidîn* made for a very peculiar elite. They were mostly very young, and few had ever been to school. They found themselves running a country that lacked the most basic infrastructure, destroyed by seven years of war, and which had been left precipitately by almost all of its former white-collar workers, as one million French Algerians 'returned' to France. Doctor Mary, a French sister who was one of the first doctors to work in the Akbou hospital after the French had left, recalls the peculiar post-war atmosphere as follows:

> The hospital was full of people who wanted to help, who wanted to construct a new country, all of them were *mujâhidîn*, everybody who had a government job at that time had to be a *mujâhid*. They had just come back from the *maquis*, where they had usually gone when they were still very young. Most of them were illiterate, and fortunately they had good intentions, because they didn't have anything else. We had to do what we could: for many years, the hospital director was illiterate, the mayor was illiterate... Sometimes, that caused trouble, because some people just got them to sign anything.

But who were these *mujâhidîn* who had come to rule the country? Some of them were indeed locally known and respected. Due to the overwhelming military success of the French on the ground, however, most long-standing local nationalist fighters had been killed. The few survivors had either joined the FLN very late, or had spent most of the war in Morocco or Tunisia. Some came from outside the area. Few were thus locally known and recognised beyond doubt as *mujâhidîn*. The suspicion of 'fake *mujâhidîn*' who had 'stolen' the national revolution and who had dispossessed the true local heroes and their families of their rewards thus seems to be as old as the figure of the legendary war hero, founder and liberator of the Algerian nation, itself.

The day I arrived in Algeria, before reaching my final destination, Arezqi insisted on introducing me to his 'maternal uncle' (his mother's patriparallel cousin), Si Smaïl. Si Smaïl, *mujâhid*, is the president of the regional branch of the nationwide *Organisation nationale des moudjahidine* (ONM) and the ex-mayor of Akbou – the 'king of Akbou' as I secretly thought of him. He himself was to confirm this impression several months later, in his own, more modern idiom: 'I am the [Algerian president] Bouteflika of Béjaïa!' As soon as he met me, Si Smaïl was charmed by my presence. For Arezqi, this was the main reason and condition for the subsequent success of my research in the area. Therefore, he insisted that I should go and visit Si Smaïl in his office in Béjaïa as often as I could, although I could not quite see what exactly I was supposed to do there, and why visits to his family home in Akbou would not be sufficient.

Once in his office, Si Smaïl showed me 'his' archives, which filled two large rooms. In these archives, 'everybody', he said, had his own file. When I ventured to ask whether it would be possible for me to have a look at them, he looked highly amused:

> No, no, these documents are not for everybody, they are too important. Everything is there: with these documents, we know everything. I see somebody in the streets, and I know: this one, he collaborated, or else: that one is a traitor, even if he has his card [proving that he is a *mujâhid*] and everybody thinks he is a *mujâhid*. I know, and I know that he knows that I know.

The fact that Smaïl, like all *mujâhidîn*, had added the prefix 'Si' to his name, which until the war of independence had been the prerogative of marabouts, did not seem a mere coincidence or mockery. Once again, 'history' had been 'stolen': it is seen as confined to secret documents, 'hidden' by a privileged class, who combined their true knowledge of what had happened with their rule over what was going to happen in the near future, and for whom the knowledge of history was as much a sign as it was a source of power. As true historical knowledge was confined to locked shelves, the knowledge of local events became either 'dangerous' or 'forgotten': the gap between what had actually happened at village level and the 'official' history was too large to be bridged. This was one of the reasons why, despite its all-pervading importance as the only unquestionable source of legitimacy, 'history' was conspicuously absent from the village, unless it did not really matter, because it was told by the 'losers' of official historiography, in this case the marabouts and the PPA party members (cf. Shryock 1997).

As indicated above, this 'ownership' of history is increasingly criticised by the younger generation, alongside the monopoly of power perceived to have been installed by the *mujâhidîn*, or, even worse, by the numerous 'fake *mujâhidîn*' that haunt Algeria's post-war imagination. Liberation from those who had confiscated history at the same time as they had seized power was often described to me as fundamental to any potential political change, and could only be brought about by the knowledge of 'true history'. This explained the growing interest in the histories of the 'losers' of official historiography; and it explains the current popularity of archaeology and pre-conquest Berber history. Yet, in most cases, these alternative histories tend to be expressed in terms similar to those of the 'official' national history: the cast might have changed, but the characters remain the same. Similarly, the notion that the truth-value of history depends on its secrecy and its inaccessibility seems to continue, as if history was quite simply too important to be known to all.

The exponential increase in literacy after independence does not seem to have changed this situation substantially. On the contrary, the fact that written history is now theoretically accessible to nearly everybody has made it if anything even more obscure, as it has devalued publicly accessible written historical knowledge. The 'truth', or rather the documents containing it, are perceived to be as inaccessible as ever, because 'the French', the 'FLN' or somebody else hold them under lock and key. This perception of history is often extended to all kinds of knowledge, which is by definition seen as located elsewhere, even if its subject matter is local. As a consequence, access to the various sources of knowledge that might be of importance to villagers is crucial in village life, and determines village hierarchies. The following chapter deals with these various paths of access to 'universal' knowledge (and other perishable goods), and their impact on village society.

5
The Centres of the World

The world of humankind constitutes a manifold, a totality of interconnected processes, and inquiries that disassemble this totality into bits and then fail to reassemble it falsify reality. Concepts like 'nation', 'society', and 'culture' name bits and threaten to turn names into things. Only by understanding these terms as bundles of relationships, and by placing them back into the field from which they were abstracted, can we hope to avoid misleading interferences and increase our share of understanding. (Wolf 1982: 3)

One of the reasons it took me so long to find my way around the village was the simple fact that at the beginning I was not left to spend much time there. Arezqi, who had carefully prepared my arrival, had set up trips to various neighbouring villages and towns, where he had fixed appointments with all the experts on Berber matters he could possibly summon. Most of these 'experts' resided in the towns in the valley. To arrange the appointments, Arezqi had activated a large part of his innumerable and very extensive networks, ranging from those established through shared political commitments and work to those based on kinship – which might, in any case, be partly identical. My lack of interest in these 'experts', whose names I could not remember and whose function I did not understand, did not seem to bother him in the slightest; nor did the fact that I never actually had the occasion to talk to any of them, as if the physical meeting in itself carried all the significance (which it did, as I realised later). As soon as I started to move in circles and along paths – within and outside the village – that were not familiar to him, and that (invisibly to me) were excluded from his area of potential contact and activity, Arezqi became increasingly angry, and would argue with other contacts I had made over the control of my time.

This tendency to restrict one's movement to 'known' places and 'known' ways of access to these places was not particular to him. I also observed it among several of my Kabyle informants and friends, who generally saw a great number of barriers and blocked accesses to nearby places, where I could not detect any. At the same time, they would freely use pathways that might lead very far and that I would never have thought of. They would always maintain that their chosen path – which invariably differed from one person to the other – was not only the easiest, but the only possible, way of approaching the world. The extent to which networks of this kind could be mobilised by individuals or groups bore directly on their position in the village and in the 'world' as a whole: the larger and more diversified the network, the more important one was. Similarly, the more two individuals' sets of connections corresponded to each other, the 'closer' they were.

As described in Chapter 3, village space is seen to reflect ideal representations of social order. Practically, however, the village escapes any neat schematisation: it appears as a continuous space with several centres rather than as a juxtaposition of clearly defined blocs. These various centres tend to be associated with certain groups of people who are, in one way or another, 'close' to them, but might easily move from one to the other. They derive their centrality from their geographical position and the use villagers make of them, as much as from their reference and privileged access to larger centres and systems that surpass village boundaries and ultimately encompass 'the whole world'. The mosque, for instance, is central because it links the village to the Islamic *umma* (and to the Ministry of Religious Affairs at the same time); the house of the marabouts derives its *baraka* from its proximity to the hierarchy of saints reaching up to God himself, as well as from its access to universal knowledge (Touati 1990); the *tajmaɛt* consciously sees itself as part of a wider system that encompasses the region as a whole; the school opens up ways to the national administration, but also to the international world of learning which is, for most villagers, ultimately centred on Paris. These and other outside connections are highly valued, and are indeed indispensable for the survival of the village, economically as well as socially and intellectually; yet they are also seen as potentially harmful, as laying the village open to 'outside interference' and manipulation. Thus the emphasis on boundaries recounted in Chapter 3; thus also the debates over where the rightful centre of the village is, debates which implicitly aim to determine what kind of connections the village should privilege or guard itself against, and thus, as is implied, what kind of village it is.

Although Kabylia is often portrayed as remote and cut-off from the world, and 'Kabyle-ness' as a result of resistance against outside influence (see Chapter 1), these connections seem to go back a long time, and certainly pre-date the French conquest. This chapter describes them in more detail, showing not only that they are essential for understanding the village, from its physical appearance to the internal social hierarchies that govern it, but also that such a long-standing 'connectedness' has certain effects on the village itself, not only economically and politically, but also intellectually and socially. Villagers constantly strive to widen or at least to maintain their access to the outside world, and village hierarchies tend to be expressed in terms of 'connectedness'; 'village elites' appear as mediators between the village and the outside, and intellectual legitimacy as derived from past or potential future movements; while notions of identity and self-definitions develop with reference to outside categories. These connections and categories have changed over the years, in orientation and partly also in kind; yet, both the fact that the village remains 'connected' and that it remains marginal to the various systems it connects with seem to be indications of historic continuity.

The economic background

A brief look at the economic structure of the region will give us an idea of the material reasons for the importance of outside links for village life. Due to its chronic lack of good agricultural land, and its relative overpopulation, Kabylia has always been dependent on migration and trade.[1] Up until independence, the cereals used to produce daily foodstuffs in the village, couscous and *aɣrum* (a round unleavened bread, which even more than couscous constituted the average Kabyle's daily fare until independence) were, according to villagers, mainly grown on the *Hauts Plateaux* or further south. They were traded in the large regional market towns against local produce: olive oil, dried figs, and various exportable handicrafts such as cloth, jewellery, weapons and tools (cf. Carette 1848; Sainte-Marie 1976: 103). Villagers say that, in former times, they used to frequent the markets of Akbou, Tazmalt, Sidi Aïch, of various villages among the Ouzellaguen, and the Beni Zikki as far as Wedris. More important commercial ventures would lead them to the larger markets in Béjaïa, Bordj Bou Arréridj, Sétif, and even Constantine and M'sila (at a distance of 300 to 400 kilometres from Ighil Oumsed).

This intrinsic dependence on trade was combined with a heavy reliance on pedlary and on seasonal agricultural or industrial labour in the large farms of the *Hauts Plateaux*. In the late sixteenth century, Haëdo mentioned the presence of a large number of Kabyles as seasonal workers in Algiers and its surroundings (cf. also Robin 1873); he further noted that Kabylia provided at least a third, if not more, of the Ottoman army recruits, and that they – and often also their wives – were to be found in all coastal towns and Turkish garrisons inland (Haëdo 1998 [1612]: 57–8). The French adopted the same recruitment policy as the Turks had done before them; at the same time, seasonal migration to Algiers or the *Hauts Plateaux* continued (cf. Devaux 1859). In Ighil Oumsed, from the beginning of military records just before the First World War until the 1950s, roughly a fifth of young men were recorded as temporarily or permanently absent, initially in Algiers or Constantine, then increasingly also in France (see Table 4). This made the village vulnerable to the fluctuations of the world economy, a vulnerability that increased even further with French colonisation and tax obligations. The world economic slump of the late 1920s was

[1] Judging by the reports by early modern travellers describing Béjaïa and its region (e.g. al-Fâsî 1956 [1550]: 361; Haëdo 1998 [1612]: 57), by the first French colonial ethnographers (Carette 1848) and administrators in the Akbou region (*Rapports trimestriels*, AOM 67K1, 70K2). Leo the African further remarks that the Kabyles were coining money (ibid. 407); Peysonnel notes that they were 'very knowledgeable money forgers' (1987 [1724-5]: 264), which indicates the area's intense and early involvement in regional trade.

therefore of immediate consequence to the village economy, as the drastic decrease in the number of marriages concluded in these years in Ighil Oumsed and the increase in the average age at marriage allow us to guess (Table 1).[2]

By the 1930s, less than half of the total income of the inhabitants of the *commune mixte d'Akbou* every year was the result of agricultural labour on their own fields. Other sources of income included paid agricultural labour on the large farms in the valley, work as *khammâs* (sharecropper) for indigenous landowners, employment in shops in the towns, seasonal labour in road construction and small private workshops. These forms of employment, put together, occupied in season almost 9000 men, or roughly two-thirds of the total workforce; most families combined wage-labour and subsistence agriculture in order to survive. The amount of cash generated through wage labour locally appears as marginal, however, when compared to the remittances sent home by emigrant labourers in France: 8 million francs in 1937 alone, which accounted for two-thirds of the area's total cash income. In 1938, a fifth of the local male adult population of the *douar* of Chellata had left for France.[3] This figure was to rise after the Second World War, increased further during the war of independence, and reached its peak in the 1970s. Since independence, the economic dependence of the region, mirrored by that of Algeria as a whole, is on foreign imports, fuelled by the export of non-refined oil and gas, often extracted through wholesale concessions given to international companies.[4] Within the country, more than ever before, access to the centralised state economy and to remittances from abroad has become crucial for economic survival (Harbi 1980, Bentaleb 1984).

In Ighil Oumsed, this dependence on outside resources can be clearly felt. Relative wealth and poverty are mainly a function of the number of emigrants or former emigrants in any one family, a criterion that has by now almost replaced more 'traditional' ways of judging wealth such as land ownership. For those who stay behind, the most sought-after jobs are 'government jobs'. Although these are generally badly paid – a problem that nobody ever failed to remark upon – they still are seen as 'real' jobs, as they at least guarantee a certain stability, such as a pension scheme, more or less punctual and regular wages, and a position in the 'system'.[5]

[2] This impression is confirmed by the local administrator: 'In the *commune mixte d'Akbou*, a country of crude and thrifty mountain dwellers, living standards have never been very high, even in times of affluence. In these last years of prolonged economic crisis, the restrictions on food that have been imposed on everybody have brought out an under-nourishment that is impossible for us even to imagine' (*Enquête alimentaire*, 25/04/1937, AOM Akbou).

[3] *Rapport sur l'émigration dans l'arrondissement de Bougie*, 1938, AOM 93/1415. Conversely, the heavy restrictions imposed on emigration by the Vichy government in Algeria (1941–3) led to the worst economic crisis the area had ever known.

[4] In 2002, 63% of the national income came from hydrocarbons, which accounted for 97% of revenue derived from exports (Economist Intelligence Unit 2002). Nationwide, 27% of the overall Algerian workforce is unemployed.

[5] This, according to Ahmed Henni's analyses (which might have to be taken with a pinch of salt, but are in their general tendency confirmed by villagers' perceptions of their own economic situation), is all important in a society where 'the strategy of social actors is not aimed at ...

'Government jobs' mainly mean positions in the local administration and in the booming educational sector, but they also include jobs in the nearby state-run cloth factory Alcovel. Most government jobs are taken by members of the elder generation. The majority of Alcovel's employees, for example, are still those who were taken on at the inauguration of the factory in 1984, and who were trained by the foreign experts who constructed and equipped the production plant. Other possible sources of employment for villagers are the newly created private factories in the industrial zone of Akbou. Some of the wealthier villagers have invested in these factories (one of the Yennat cousins used to be assistant director of the local Danone production plant), and a large number of younger villagers work there. Working conditions are said to be much worse than in government employment, salaries infrequent and variable, and recruitment allegedly always based on *piston* (string-pulling):

> I used to work as a technician for Alcovel, but I didn't like it, there were too many restrictions. That's why when one of my wife's cousins opened a factory for industrial packaging right next door to my house, I quit my job and started to work for him. But that wasn't ideal either: at the beginning, he told me to wait for my salary, because everybody knows that at the beginning, things are never easy. After a year, it was still like that, he paid me when he felt like it, and that was it. After a couple of years, I left. Since then, I work for myself, as an electrician, and I harvest my own olive trees. Overall, I earn more than before, and I can do what I want. (Fodil Ihamlalen)

For the younger generation, '*bricoler un peu*' ('doing odd jobs'), seems to be the most common job description. This can mean anything from working as an electrician, or as a builder paid on a daily basis on building sites in the valley, through doing the occasional agricultural job, to becoming rich through officially illegal small-scale import-export businesses (*trabendo*). *Trabendo* soared throughout the 1990s. Although it recently seems to have lost some of its initial importance, it has impregnated the local and the national imagination of a whole generation with the idea of the 'self-made man' who, despite his young age, 'succeeds' in life, that is to say, manages to make a lot of money very fast. When asked, villagers in Ighil Oumsed could give me a list of about twenty young *trabendistes*, or former *trabendistes*. Like trade and hawking in former times, being a successful *trabendiste* requires mobility, extensive networks, access to sources of illegal imports, and intimate knowledge of the region and beyond. As recounts Djamil Benhamidouche, who is now in his early thirties and owns the village jewellery shop:

> There are a lot of things that you have to learn when you start: how to talk to people, where to find what, and so on. There are differences between here and Sidi Aïch, for example, and even more between here and the Arabic-speaking

---

[5] (cont.) obtaining a maximum of revenues through a productive effort, but at obtaining a good position in the distribution mechanism' (Henni 1990a: 237); and where 'the factory is not an institution of temporary, but of permanent redistribution. The workforce is in actual fact a group of clients in the strict sense of the word. Employment is a means of redistribution and of the recruitment of clients' (Henni 1990b: 221).

areas... For those who are into gold, there are big markets, around Sétif, and in Batna, that's the biggest, just for *trabendistes*... When I go to the black market in Tizi-Ouzou, I take somebody from the village with me. I keep the money; I stay in the car, with my mobile phone. The other person keeps a look-out, and those who have got something to sell get into the car one by one: what have you got, show me, I like that, I'll take it. It's very dangerous, but once you know what to do, once you know the people you have to know, it's OK.

Recently, some of the money made in the 1990s by the *trabendistes* in the village has been reinvested in more stable and more 'traditional' economic ventures, such as shops, buses, or even agriculture or livestock. The village now counts a proud fourteen shops of all descriptions, and nine privately run buses. This, however, has not lessened its economic dependence on the outside, as these shops mainly seem to act as signs of past rather than as guarantees of future economic success; true economic ventures, everybody seems to agree, or 'proper jobs', can only be had outside the village, and it is towards the outside that virtually every young villager's career is geared.

Grandfathers and brides

Nevertheless, the intrinsic value attached to outside connections in contemporary village life cannot merely be explained by economic interest, and attempts to position oneself closer to one of the various centres of the world clearly go beyond the purely economic sphere. Family histories, for instance, in particular those of the less influential families in the village, tend to stress the role played by their ancestors in world-historical events. Thus, the Berri family, one of the smallest families in the village, most of whose relatives live in the neighbouring village of Felden, explain their presence in Ighil Oumsed as follows:

> My grandfather came from [the neighbouring village] Felden. He was a famous *bandit d'honneur*[6] in the area; he was so famous that he had to run away from the French. One day, he took his wife, who was pregnant with their first son, to Ighil Oumsed, which was seen as safer than Felden. Then, with all his men, he took the road to the East. Nobody ever heard from him again, but he certainly went all the way to Lebanon: have you ever heard of Nabih Berri?[7] He is one of our family. (Mouloud Berri)

Every family in the village has a similar story of origin, which situates them firmly within the world – and within the village. These family histories speak of a society marked by movement and by the secession and fusion, or even the emergence and disappearance, of villages and families, as much as by the pretence of permanence and of geographical anchorage. Some families

[6] Algerian 'honour bandits' were famous in the first decades of the twentieth century. They caused many sleepless nights among European settlers (AOM 93/20066; 93/5329) and became a fashionable subject of romantic French novels (Mahé 2001), before they were recycled by the independent Algerian film industry as precursors of nationalist guerrillas.

[7] Born in Sierra Leone to a family of Lebanese expatriates, Nabih Berri is now head of the Shi'ite political organisation Amal in Lebanon and currently speaker of the Lebanese Parliament.

still claim ownership of land they had once settled, although it might be too far away even to think about working it or 'owning' it in any practical way. The criss-crossing itineraries attributed to the family ancestors would, if drawn on a map, cover the mountain range with a dense net of 'known places', which in many cases would extend far into the Arabic-speaking areas of the *Constantinois* and the *Algérois*. These itineraries often influence – at least theoretically – the relationships between families in the village, and are partly still revived through religious pilgrimages and marriage arrangements. Although sometimes forgotten by the younger generation, they are still alive in family names (such as Azouaou, after a tribal federation in Greater Kabylia, Aouzelleg, those from Ouzellaguen), and in topographic names that often take the names of the people who used to live there. Due to their repetitiveness, these names only ever give an illusion of precision, however, and could easily be interpreted in a different way by a different narrator – to the point where the confusion itself seems functional, the only reasonable way of firmly integrating all of the land in one logical scheme without causing too much friction between conflicting claims (cf. Berque 1974).

These historical 'connections' between families, villages and places are frequently doubled up by repeated patterns of economic and matrimonial exchanges.[8] The formerly most influential family in the area, that of the *bach-agha* Ben Aly Chérif, provides an example of the conflation of historical, economic and political links with marriage arrangements, and of the attempts to maintain a balance between the necessary local attachments and links to other large and influential families in the valley and beyond. The first marriage their saintly ancestor is said to have concluded locally was with one of the maraboutic families from Ighil Oumsed. It was followed by repeated alliances with the Benbélaïd family from another nearby village, Sidi Amar – the same family that is known for its frequent intermarriage with the Ouhaddar family from Ighil Oumsed – and with influential maraboutic families in the region. From the early twentieth century onwards, spouses for the Ben Aly Chérif's male and female children increasingly also included members of the locally emerging French-educated *intelligentsia* such as Salah Mesbah, a lawyer from El Kseur and delegate to the Algerian assembly in the late 1940s and 1950s; descendants from other, less influential maraboutic families who had successfully secured posts in the French administration, such as the *caïd* Larbi Smati from Amalou; and the two

---

[8] In anthropological writings, the whole of North Africa is seen as a region generally favouring 'endogamy'. However, due to the inherent ambiguity of the category of 'one of ours' (as opposed to 'foreigners'), this 'endogamy' can be defined in varying ways: marriages create endogamic groups as much as they are claimed to be concluded within them. As Pierre Bourdieu noted: 'One immediately understands how strange the project to calculate the percentage of endogamy is in a case where, like here, the notion of the endogamic group itself, thus the basis for the calculation, is at issue' (1972: 76). In Ighil Oumsed, this group-defining 'endogamy' has often led to repeated marriages with certain families outside rather than within the village, especially among the larger and more influential families, and especially the maraboutic families who generally do not marry into non-maraboutic families.

daughters of the former Tunisian Minister of the Interior in the 1940s.[9] In 1953, the French administrator of the *commune mixte d'Akbou* described the family's overall web of influence, partly established through matrimonial alliances, as follows:

> There are: under the direct influence of Ben Aly Chérif, the *douars* Chellata, Bouhamza, Ighram; under his indirect influence: the *douar* Amalou, whose *caïd* Smati is linked through marriage to the family; the *douar* Tamokra, whose *caïd* El-Hadi is from a family that is allied with the Ben Aly Chérif, but who only waits for an occasion to betray him; the *douar* Ouzellaguen, whose *caïd* Méziane Larbi shows a personal devotion to Ben Aly Chérif.[10]

The Bou Daoud family from the neighbouring village of Tasselent, also marabouts and hereditary masters of a prestigious *zâwiya* (Islamic teaching institute), similarly opted for a broad range of alliances. However, as with the Ben Aly Chérif, kinship and marital relations only enter the picture as one among many ways of constructing a dense and polyvalent web of relationships. Other ways of establishing and maintaining these numerous and heterogeneous 'connections' include the Bou Daoud's claim to 'ownership' of the extensive religious endowments on the *Hauts Plateaux* and around Bordj Bou Arréridj pledged to the family *zâwiya*; and their extensive network of former students, who now very often occupy important positions in the national government. A large number of these claims are 'proved' by the family's photo album, which I was shown on my first visit to the Bou Daoud family house in Akbou:

> This is my grandfather, who died a *shahîd*; this is my father, who died a *shahîd*. This is my grandfather with Colonel Amirouche [one of the best-known FLN officers], who often came to the *zâwiya*. This is Ben Aly Chérif who was a good friend of the family. This is the *shaykh* Ben Badis [the founder of the reformist *Association des oulémas*], who often came to the house for weddings. This is one of our *talba* [students] who used to work for the government. (Si Mohand Tayyeb Daoudeddine)

The range of marital choices was more limited for smaller, but nonetheless status-conscious maraboutic families. Shaykh Tahar, the 'grandfather' of the Ouhaddar, married on his arrival in Ighil Oumsed two sisters from the Benbélaïd family from the neighbouring village Sidi Amar. He thereby started a close relationship between the two families, which also involved their respective villages: Sidi Amar, several kilometres further up the valley, remains a favourite destination for pilgrims from Ighil Oumsed. At the same time, the Ouhaddar family also established alliances with other, more 'modern' maraboutic families throughout the Soummam valley, mainly in the area of Tamokra, where until the 1960s all of their sons completed their education.[11]

---

[9] *SLNA Famille Ben Aly Chérif* AOM 93/4244 (restricted access).

[10] Letter from the administrator of the *commune mixte d'Akbou* to the subprefect of Bougie, 24/02/1953 AOM Akbou. Peters (1990) points to similar marriage patterns followed by high-status families in Cyrenaica.

[11] After independence, the *zâwiya* of Tamokra was converted into a state-run Islamic teaching institute. It succeeded in maintaining its reputation of excellence, and today counts a large number of high-ranking government officials among its former students. It therefore remained an important node in regional and national socio-political networks.

Non-maraboutic families remember less of their family's past marital choices, although these do not seem to be substantially less diverse or flexible than those described above. The analysis of marriages concluded in Ighil Oumsed since a rudimentary *état-civil* was established for the area in 1891 leaves us to guess at certain recurrent patterns (see Appendix 1A, p. 151). Several of the larger and higher-status families, such as the Imessaouden and the Ihamlalen, stand out for a higher degree of 'endogamy' (in the sense of marrying people who bear the same family name, or the name of families referred to by today's family members as 'cousins') than others. A certain hierarchy of families that corresponds to people's memories and archival data is confirmed by the pattern of 'possible' and 'impossible', of frequently repeated and 'extraordinary' alliances. A thorough understanding of these categories, however, would need more, often long forgotten, information on the actual circumstances of the marriages in question (cf. Bourdieu 1972: 100). Certain 'extraordinary' cases are still remembered, often as means of integrating high-status outsiders into the village community. As the maraboutic Aït Ahmed family recounts:

> Our grandfather first arrived in Chellata, where he worked for Ben Aly Chérif. When it was time for him to marry, Ben Aly Chérif found a wife for him in Greater Kabylia and brought her to Chellata, to bind my grandfather even more to his house. At this time, however, one of the larger families in Ighil Oumsed, the Benhamidouche, had problems with some people, and asked my grandfather to come and help them – they offered him a very large house in return.... He worked very hard, and after a while, he managed to buy some land, and then married his sons to girls from the village: a girl from the Aït Cheikh, one from the Ihamlalen, the largest family in the village, because my father's business started to become more important, and he had to make friends with everybody. (Si Messaoud Aït Ahmed)

Judging by the *état-civil*, historical developments such as the war of independence were frequently marked by short-term dramatic changes in marriage patterns. Thus, in the 1950s and 1960s, the number of mixed maraboutic and non-maraboutic marriages increased dramatically, as a new group of high-status people emerged: the *mujâhidîn*. Nevertheless, and despite these short-term upheavals, notable permanent changes within the marriage registers seem to be caused by individual families' change of positions within the village hierarchy rather than by a fundamental restructuring of the hierarchy as such. Several permanent changes nevertheless seem beyond doubt: the number of marriages concluded within the *iderma* and within the tribe has decreased over the years, to the benefit of marriages concluded within the family, the village or with inhabitants of nearby Akbou (Appendix 1A, p. 151, cf. also Basagna and Sayad 1974).

More generally speaking, the geographic range of marriage alliances has been reduced as time goes on. At the same time, networks established through marriages have also been reduced in their social scope, as the younger generation have partly 'opted out' of the larger system of 'connections' of which they were an integral part, in particular if their social position – an independent flat and employment outside the village – allows them to do so. Today, marriages have increasingly become an individual venture, whose aim is individual happiness and fulfilment rather than the strengthening or maintenance of the extended family. Ideas about good 'connections' persist, however, and marriage choices are only rarely made without the consent or the mediation of the family. Similarly, my daily experience during my fieldwork showed that the web of past and present 'kinship', carefully tended and maintained through mutual visits, gifts and services, remains crucial to the way the world opens up to villagers. This is especially true for women and girls, for whom visits to relatives often constitute the only opportunity to travel and to acquire direct knowledge of places and people outside their immediate neighbourhood. The contraction of kinship networks therefore seems to indicate a more general contraction of the field of the 'familiar', which will be discussed further throughout this chapter.

The circulation of knowledge (I): the *shuyûkh*

Alongside connections established through kinship, Ighil Oumsed has always been situated within several overlapping networks along which knowledge and ideas were circulated. Until the 1930s, most of these networks were part of one or several of the various local religious traditions: the veneration of saints, the links maintained among the local maraboutic families, and the dense network of educational *zawâyâ* and Sufi brotherhoods that covered the area.[12] These networks, the knowledge they conveyed and the intellectual hierarchies they produced were central to the region's social, political and even geographical structure, as much as to its self-perception. From a local point of view, however, it seems that they also gave rise to a certain ambivalence, which still informs contemporary perceptions not just of Islam, but also of 'universal' sources of knowledge and their local representatives more generally.

The local saints are said to have come from Morocco, and to have led lives of wandering and searching, until they settled down to establish a village or open a *zâwiya* (in Kabyle *taɛmamart*, from the Arabic *'amara*, to settle or civilise). Much as the itineraries of the village families recounted above are dotted with places inevitably connected to them by their family history and names, the saints' itineraries, as they appear in local legends, are marked by the physical proof, the *burhân*, of their passage: a spring they caused to yield water, a village they established, a rock they displaced. Through this emphasis on the saints' individual itineraries through 'known' places, and on their faraway origin, the saints appear as mediators, or, in

---

[12] In the following, these various traditions will be described in distinctive sections for reasons of clarity rather than because the distinctions between them appear pertinent on a local scale. Local perceptions and terminologies treat them neither as perfectly identical, nor as truly distinctive: similar images and patterns of religious practices and holiness pervade all of them, and are recognised as such. As a general rule, the individual local holy men or *'ulamâ'* tended to be part of several of these traditions at the same time. For a similar observation, see Cornell (1998) and Filali (2002).

terms of local stories of saints' lives and deeds, literally as 'go-betweens' that link the region to the wider world of Islam, and make it become part of it (cf. Touati 1990: 152). The legend of the local saint, Si Mohand ou Messaoud, runs as follows:

> Si Mohand ou Messaoud belongs to the house (*axxam*) Ben Aly Chérif. Like them, he came from Morocco, he went through the Aït Waghlis, via Smaoun, and he came along the path above the village. He stopped at Si Moussa ou Ali and sat there for some time. He made water flow at Si Mohand ou Messaoud, and then he stayed there and founded his *zâwiya*.

The saints thereby link the area to the centres of the Islamic world, such as southern Morocco, Cairo and Mecca, and, ultimately, to God and all his saints; and the origin of the *zawâyâ*, the most visible localities in the area, is seen as the result of past movement, channelling a central force – God's *baraka* – to a place that thereby becomes specific, and named.

The saints' itineraries are still partly re-enacted nowadays through pilgrimages to local saints' tombs.[13] Although saints' tombs offer a sanctuary to all pilgrims without distinction, the choice of the date and place of a pilgrimage and the way it is conducted define and re-confirm certain attachments held by different tribes, villages and even families within a village. Some of these groups also hold different claims over, and have a variety of well-defined responsibilities towards, the saint's tomb (cf. Hadibi 1999, 2002). The annual spring pilgrimage in Ighil Oumsed, for example, might lead different women from the village either towards the saints of the Ouzellaguen, or towards Si Mohand ou Messaoud, halfway to the neighbouring village of Felden. Pilgrimages also maintain and re-confirm links with neighbouring villages and tribes, as saints' tombs are, apart from their initial function as places of worship, one of the rare 'public spaces' where women can meet, spend time and exchange news.

The regional maraboutic families, alleged descendants of the saints, are thus in a sense living reminders of the region's integration into the world of Islam and Islamic scholarship. Until recently, as teachers and preachers, they also actively furthered this integration, and maintained links with the centres of Islamic scholarship where they could and were inclined to do so. It seems that, in the past at least, their religious reputation depended not only on their past genealogical closeness to one of the regional saints, but also on their own travels or access to manuscripts from these centres, and thus to 'universal' scholarship, knowledge and moral standards (Bargaoui 1999; cf. al-Wartîlânî 1908; Urvoy 1993; Katz 1996). Thus, although the bulk of manuscripts that I found in the Ouhaddar collection in Ighil Oumsed (see Chapter 4) were produced locally, that is to say, in an area spanning

---

[13] Although pilgrimages and the veneration of saints have been heavily condemned by the national government's modernising agenda and even more so by today's Islamists, they are still – and even increasingly – very popular (see, for example, Andezian 2001; Hadibi 1999, 2002). This is especially true among those women, who, old or young, do not have any other occasion to leave the house or the village, that is to say, those who do not go to school or university. For more detail on pilgrimages and the veneration of saints, see below.

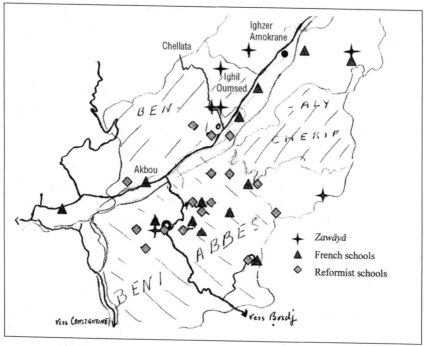

Map 5.1 *Zawâyâ*, French and reformist schools in the Akbou area (1950s)
(based on *L'Enseignment privé réformiste et l'Association de oulémas d'Algérie*, n.d., ACED)

the regional centres of learning such as the Zaytûna in Tunis and Fez and Marrakech in Morocco, the collection also contains books from as far away as Egypt, and various copies of standard works known and used through-out the Islamic world (Appendix 1B, p. 152). This library is by no means a rare phenomenon in the area: most maraboutic families in the area own at least some manuscripts or talk about a family library that was lost or is still held by other members of the family (cf. Aïssani and Mechehed 1998).

Many of these private libraries were constituted within the numerous regional Islamic teaching institutes or *zawâyâ*, for which the Soummam valley was particularly well-known (Merad 1967, see Map 5.1). The *zawâyâ* were usually built around the tomb of a founding saint, and run by the saint's descendants. The individual *zawâyâ* could generate considerable wealth, as they came to control an important amount of lands that were *ahbâs* (sgl. *hubus*, religious endowments). They were also more often than not part of one of the extensive Sufi networks that covered the area and that linked it to the world beyond.[14] The number of students in the *zawâyâ*

[14] In 1916, at a time when the influence of the orders was already said to be diminishing, the French administrator of Akbou estimated the number of Sufi adepts in the *commune mixte* at over 3000, that is to say more than one fifth of the male adult population (AOM B3 150). Sufi thought has evidently had a strong influence on Shaykh Tahar's collection of books in Ighil Oumsed (see Table 2), and he is remembered to have led Sufi prayer sessions (*dhikr*).

varied from ten to more than a hundred, studying Arabic grammar, the exegesis of the Qur'ân, and Islamic jurisprudence. Although the teachers seemed to have been mostly of local origin, and many belonged to the families that 'owned' the *zâwiya* where they were teaching, most of the *shuyûkh* spent an important part of their career studying and teaching outside their *zâwiya* or village. The same high degree of mobility was common among students.[15] Through studying, teaching and travelling in search of knowledge, as much as through economic relations and marital alliances, the *shuyûkh* of the area thus developed a tight web of relationships that was essentially rural and largely concentrated on the Soummam valley and the neighbouring Arabic-speaking areas, but that could on occasions extend as far as Cairo or Mecca.

Before the arrival of the French school, Ighil Oumsed had two schools: a Qur'ânic school where children were taught in the mosque by the local imam, who since the arrival of the Ouhaddar family was usually recruited from among their descendants; and, slightly outside the village, a *zâwiya*, constructed around the tomb of the local saint, Si Mohand ou Messaoud, whose legend was recounted above. This *zâwiya* is said to have been a proper teaching institute, related to the *zâwiya* in Chellata, where 'foreigners' would come and study the Qur'ân, perhaps fifteen to twenty at any one time. It used to own land, which has passed into private property with the *sénatus-consulte*, but whose sacred nature is still respected. Although the *zâwiya* was destroyed during the war of independence, the tomb at the heart of the *zâwiya* is still open to all as a place of worship (Photo 5.1). Pilgrimages to it are frequent, and especially popular among women (Photo 5.2). The tomb is also visited by pilgrims from the neighbouring village of Felden.

Descriptions of the *zâwiya* when it was still functioning as a place of teaching are rare, as much more interest seems to be accorded to the saint's legend and miracles and the different occasions for pilgrimage. The one more detailed story that survives presents the *zâwiya* less as a place of learning than as hosting a group of young 'foreign' men:

> The *zâwiya* of Si Mohand ou Messaoud? I remember a song about it, because of something that happened there: a woman from the village ran away with one of the *talba*, it was a great scandal at the time, and we still sing about it to have a laugh... (Nana Hajja Bennoune)

A similar story, here linked to accusations of embezzlement, appears in the French archives with reference to the neighbouring *zâwiya* Sidi Saïd:

> The *adjoint indigène* of the *douar* Ouzellaguene... had taken under his protection two students (*talbas*) of Arabic origin.... As soon as they arrived in our *douar*, the two *talba* started to behave like Don Juan with our women[16]... They took control

---

[15] As shown by requests for teaching permits made by religious scholars to the French authorities, tracing their educational and professional careers (AOM 93/1393): and by demands made by students from all over Algeria for permission to travel to various *zawâyâ* in the area (AOM B3 246).

[16] '*Ils ont pris des allures de Don Juan auprès de nos femmes*'. That the tribal elders of the Ouzellaguen – or the scribe who wrote or translated their petition – should be familiar with Don Juan shows the close intellectual intermeshing of local and French imagery even at such an early date.

Photo 5.1 Interior of the village saint's tomb, with candles lit and headscarves draped over the tomb for *baraka*

Photo 5.2 Pilgrimage to the tomb of Si Mohand ou Messaoud, to celebrate the first day of *tafsut*, the Kabyle spring (note Berber writing and symbol on outer wall)

over the income of the *zâwiya*... everything they pocketed in this illegitimate way, they handed over to the *adjoint indigène*.[17]

From the local point of view, then, the status of the *zawâyâ* was ambiguous. On the one hand, they were nodes in a prestigious network that linked the local to the regional centres of learning, and, ultimately, to the centres of the Islamic world. As representatives of Islam, the *zawâyâ* procured 'universal' knowledge, morality and *baraka* (blessing) for the locals. On the other hand, they partook in the ambiguous status of the 'outside' in general: as abodes of 'foreigners', they were outside the village's moral boundaries, and thus potentially threatened village order. At the same time, they taught 'universal' moral categories that did not necessarily correspond to village norms as they were practised, and, as they constituted considerable local assets given over to 'outsiders', they were permanently in danger from 'corruption'.

Contemporary debates over the *zawâyâ*'s legacy, and the role of the local intellectual heritage more generally, still echo this ambivalence. Condemned by the reformist discourse of the 1930s onwards, and, by official governmental policy after independence, frequently accused of collaboration with the French, the *zâwiya* tradition seemed to have died out, and former rural networks were replaced by hierarchies based on the cities of the coast and increasingly on the state and the Ministry of Religious Affairs in Algiers – at least if we believe official rhetoric and records. Yet replacement was never total (see Scheele 2007a), and if most *zawâyâ* indeed stopped functioning as teaching institutes, they were still considered as pilgrimage sites by locals, and seem to have become especially popular since the late 1980s, in a development that mirrors the emergence of Islamism in its rejection of the state's postulated monopoly over religion, while at the same time opposing it as an assertion of local 'traditions' (see also Chapter 6). Thus, since the early 1990s, efforts have been made to reconstruct several *zawâyâ* in the immediate neighbourhood of Ighil Oumsed that had been destroyed during the war of independence. Most of these were made by the descendants of the families that still 'own' them, or by their former students:

> For several years now, we have been trying to reconstruct the *zâwiya* like it used to be, following old drawings, the memories of former students, and old photos. The money and the initiative mainly come from former *talba*, who today work for the government or have other important positions in Algiers. We thought: as long as we still had our *zawâyâ*, there weren't any Islamists; as soon as our *zawâyâ* were destroyed, we started to have problems – that means that we have to rebuild at least one of them, and that's what we are trying to do. But this turned out to be very difficult, we got into a lot of trouble, there is a lot at stake in the *zâwiya* and its landholdings, we had problems within the family.

The maraboutic families' manifest interest in the reconstruction of the *zawâyâ* has been shared by the national government, which is eager to

---

[17] Petition by the notables of the Ouzellaguen for the re-opening of the *zâwiya* of Sidi Ahmed ou Saïd, 7/06/1912, AOM B3 246.

reassert its long-lost control over Islam,[18] much to the detriment of the zawâyâ's local reputation, and by local academics keen to re-write the history of the valley. The 1990s saw a project to reopen the zâwiya in Chellata, which was instigated by an association that mainly comprises highly educated, urban Kabyles from Béjaïa (cf. Aïssani 2002). In their eyes, the zâwiya was primarily a teaching and research institution that proved that the region as a whole had been part of a larger, Mediterranean rather than purely Islamic intellectual tradition, and that this intellectual tradition was compatible with Islam – an Islam whose centres would be Granada, Fez and Béjaïa rather than Mecca and Cairo. Their project, however, was met with resistance by the villagers, whose relationship with the tradition represented by the zâwiya and thus by extension also by the Ben Aly Chérif family is less academic than social: here as elsewhere, the re-establishment of the zâwiya would unearth ancient conflicts and unpleasant memories. It could be seen as an attempt by the formerly influential families associated with the zawâyâ to reclaim the 'territory' they had lost during the Algerian war, and as a more general attempt by the new and old 'upper classes' to re-establish past 'feudal' structures in the area.

On a smaller scale, these efforts are also reflected in Ighil Oumsed by attempts to reconstruct the local zâwiya of Si Mohand ou Messaoud, undertaken on the initiative of a group of four villagers, who have all been very active in village life through the years. Many others in the village were critical of this project, not only because of its religious, 'superstitious' or 'non-Berber' nature, but also because of the monopoly over the zâwiya and maybe even over its former landholdings claimed by the authors of the project. Others tried to reclaim the zâwiya as a sign of a purely local tradition, by painting it with Berberist symbols (Photos 5.1 and 5.2), and thereby integrating it into a whole new set of transregional networks and redefining it as a symbol of local resistance to 'Islamism'.[19] Many local women, on the other hand, use it as a meeting place and implicitly associate it with the 'zâwiyas' or Sufi-inspired dancing and trance sessions that are increasingly popular among women, especially those residing in the towns of the valley.[20]

---

[18] The government started officially to pay attention to the zawâyâ with the forceful emergence of political Islam onto the political stage in the late 1980s: see for example the articles in the official newspaper *El Moudjahid* of 17 August 1989 and 24 April 1990 (Salhi 1999a). In March 1991, the government organised a seminar about the heritage represented by the zawâyâ (see Hadj Ali 1992). More than ten years later, the current Algerian President Abdelaziz Bouteflika mobilised the network of traditional zawâyâ and Sufi orders during his election campaign in 2004.

[19] Most Islamist groups tend to condemn the veneration of saints, although, more recently, groups like the Hamas have tried to take gain control over some of the most important zawâyâ in the area in order to reform them from within.

[20] Such Sufi sessions have recently become popular, often in recently constructed quarters of the rapidly growing towns in the valley. They are generally run by groups, mainly of women, who probably have existed for much longer, but had been afraid to come out into the open. Their main emphasis is on trance experience and on capacities to heal illnesses and exorcise the 'spirits' that take possession of bodies and souls. For similar cases in Western Algeria and Tunisia, see Andezian (1993) and Ferchiou (1993) respectively. In Ighil Oumsed, Sufi chants continue to be performed at funerals by a group of men known as the *ikhwân* ([Sufi] brothers).

The *zâwiya* remains thus defined by the networks to which it gives access, but the nature of these networks continues to be hotly debated.

Religion has long provided the foremost means of integration of the village into the outside world. Through Islam, villagers have been able to access a vast scriptural, legal, historical and theological tradition, and have known themselves to be part of the 'world'. Yet Islamic scholars and their institutions were and still are qualified as 'foreigners', and local attitudes to their legacy and the knowledge they represent remain ambivalent until today. Nevertheless, control over religious institutions and over sources of religious legitimacy is clearly a preoccupation that has lost none of its importance, although the nature of religion itself has changed profoundly over the last century. In the village as in the region as a whole, the current revalorisation of the religious heritage, conducted by an uncomfortable alliance of secular academics, traditional *shuyûkh* and hesitant representatives of official religious institutions with Islamist sympathies, thus appears as one facet of an ongoing debate over local, regional and national 'identity', and over the role played by various 'legitimate' and 'illegitimate' outside connections, networks and forms of 'universal' knowledge.

The circulation of knowledge (II): the *instituteurs*

From the early twentieth century, the legitimacy derived from religious knowledge co-existed with, and for many was gradually replaced by, another form of learning: the French schools. Although Kabylia as a whole is generally seen as the only rural area in Algeria where French schooling was successfully introduced at a very early date (the first schools date from the 1880s, see Chapter 1), not all areas in Kabylia were equally well covered (Colonna 1975). Thus, until the beginning of the war of independence, almost the whole Akbou area, with the notable exception of the Aït Abbas on the far side of the river, had been neglected from the point of view of schooling, especially when compared with the neighbouring tribe of the Aït Waghlis or with those of Greater Kabylia. The first permanent school in Ighil Oumsed was built in 1958, four years after the beginning of the war of independence, as part of the 'pacification' of the area. By then, the FLN had proclaimed a general boycott of French schools. As the French army obliged each village to provide a certain number of children for their schools, the choice often fell on children in a more marginal position within the village community: 'My father had died, and I was his only son. My mother didn't know what to do with me, so she sent me to school' (Smaïl Yennat). This was also valid for the few girls who attended classes during the war: 'At that time, I was living with my mother, who had just divorced from my father. We lived by ourselves, the two of us, that's why I went to school' (Ouardia Hamlal).

After independence, the primary school in Ighil Oumsed continued to function. Qualified teaching staff were lacking, however, because the vast majority of teachers, who had been of European origin, had not returned to their work after summer 1962. Very few of the first generation of pupils from Ighil Oumsed continued their studies after the war:

> I was in the first class that got through to the final exam, but after that, we didn't know what to do. We had been told that now we should go to Akbou, to the *collège* [secondary school], but seeing as in the village, nobody knew how these things worked, we arrived too late in Akbou, when the enrolment for the *collège* in Akbou had already been completed. We wanted to go to school anyway, so we went to the missionary school that was still there at that time... There were no buses or cars, and we couldn't walk to Akbou everyday, and come back in the evening. We rented a small room, all three of us together, with the help of our parents. We were fifteen years old, we didn't really have any money, so we had to get by somehow, find food, learn how to cook, how not to be treated just like children, and so on. That wasn't easy. (Smaïl Yennat)

Of the three pupils who made it to the town and through the *collège*, none is living today in the village. One of them returned as a teacher to his home village shortly after having finished the *collège* in Akbou, but he has now moved away to one of the new villages in the valley and commutes to work. Smaïl had to struggle to be able to carry on his education, which was frequently interrupted by spells of office work in order to help out his family. The break-through to 'proper' study came when he managed to obtain 'sponsorship' from one of the major factories in the area, at that time run by the government. Smaïl now prides himself on being the first villager to have obtained a university degree. He has established his private accountancy office in nearby Akbou. His relations with the village are sporadic, and relations with some of his cousins strained, as one of the latter explained to me:

> We don't really talk to each other anymore, since he took some of our land from us. It's always like that: Smaïl, at the beginning, was just a little orphan, very poor, everybody had to help him. Now that he is rich, that he has his office in Akbou and connections where he needs them, he has forgotten his poverty. Things had just started to work out for him when our father died, and suddenly we were the orphans, not him anymore. He took advantage of our difficult position to take our lands, saying that before, they used to belong to him. Since then, our case has been waiting to be judged in Akbou. Do you see now what these people are like? (Hamid Yennat)

Smaïl's ascent through the village hierarchy is emblematic of how, as education became crucial to social advancement in the years after independence, this often led to a radical change of status of individual villagers or even families, whose low status had led them to send their children to school before anybody else did. The position of those who thus succeeded remains nevertheless ambiguous, as attitudes towards them, as towards any other kind of 'intellectual', oscillate between jealousy and admiration.

For the first generation of educated villagers, ascending through the school system thus meant to travel further and further, and to get 'closer' to the centres of knowledge and regional and national decision-making. It meant spending several years as a boarder in the regional *collège* or *lycée*, together with a broad selection of students from villages all over the area, while for the first time encountering the benefits of town life, such as weekly visits to the then still functioning cinemas. For those who went on to university, it meant moving to Algiers, and for those who benefited from a grant, it then meant going on to study abroad. These ever increasing circles of movement, along well-traced and well-trodden paths following the administrative structure of the region and the country, educated a particular kind of intellectual, evolving within his own, newly created network of known places and known people, which often overlapped with those created by the administration (cf. Anderson 1983).

Times have changed since then. Despite an extraordinary increase in the number of students, careers like Smaïl's do not exist any more. With a high rate of overqualified unemployment, education has lost its almost magical quality of being able to change radically the fate of the poor man. Trajectories like that of Smaïl nevertheless still influence the imagination of how social mobility should be working and especially to what degree it is seen to depend on the state and on state education. Thus the lack of recent similar cases of successful upward social mobility through state-sponsored education is often cited as an example of the failure of the state, but also of the 'poor quality' of teaching dispensed by today's national educational system:

> No wonder our schools don't get you a job any more. The teachers we have, they don't have the slightest idea what they are doing; they are neither qualified nor proper teachers. I know some girls I went to school with, and now people tell me that they have become teachers, and I know perfectly well that there is no way they are capable of teaching anything. (Nabila Hamlal)

Due to frequent strikes and boycotts, the average school career is lengthy. It is often further prolonged by several repeated classes or failed attempts to pass the final exam to obtain the baccalaureate, which, in Algeria as a whole, is obtained on average by only little more than 15% of students each year (Benghabrit-Remaoun 1998: 18). The frequently evoked 'failure' of the national education system, and the fact that so many of the recent protest movements in Algeria and Kabylia have turned on the nature of the educational institutions in the country, seems to be symptomatic of a widespread lack of confidence in the current national education system. Many villagers feel that the knowledge they might acquire at school is of no consequence in the wider world, that they thus wilfully remain excluded from universal knowledge, and that they are thereby forced to live in an intellectual, educational and cultural void, which needs to be filled by 'authenticity', whatever that might mean. This sentiment leads to an almost physically felt thirst for 'history' outside the official history, 'culture' outside the officially promoted 'Algerian culture', and language – French and Kabyle – outside the officially spoken and taught '*langue de bois*' ('wooden', i.e. stereotyped and meaningless language) which, in Kabylia, is often associated with classical Arabic. As the youngest descendant of the local maraboutic family, and the village doctor, complained:

> Islamism was produced by the Algerian school system, because everything that is taught there is empty, uninteresting, dull, useless. It's empty and made

elsewhere; it has nothing to do with us, but it doesn't allow us to communicate with any body else either. Everything that we have got, ourselves, nobody wants it anymore, we have thrown everything away; it's thus not surprising that we don't have anything left. It suits the government, and our children go to waste, because everything that is left is devoid of sense.

For girls, however, schooling is still perceived as the only 'way out' of the village. The education of girls, especially past the six years of primary school, is a quite recent phenomenon in the village. In 1995, there were still twice as many boys as girls in the primary school of Ighil Oumsed.[21] Since 1997, however, almost all families have started to send their girls to school, and by now girls outnumber and often also outperform boys in all subjects and on all levels. Villagers generally attribute the exponential increase in the number of female students to the slightly delayed effect of the paving of the road in 1985 and the privatisation of transport in the 1990s. It also seems, however, to indicate a more profound change in the idea of female skills and activities that are considered valuable:

> I stopped going to school after the cinquième [first year of secondary school]. I was a good pupil, but it was too difficult to get to school, all the way to Akbou. The road hadn't been paved yet, and there was only one bus, twice a day, from Akbou to El Firma: you miss it, you walk. We would leave the village in the morning before sunrise on foot, to get back late in the evening. There weren't many students who wanted to do this, and especially not many girls, and people would talk if they saw you like this walking in the dark. That's why I dropped out of school. Today, it's much easier for girls, there are buses all the time, and nobody bats an eyelid when girls take them – there are so many of them by now, and if you haven't been to school, you can't even get married any more. (Fadila Yennat, born in 1972)

The decentralisation of secondary and higher education since the late 1970s, which among other things allowed more girls to benefit from schooling and university, has nevertheless also reduced the mobility of students. As seen above, in the decades after the war of independence, education was about movement, and literally opened up new paths leading to the 'centres' of the country, if not of the 'world'. Today, going to university usually means only travelling as far as the regional capital, Béjaïa, or maybe Tizi-Ouzou. The contact of the average student from Kabylia with their Arabic-speaking neighbours has thus been reduced drastically, much as has the knowledge village youth might have of Algiers or any other Algerian city. This has changed the status and experience of students profoundly: in nearby Béjaïa, students, and especially girls, are still under parental control even while living on their own in closely supervised student halls. Despite these restrictions, the dream of studying is still virtually identical to the dream of leaving, of travelling as far as possible:

> At the moment, I am studying in Béjaïa. I am the first in my family to go to university. If I had a brother, I am sure that I would never have been able to do it. Béjaïa is not very far away, we have family there; that's OK, my father allowed me to go there. If all goes well, after my degree, I'll carry on with my studies, I'll do a master's, in Algiers, maybe even in France, or in Canada... (Karima Hadid)

---

[21] PDAU, *Commune de Chellata*, ACC.

Most of these dreams fail, and those who do make it as far as Paris generally have a rather complicated itinerary, and often end up disappointed. One of the villagers who has 'made it' in this way is Yahia Hadid, the fourth son of a former emigrant to France:

> I chose my subject to be able to go to Algiers – Bougie and Tizi [Ouzou] didn't appeal to me at all. It was rather something to arrive at Algiers, especially because it was right in the middle of the 1990s, during the years of terrorism. I could hardly understand the Arabic they speak in Algiers, and you can tell that I am Kabyle just by looking at me... I found a job in a bank in Algiers as soon as I got my degree – and I can tell you, we had a good life in Algiers, despite everything. I made a good living, I could buy everything I wanted, I would see a pair of jeans, I'd like it, I wouldn't even look at the price, I'd just take it... The bank went bankrupt, and I had to leave before everybody else. To avoid having to do military service, I enrolled at university to do a masters, I wanted to go France after that. I have always wanted to go to France, since I was little. You won't ever succeed in anything if you stay in Algeria, not in your studies, nor elsewhere... At the beginning, I stayed in Paris without doing anything, working in bars, earning a bit of money, doing nothing at all. At the moment, I am doing a master's here in France, and next year, if all goes well, I'll find a job here in France – or else I'll enrol somewhere to do a PhD, for the residence permit – I call it *mobicarte* [rechargeable phone card], you always have to recharge it, and that's usually very expensive... Living in Paris isn't easy. I am staying at my sister's in the suburbs. Just to think that I used to have a flat and a car for myself. Algiers isn't too bad, otherwise; the village is a bit difficult, you never go back the same as you left, but people always try to catch you anyway. (Yahia Hadid, in Paris)

This, however, does not stop these almost mythical success stories influencing the imagination of those who stay behind, as the general consensus by now seems to be that national networks of education have failed, and that 'true' education – and peace, happiness and money – can only be obtained abroad.

The importance of being French

Emigration from Ighil Oumsed was mainly concentrated in Northern Paris and in Sedan or other mining towns of the Ardennes (see Table 4). It initially relied on family and village networks, which still function today. It soon also led to the creation of new networks of solidarity and dependence that transgressed 'traditional' boundaries and accorded more and more influence to the 'brokers' of emigration: café- and hotel-owners and foremen from neighbouring tribes and *communes*, who had come to France previously. As most families seemed to prefer to keep their older and more experienced sons in the village, the first generation of emigrants from Ighil Oumsed to France were mostly very young, inexperienced and illiterate:

> On arrival, I didn't speak a single word of French; everything I had done so far was herding sheep. I arrived in a hotel in northern Paris, owned by a Kabyle, who was not from the village – I think he was from the Aït Abbas... I went out trying to find a job, but every time I tried to find my way back to the hotel, I got lost, and I had to take a taxi to get back. It became so expensive that I

decided to stay at the hotel. After a couple of days, the landlord asked me what had happened to me, and then he explained to me how Paris worked... At the beginning, I was sleeping in the cellar; there was no room anywhere else. It was very wet and there was no light. The landlord promised me that he would give me a room as soon as he had one, and then, a room was vacated, and he gave it to somebody else, maybe his cousin. I left and I went to stay with somebody I had met at work, from Ighram [a nearby village belonging to a different douar but to the same tribe as Ighil Oumsed]. (Yahia Ihamlalen)

As financial power locally was increasingly generated through remittances sent home by emigrants, but also as access to knowledge and the mastery of 'modernity' that came with emigration became essential to village life, this first wave of emigration led to the partial emergence of a new 'village elite'. However, although the development of this new elite in some individual cases allowed poorer members of the less influential families to better their position, and younger brothers to take precedence over older ones, it did not lead to a total reversal of village hierarchies. As a general rule, the larger families were the only ones that could truly benefit from the opportunity to emigrate, while also maintaining close contact with the French, keeping enough men at home and investing in modern economic structures, education systems and nationalist parties (cf. Mahé 2001: 249). For most, emigration remained part of village life, and subordinate to the family household (cf. Sayad 1977, 2004). Most first-generation emigrants affirmed their communal link to the village through the institution of a village committee in Paris, which saw itself as a mere executive arm of the village community as a whole.

Emigration increased steadily until the 1970s, when French immigration laws became more restrictive. By now, legal emigration is extremely difficult, if not impossible. Many conflicts arise in families where the father could have had a French passport, but refused it because he wanted his children to stay in the house he built for them – and in the country he 'liberated for them' – whereas the children try everything they possibly can to get away:

My brother Mouloud always wanted to go to France, and my father, who had lived and worked in France for more than thirty years, could easily have obtained a [French] passport for himself and then Mouloud could have had his papers – but he refused. That's why Mouloud went to the Ukraine to study, it's easier to get in. After that, he spent two years as an illegal immigrant in Paris, but he didn't manage to find a job – it's not easy if you don't have the documents you need – and he came back to the village. He has now found a job in a factory; can you imagine, all these years of study for nothing? (Yamina Khebbache)

However much longed for by almost all of the village youth, the new life in France often proves to be a disappointment for those who finally manage to get there:

My brother Yacine and I were born in France – that means that we have got French passports. My father left us in the village with our mother, he didn't really want to have anything to do with us, I think, but as soon we had finished school, we turned up in his flat. He was very angry, but what could he do? The first three months after my arrival here in Paris, I hardly ever went outside. I didn't see anything of Paris, and it was already too late to enrol at university. I just stayed at home and grew fat. After three months, I went back to the village, and I went to university in Tizi-Ouzou. I stayed for two years, and now I study here in Paris. But I miss the village, I want to go back so much, you can't even imagine. I don't have any friends here, really, the French girls at university are so much younger than I am, and they are very different, it's not easy. I want to go back and do something useful, there is nothing for us to do here really. (Nabila Ihamlalen, in Paris)

Today's emigrants can be divided roughly into three groups: the older generation who left the village in the 1950s or 1960s; their children (if they have been brought up in France), who have French nationality and have mostly become part of France's *banlieue* culture; and a new generation of emigrants who have made it to France through study or hard work, and who tend to keep away from their elders and from the existing village institutions in France as much as they possibly can.

The first group, mainly composed of retired men, tend to live in Northern Paris, mainly in one street and often in the same houses indicated almost a decade earlier in the French military registers as their fathers', uncles' or cousins' residences, or in the mining towns of Sedan and Charleville-Mezières. From the point of view of the village, these emigrants, and to a lesser degree their children, form an important part of each family, and of the village as a whole, the very part that still allows for a certain opening to the world. The 'world' – in its directly experienced rather than digital and televised format – is thus constituted of certain 'familiar' places: the nineteenth *arrondissement* and Aubervilliers for Paris, and the Ardennes, especially Sedan and Charleville-Mézières. These places, associated with known people, stories and photographs, appear much closer than neighbouring North African countries, but also than the neighbouring Arabic-speaking cities of Algeria.

Many of the first-generation emigrants are very active in the Parisian village committee, which now has as its main purpose collecting funds to repatriate the bodies of those who die abroad.[22] Membership in the committee is voluntary, but refusal to be part of it, and thus to maintain privileged links with the village community, is irrevocable:

> If you don't pay three times, you are excluded: if you die, we don't know you; if you are ill in hospital, you'll be on your own, and that's the end of it. Even my own brother-in-law, he never pays; if he dies, he has to pay for himself: at least 1,500 euros [£1,000] per funeral. Even my nephew, he had never paid, so we didn't help him at the end: either you are with us, or you aren't, family or not. If we weren't strict like that, we'd never cope... The young people today, they don't realise, but we hang on to them. We let them run a bit, but they are on the end of a lead, and we always hold on to that lead, even if it is long.

The committee member who finally agreed to talk to me had been in France since 1948, but had left his wife and children in the village. He still

---

[22] The current amount for participation is 20 euros per male adult per funeral, 15 euros per adult woman, and 10 euros for each of the children under eighteen years of age. Villagers are supposed to keep themselves informed or to be informed by the relatives of the deceased (which presupposes a constant close contact with the village and other village members in Paris), and come and pay the money of their own accord. Lists of payments do exist, but I was not allowed to see them.

lived by himself in one of the Kabyle 'hotels' that are common in Northern Paris. He estimated the number of 'Aït Ighil' in France at 80, of whom 65 are retired. The number of people linked in one way or another to Ighil Oumsed who live in France is far higher, but, from his point of view, 'emigrant' means much more than just somebody from the village who lives in France. It is an almost honorary title that indicates a certain mode of behaviour towards other members of the village, a readiness to spend time, effort and money on Parisian and Algerian village structures, and a certain style of living depending on and confined to the world of emigrants from the village or the neighbouring villages. He often quoted the latter as a reference for his own attitudes – and as spatial references for the description of his Parisian *arrondissement*. As the support young people give to the village committee is feeble, he deliberately gives the impression of defending an institution that is doomed to die out, as according to him the values it is based on 'die out' themselves:

> Before, even when you were rich, you wouldn't show it. You'd behave just like the poorest among us, you have to, because everybody has to stick together: we are all the same, and God knows best. In any case, here in France, you are not in your own country, you never really have anything: your wife isn't here, your children aren't here, you are nobody. It's just you in an empty room. You have to stick to your people; otherwise, when you fall ill, you will be on your own in hospital. The young people don't understand these things.

The attitudes of second-generation emigrants towards the village committee are as diverse as their profiles. Many of them – and it seems especially those who seem most 'integrated' into French society and over whom the elders' 'hold' is least effective – still pay their contribution to the village committee. They also try to spend at least one holiday out of two in the village. This, however, seems to be less an essential act of social existence than a voluntary sign of a continuous attachment – not the only and most vital attachment they entertain, but one among many. As a group, they are nevertheless very active in shaping the image of Berbers abroad: a large proportion of students at French universities who conduct research on Kabylia are by now second-generation emigrants; the numerous 'Berber associations' in Paris are mainly run by Kabyle emigrants of a similar profile, with the occasional help of more recent immigrants; a large percentage of the equally numerous web-sites that deal with all sorts of matters relating to Kabylia and Berber culture and language are set up by young second-generation emigrants; and they are also responsible for the large number of re-editions of nineteenth-century descriptions of Kabylia. Although these second-generation emigrants are somewhat detached from village life, and tend to take care to emphasise their 'French' way of life, as the most educated and successful 'villagers', they are crucial for the self-definition of the village, and the region as a whole (cf. Chapman 1978).

Open conflicts arise mainly between the elders and the third group of emigrants: those who made it to France 'on their own account'. When I went to see the member of the village committee quoted above, I was accompanied by Yacine Ihamlalen, whose father had lived in France for a long time, and Yahia Hadid (whose career was described above), who had already been in France for a year to study for a master's degree in economics. The meeting was not free from tension, and Yacine and Yahia continued the discussion even after we had left the Kabyle-owned *café* where the meeting took place. During the discussion, Yacine had been busy establishing a list of all the money his family still owed the committee, whereas Yahia, the 'tourist' as the 'old man' had called him, seemed very discontented with this criticism and the general 'pretension' of the old man to meddle in his private life. For him, the first-generation emigrants were far too oppressive:

> You see, even here in Paris, they don't let go of you. The old men never leave you alone. I came up here once to see the committee, just to see the old room where my father used to live, to see where he started from – but all this is over now. Even the young people, those who are born over here, we don't have anything in common with them: we slaved away to get here, we worked hard at university, an endless struggle. As for them, they are born here, they don't have any education, they just don't care, everything is far too easy for them. We just don't live in the same world, it's as simple as that. (Yahia Hadid)

Yacine, himself not a 'tourist' but an 'emigrant' by virtue of his father, who was still living in Paris, was very critical of this attitude:

> In any case, we know what you are interested in: to have a small job, and that's all: a true Parisian private life and so on. But who will look after our village? You can't go at a hundred miles per hour if everybody else goes at thirty, and you can't just cut yourself off. (Yacine Ihamalalen)

Emigration still remains of crucial importance to Ighil Oumsed, as do other kinds of 'outside connections', be they economic, kin-based, social or intellectual, and villagers constantly strive to maintain or even to extend their own access to these connections. The village thereby is not only consciously part of a larger whole, but this whole has also partly made it what it is, and continues to do so, as the village's economic and intellectual dependence on the outside world, far from diminishing, has further increased with the current economic and political crisis. Recently, however, the range of movement open to villagers has been reduced rather than enlarged, through members of the younger generation who 'cut themselves off', but mainly due to practical reasons such as visa restrictions, unemployment, insecurity and decentralisation, as outlined throughout this chapter. For the younger generation, access to outside resources – a necessary pre-condition for a good position within village society – has thus been severely restricted: although the world seen on satellite TV and on the internet might have enlarged a hundred-fold over the past decade, most of today's twenty-year-olds have hardly ever left their immediate neighbourhood. Hence, the 'world' as an abstract quantity might be better known to villagers, but it is also less accessible than it used to be – a fact which, as I shall argue in the following chapter, needs to be kept in mind when trying to analyse the successive social movements that have shaken Kabylia since the 1980s.

6

Speaking in the Name
of the Village

Jealous of its honour, proud of the help it gives to the weak who call upon it, rich already through donation and some fines, run by its *jamâ'a*, protected by its law, the African *polis* exists in principle without walls or buildings. In order to be and to reign, it does not need to be built on the land, to be visible, material, limited by a Romulus or a Theseus. It is in the heart of all the free men who compose it. (Masqueray 1983 [1886]: 80)

The outstanding feature of Kabyle villages, as all anthropological and historical works on Kabylia seem to agree, is its village assembly, or *tajmaɛt* (see Chapter 1). According to all authors, and to many Kabyles themselves, in Kabylia, the *tajmaɛt* is what turns a mere agglomeration of houses and people into a village. It is what truly 'makes' a Kabyle village; and from a male point of view at least, 'village' and '*tajmaɛt*' are practically synonymous – or at least they should be.[1] Looking for the *tajmaɛt* in Ighil Oumsed, however, proved to be as difficult as looking for the village's spatial boundaries and for its history. All that seemed clear is that since the late 1980s, the village *tajmaɛt* has been 'replaced' by the various associations in the village. But by which one? Most villagers would point towards the *association sociale*. Others, however, flatly denied the latter any right to represent the village, and favoured one or several of the other political institutions in the village, which all claim, in one way or another, to be representative of the village community.

In the present chapter I shall try to show how the various political movements that have succeeded each other in the area construe their arguments for representation and legitimacy. I thereby aim to show the relationship of these 'modern' groups to more 'traditional' village institutions such as the *tajmaɛt*, and to the state, the assumptions about the nature of collective action, politics and community that underlie them, and the permanence of certain characteristics of village elites that can be observed throughout them. These characteristics include the position of the village elite as intermediaries that was already touched upon in Chapters 4 and 5; their accumulation of various sources of legitimacy that for the outsider might appear as contradictory; and their constant efforts to represent and thereby define and 'make' the village as a community.

[1] Although the *tajmaɛt* is often described as a unique Kabyle institution, similar institutions can be found throughout village-based peasant communities in Europe, the Mediterranean and the Middle East: see Behar (1986) for a case in Northern Spain, and the collection of essays in Richards and Kuper (1971) for various examples from sub-Saharan Africa. For a detailed account of recent developments within a Kabyle *tajmaɛt*, see Kinzi (1998).

The village council and the social association

Villagers maintain that the oldest form of independent social organisation in Ighil Oumsed was indeed its internal self-administration through the *tajmaɛt*. The *tajmaɛt* used to be a meeting of all male adult villagers, and would, until the 1970s, generally take place once a week, on Fridays after the weekly communal prayer. Participation used to be obligatory, and absences were punished by a fine. This weekly assembly would 'elect' a village head (*amɣar* or 'old man'), for as long as the selected person was willing to do it, and for as long as no complaints were brought against him. The village *amɣar* would represent the village to the outside, and act as an arbiter in village affairs, assisted therein, for more important matters, by the *tajmaɛt* as a body, or, more frequently, by a restricted assembly which would – at least notionally – include representatives of all families or extended families in the village. 'Village affairs' included land conflicts and transgressions against village customs and morality. A prolonged failure to comply with village directives would lead to exclusion from the village, either through social ostracism, or, if the person had moved away from the village, the denial of the right to be buried in the village cemetery.

In Ighil Oumsed, these 'village customs' have never been written down, and only little of them is now remembered. The habit of pronouncing fines against those who wilfully act against the interest of the village community, or endanger it by their 'asocial' behaviour, has been maintained, however. It is now mainly applied to failures to attend village funerals, or communal village labour. Communal workdays were called to construct the necessary infrastructure for the electrification of the village in the early 1980s, the construction of fresh water pipes to all houses in the village at roughly the same time, and, more recently, the paving of the village's mud roads and urgent repairs. The list of former village *imɣarin* (plural of *amɣar*) reads like confirmation of the changing fate of the village's large families: during and after the war of independence, several traditional influential families appear to have become marginal to the official positions of responsibility, although they often maintained a more indirect influence on village politics. The educational and professional background of official elders also changed gradually, as 'modern' knowledge and skills (such as mastery of the written word and of administrative forms and rhetoric) and privileged contact with the national administration became more important.

In addition to physically constructing the village as a community and as a communal and inhabitable space, the *tajmaɛt* also aimed to present a more united and thus powerful front to the 'outside', in this case, the non-governmental institutions of the area and, most importantly, the national administration. As a general rule, administrative divisions, which in the Akbou region often correspond at least partly to former tribal boundaries, have replaced the latter even for meetings and collective movements independent of the government. 'Tribal' or 'administrative' solidarities, in any case, are not described as fundamentally different or as belonging to two mutually exclusive systems, but rather as co-extensive or even identical. Thus, the last 'tribal assembly' remembered in the village dates from the 1970s, when the last village shepherd was killed by people from the neighbouring village Chellata, of the same tribe, the Illoula Ousammeur. In order to avoid an ongoing vendetta, the *tajmaɛt* of Ighil Oumsed called for a 'tribal meeting' (*jamaɛ*), to which not only members of the Illoula Asammeur were invited, but which also included elders from all tribes in the *commune d'Akbou*, to which Ighil Oumsed then belonged.

The main outside institution that impinges on everyday village life and thus has to be dealt with continuously, however, is the national administration. Much of the outside representative action of the *tajmaɛt* is directed towards it, to channel funds towards the village, and inversely to protect the village against the 'meddling' of 'outsiders'. Representation of the village community as a 'united front' to the state and privileged access to state institutions were often described as central to the functioning of the *tajmaɛt*:

> You have to get together, you have to be many, or else you won't get anything. The government only ever gives when you force them to do so; for everything, you have to go and ask them. When you go by yourself, they don't even let you into the mayor's or the *wali*'s [president of a *wilâya* or department] office. But if you come from the *tajmaɛt*, they respect you. We, the *tajmaɛt* from Ighil Oumsed, used to be known: once, I remember, we went all the way to Béjaïa, to see the *wali*. Everybody else was queuing in front of his office, but as soon as he heard that the village assembly from Ighil Oumsed wanted to talk to him, he let us in before everybody else. (Yahia Benallaoua)

This description of successful interaction with the state – probably coloured by nostalgia and local pride – is reminiscent of the way the *tajmaɛt* itself used to function: as a body composed of different families and their spokesmen, where, despite the official rhetoric of equality, the most influential and 'united' families would be heard first and most. From independence until the 1980s, the state appears to have been conceived of along similar lines, and was generally expected to act accordingly (cf. Roberts 1993).

With the increasing involvement of villagers in the national administration and other public services, the boundaries between interior and exterior village affairs, and between local and regional, or even national sources of influence, became blurred. Leading members of the *tajmaɛt* might double as village elders, government officials, representatives of the FLN or other political parties, and as government employees with a certain local influence such as teachers in the local primary school or engineers in state-run factories. Events, decisions and solidarities at village level could therefore always be interpreted in various ways. Thus, in all the collective building projects cited above, the government was involved in one way or another, furnishing the necessary materials (as for the electrification of the village in the early 1980s) or funds, generally through privileged contacts some villagers entertained with government officials. The manual labour, however, was done by the villagers. These projects are nevertheless generally referred to as 'village projects', and often cited as examples of village solidarity as opposed to the general neglect of the village infrastructure by the state. Hence, the relationship of the *tajmaɛt* with the state remained ambiguous. Although the *tajmaɛt* derived some of its power from its privileged access to state resources, to become too close to the state would have deprived it of its legitimacy as representative of the village community (cf. Bloch 1971).

Despite changes in personnel and orientation in order to stay in touch with political developments in the region and in Algeria as a whole, the *tajmaɛt* had ceased to perform most of its functions by the late 1980s. By then, it had lost its authority and legitimacy in the eyes of many villagers, especially those of the younger generation. In 1989, following the riots of 1988 (see Chapter 2), non-governmental organisations were legalised throughout Algeria. Six years later, the *tajmaɛt* in Ighil Oumsed was re-established under the new name of *association sociale*. The outside event that triggered this was the project proposed by the neighbouring village of Felden to establish a 'social convention' applicable to every village in the *commune* of Chellata (see Appendix 2B p.159). Such conventions were very popular throughout Kabylia at that time (cf. Kinzi 1998; Mahé 2001: 548-9), and the draft text of the Chellata social convention was probably based on an idea taken from the neighbouring *commune* of Chemini.

Throughout the region, all social conventions that were thus agreed upon were similar, although the self-description of the instigators of the conventions varied, from 'religious delegations' via 'social associations' to *tijmaɛtin* (plural of *tajmaɛt*). They all positioned themselves as guardians of collective morality, 'corrected' to fit modern living conditions in the name of tradition and of 'religious' (a word of high political significance in Algeria in the late 1980s) and social values. They do not seem to have perceived their efforts as directed against the ideal nation-state, but rather as part of it. Thus, the convention of the *commune* of Chellata is calqued in its very format on official documents. It is headed by the title '*République Algérienne Démocratique et Populaire*', and copies the idiom of officialdom:

> In the year nineteen hundred and ninety-five, on the twenty-seventh day of the month of July, at the town hall of the *commune* of Chellata, was held a meeting of the committees of all of the villages in the *commune* in order to discuss the pre-project of a convention regarding celebrations and ceremonies.[2]

The convention enumerates and limits in detail all expenses that might be connected to any kind of event or celebration. It deals with religious celebrations, funerals, wakes and births, and deliberately positions itself as a guardian of both Islamic and 'Berber' traditions. The largest part, however, is taken up by the regulation of wedding customs:

> Heading 1: Marriage
> Chapter 1: Engagement ceremony (*tahbult*)...
> Art. 2: the fiancé is asked to bring seven items by way of presents as listed below: two suits as well as two pieces of cloth

---

[2] *Procès-verbal de réunion, avant-projet du pacte social de la commune de Chellata*, 27 July 1995.

one pair of shoes
one bottle of perfume
one packet of henna
six small bars of soap
one engagement ring.

These objects should under no circumstances be subject to an exhibition during the engagement ceremony ...

Chapter 2: Wedding ceremonies (*assensi*)...

Art. 6: the wedding procession (*tikli*) inside and outside the village is regulated according to the customs and traditions of the village as well as according to the ability of the groom to offer a reception or a dinner to all the citizens of the village, or only to his relatives (*proches*) and guests.

Art. 7: in addition to this, the use of firearms during and after the ceremony is abolished.

Thus, the convention tried not only to formalise the very varied pre-existing customs, but also to incorporate more recent changes in the wedding ceremony, such as wedding rings, and to abolish customs that might be seen as outmoded and potentially dangerous, such as the use of firearms.[3] It also sanctioned formerly 'shameful' or 'asocial' behaviour in the name of the good of the community: the groom (significantly not his family) is held to provide food only for as many villagers as he can possibly afford. This socially sanctioned reduction of the scale of weddings followed a general 'privatisation' of weddings, as if to avoid their 'dropping out' of the village altogether.[4] As I noticed during the numerous weddings I was invited to (and of which not one was like the other), the details of how a 'proper' wedding should be celebrated were generally the object of passionate debate, turning around necessary and unnecessary expenses, but also around the introduction of 'Western' or 'Arab' custom and symbols.[5] The social convention thus not only functioned as a practical regulator of expenses and social practices. It also attempted to affirm village authority in reaction to the threatening encroachment of 'outside' customs and sources of legitimacy and moral 'systems', of which the 'Islamism' of the 1990s (or the increasing 'individualism' of the younger generation) was but one symptom.

In order to be able to participate in the negotiations leading up to this

[3] By this time, most private firearms had been confiscated as part of the government's 'pacification' programme, with the exception of local militias.

[4] Younger generation villagers in Ighil Oumsed and elsewhere now sometimes conduct their wedding outside the villages, in the regional cities or even in Algiers, in order to be more independent of village restriction, to be able to have 'mixed (sex)' celebrations, and to avoid the high costs of a village feast. This is widely criticised by the older generation as 'weddings without the couscous', thus as socially invalid, and some outside weddings had to be followed by village feasts (sometimes up to a year later) in order to be acknowledged.

[5] At the first wedding that I was invited to, the couple had decided to join a birthday celebration to the wedding, thus cutting a cake at midnight. Gossip then affirmed that the bride had soon after felt sick, and that therefore the wedding was not even consummated that night, a fact which some put down to witchcraft, others to this breach of 'custom'. I felt that some of the criticism might be due to the fact that the wedding was generally said to have been concluded out of love, and without the initial mediation by the two families, and that the groom was from a rich family and much envied. At the same time, another innovation, the fact that both the groom and the bride arrived on horseback at the groom's house, was generally appreciated as 'good' and 'beautiful' and a 'return to the past', although this was, strictly speaking, probably not true.

convention, and in order to sign and stamp it on behalf on the village, Ighil Oumsed had to organise itself in an *association*. As the now president of the *association sociale* told me:

> The *tajmaεt* hadn't really been working for quite some time by then. The idea of a social convention seemed like a good occasion to reform things a bit, although the change was only superficial: the village assembly is still the village assembly, just with another name. (Mohand Ramdani)

Despite this assurance of continuity – which appears as rather a claim to legitimacy – the change of title indicated a series of more profound changes in the institution. It consolidated the shift of influence from the elders to a younger generation, while formally avoiding a clear break or intergenerational conflict. It was often interpreted, especially by former members of the *tajmaεt*, as symptomatic of a more profound transformation that had taken place in the Algerian political and social landscape:

> Times have changed, the *wali* has changed, and for the new *wali*, the *tajmaεt* is nothing. An association is more modern: now we have a stamp, we can send out letters and everything, and it's more attractive for the young people who went to school. For our generation, it didn't really matter, but now, to get anything at all, electricity, water, a road, you need a letter, don't you? (Yahia Benallaoua)

The founding members of the *association sociale* were almost without exception relatively young (then in their thirties and forties, that is to say, mainly the post-war generation). They had a certain level of education, but none of them seems to have pitched their life plans outside the restricted space of the village, which, at least at the time when the association was founded, still served as their main point of reference. A large number of them were government employees. This was still true of the most active members of the *association sociale* in 2004, who almost exclusively seemed to be teachers at the local primary school. The trajectory of the president of the *association sociale* and local school director Mohand Ramdani exemplifies the general profile of the now most influential members of the association:

> I was born in 1960 in Ighil Oumsed. I went to school in Ighil Oumsed, and to the *collège* in Akbou. Then I had to stop school in order to earn money for my family. At that time, they were looking for primary school teachers, and I decided to become a primary school teacher of Arabic. I mainly worked in schools in the Akbou region. After several training courses, I was promoted school director. That's when I went back home to take over the school in the village, more than ten years ago now. As I was the oldest son in the family, I got married very early to somebody from the village. I helped my younger brother to open a shop in the village, in the family house. I have always been active in the village, and especially since we founded the *association sociale*. The *association sociale* is very important: we are the only ones who do anything, and we are the only ones who really know the village, all of it, land-rights and conflicts and everything. Since I became school director, I have tried to make the school better, I read a lot of books on pedagogy, I collaborate with the *association des parents d'élèves*, and I help the *association sportive* for the young people in the village. (Mohand Ramdani)

The *association sociale* tends to be associated with the newly constructed meeting hall or *tajmaεt*, where it keeps all its paperwork, and the key of

Photo 6.1 *Tajmaɛt* or village assembly hall; note the pulpit, the Algerian flag and the Berber symbol

Photo 6.2 Office of the cultural association

Photo 6.3 Monument in Ighzer Amokrane to victims of the riots of 2001

which is kept by its leading members. The interior design of the new meeting hall sums up the various levels of legitimacy the social association tries to draw upon. The lay-out of seats, long benches in a circle, resembles the former open-air *tajmaɛt*. To this have been added large shelves on the walls to contain the association's paperwork, which is generally kept under lock and key, and access to which is heavily restricted, and a raised pulpit to address the meeting, thus installing or at least admitting to a certain hierarchy within the meeting. This pulpit is decorated like that of the Algerian parliament, with the addition of the symbol of the Berber movement (Photo 6.1).

The status of the *association sociale* within the village community remains ambiguous. On the one hand, it conducts general operations and fines those villagers – members of the association or not – who do not turn up to assist in their execution, much as the *tajmaɛt* would have done in former times. It also retains control over village communal property such as the spring and the war monument. It thereby defines itself as the representative of the village community, in internal as well as external matters. On the other hand, it is an *association*, which means that membership is a choice and is no longer identical with being a villager, and village support for it is by no means total. For its critics, the *association sociale* does not represent the village as a whole, but a group of people furthering their personal interests:

> We call them the 'four Larbi': Yahia Benallaoua [Oularbi in Kabyle], Larbi Mouhoubi, Larbi Ramdani, Larbi Hargous. You have to stay away from them; they are dangerous. They pull the strings in all matters. The village mafia. (Farid Yennat)

The tensions thus expressed indicate the failure of the *association sociale* to maintain the balance between identification with the state and opposition to it, on which the *tajmaɛt* used to depend. They also show a more profound dissatisfaction with the power relations within the village community, which are seen as symptomatic of those that govern Algeria as a whole. These tensions partly find their expression in the various village associations. They are most clearly exemplified by the complicated, but always confrontational relationship that the *association sociale* maintains with its nearest 'competitor', the *association culturelle*.

The *spécialistes de la casse* and the cultural association

When the *association sociale* was founded in 1995, the first association in Ighil Oumsed, the *association sociale et culturelle Amsed*,[6] had already existed

---

[6] Throughout what follows, I shall refer to this association as the '*association culturelle*'. The distinction between 'social' and 'cultural' associations can be found in a large number of Kabyle villages, and tends to be perceived along similar lines. The *association culturelle* is generally associated with the younger generation, and with the Berber movement (see Mahé 2001: 546). The fact that the *association culturelle* in Ighil Oumsed decided to include the 'social' in its title might point towards an attempt to avoid this dichotomy in the village, and to play a more central part than that generally assigned to an *association culturelle*.

for four years. It had been created in the wake of the Berber movement that
had started at the universities of Tizi Ouzou and Béjaïa in the early 1980s,
practically as soon as the creation of non-governmental associations had
been legalised. Although many of the most active members of the *association culturelle* were also among the initiators of the *association sociale*, the
relationship between the two associations soon became strained. They are
now generally conceived of as two opposite poles of village activity, and as
representing two different social groups within the village. These two
groups in turn relate to social and generational cleavages in the village, in
Kabylia or even in Algeria as a whole. In order to describe the development
of the *association culturelle* in Ighil Oumsed, its position within the village
community, and the constitution of its membership and the members' motivations, the following will briefly sketch the trajectories of the first militants,
and of its most influential president.

The first and best-known early 'Berberist' activists in the village were
Arezqi's cousin Fodil Ihamlalen, and Arezqi's older brother Hamid. Since
they were teenagers, several years before the 'official' emergence of Berberist
currents in 1980, they had stood out as local troublemakers using Berber
symbols to shock the 'establishment':

> In the village, they were afraid of me, because I wasn't afraid of anybody, and
> especially not of the FLN people. I had a shirt made, embroidered with letters in
> *tifinay*,[7] the branch of an olive tree and some figs, and Fodil and I had found an
> old German army helmet that we had painted with *tifinay* letters. Dressed like
> that, we would walk all the way to Tizi-Ouzou, to watch the football. Everybody
> in the village would walk there, but we had to go by ourselves, because every-
> body else in the village was afraid that I might cause them trouble – just because
> of the helmet. Everybody was afraid of us, they called us the 'shock troops'.
> (Hamid Yennat)

Both were pupils who, despite their obvious intelligence, failed in the state
school system, and they both blame this failure on the obligation to use
Arabic in class.[8] They are both from formerly influential 'old families' which
had lost a large part of their former influence during and after the war of
independence. In both their extended families, several of their close cousins
had nevertheless been much more successful in joining the 'system'. Both
young men had only ever experienced the state, locally identified with the
village 'establishment', as a constraint, and both spent time in prison, one
because he deserted several times during his military service, the other
because he had burnt down the local office of the FLN.

During their imprisonment, they had been in contact with the first

---

[7] *Tifinay* is a script based on Touareg inscriptions found in the Sahara, but which was probably
never used in Kabylia itself. It was taken up by the Berber movement in the 1970s as a proof
of the antiquity and high status of all Berber languages. It can now be seen all over Kabylia
on graffiti and shop windows. Only very few people master it, however. The standard Berber
which is now taught in Algerian schools and in French universities is usually transcribed in
Latin script.
[8] Their time of schooling, the late 1960s and early 1970s, coincided with the first, often very
experimental, period of the Arabisation of the national school system (see Grandguillaume
1983: 96–105).

generation of political Islamists and Berberists, but they had never truly become part of either of these two groups. They both had subsequently been refused a passport for several years. After their failure at school, they both left the village as soon as they could, looking for work in Algiers and elsewhere. For both, their prolonged stay in Algiers, and for Hamid his travels around the whole of Algeria – mainly on foot, it seems, as he was deprived of any identity papers after his desertion – were formative and furnished the elements which were then, for the following generations of their younger brothers and cousins, to become the main tenets and signs of 'Berberism':

> I was working in Algiers, with Kabyles, but we were afraid to speak Kabyle in the streets; French was fine, Arabic was better, otherwise, you would be in trouble. If we spoke Kabyle at all, we were whispering, very quietly, we were afraid... In Algiers, I started to follow Mouloud Mammeri's evening classes at university,[9] and that's where I discovered that we Kabyles had a long history and spoke a real language. (Fodil Ihamlalen)

> I was in Algiers when the JSK [*Jeunesse sportive de la Kabylie*, the regional football team] won the national championship for the first time – we had never thought that anything like this could ever happen to us. We were so happy that we went crazy: suddenly, everybody in Algiers was speaking Kabyle, everybody, I swear! For three days, Algiers was ours. We methodically smashed everything, stole everything. Chadli [the former (1979–91) Algerian President] was much cleverer than Boutef [Abdelaziz Bouteflika, the current President]: he held back his policemen, and just waited for us to finish. After three days, we got tired, we went back home, and everything calmed down again. (Hamid Yennat)

On his return from Algiers, Fodil became known for leading small-scale riots and erasing Arabic writing on signposts and shops:[10]

> Once, I really got into trouble, because I had painted over the sign for a shop in Akbou, which belonged to an old *maquisard* from the village. For the police, this was a criminal act because I had attacked Arabic, and thereby also Islam and the state. For the people, it was even worse: I had attacked one of the elders, one of the 'heroes' of the village. (Fodil Ihamlalen)

His own description of his 'crimes' shows the various meanings they may have at different levels. It also indicates Fodil's conflation of a general sentiment of exclusion from the state at all levels – political, social, cultural, linguistic, and economic – with grudges against local privileges. To use any 'Berber' symbols, such as *tifinay* and JSK football shirts, and to speak Kabyle in Algiers, the seat of national power, meant to reject a whole system experienced as oppressive, exclusive, made for others and by others, based on lies, 'fake' identities and corruption, and intellectually and culturally 'empty',

---

[9] Moulod Mammeri, a writer, novelist, university teacher and anthropologist, is still regarded, several years after his death in a car accident, as Kabylia's leading intellectual. He brought the archaeological research centre in Algiers (CRAPE) to its former glory, and inspired a whole generation of Berberist intellectuals (see Chapter 2).

[10] After independence, public signposts had for more than a decade continued to be French or bilingual. A massive 'Arabisation of the environment' was launched as late as 1976 (that is to say, not long before Fodil started to cross them out again). It had led to an 'anarchic Arabisation' in Algiers, where FLN party-members were sent out at night to tar over all the French writing they could find (Grandguillaume 1983: 113).

grey and uninspiring. It was a rebellion against authority, but thereby also against the basis on which this authority rested.

In the meantime, more and more militant Berber groups sprang up among emigrant Kabyles in France, from whence their ideas spread to the two regional universities in Kabylia and beyond. During the 1980s, several young villagers from Ighil Oumsed started to meet out in the fields to discuss the little material that was available on Berber culture, and – as some say – even to dream of a Berber revolution. Like Fodil and Hamid, many of the early militants had first encountered Berberist ideas and materials during periods of absence from the village, at school or during military service:

> I was in the army, and seeing as I can't write very well, I one day asked one of my friends, who was also Kabyle, to write a letter to my family for me. He asked me in which language I wanted him to write it, maybe in Berber so that my mother would understand it too? I had always thought that Kabyle was just a dialect, bad Arabic, and that you couldn't write it – I thought he was just making fun of me. But he wasn't: he drew some letters for me in *tifinay*, and that's when I first understood that they had always lied to us about our own language, our own culture, our own history. I started to ask more people, to learn everything I could. At that time, that was still very difficult.

In 1991, these first 'Berberists' publicly claimed their own status and space in the village community with the founding of the cultural association. It was instigated by a group of ten to fifteen 'youths' (generally in their mid-twenties or early thirties), who mainly came from families that were less closely associated with the 'establishment'. They were rarely those who, by a simple outbreak of anger, had been known as 'activists' beforehand, although ties between the groups remained strong.

Probably the person in the village who was most clearly associated with the *association culturelle* was my host, Arezqi Yennat, Hamid's younger brother. He was one of its founding members, he had always been more or less active within it, if only as an adviser to those who were officially running it, and he was its president during its 'golden year' in 1997. He is now in his late thirties, but still unmarried. He is the second son of a large family, which counts as among the oldest – and the poorest – families in the village. Although, according to all accounts, he was a brilliant pupil at school, he failed his baccalaureate, because he had to work to provide an income for his by then fatherless family at the same time as studying. Most of the knowledge and the 'connections' that constitute his status as village intellectual are self-acquired, mainly during his long career as a parapolitical activist. He is active in several associations in Akbou and in the first non-governmental labour union (the SATEF). He also sympathises with the FFS (*Front des forces socialistes*, one of the two 'Kabyle' parties). His attitude to all these institutions, like his attitude to the state itself, remains ambivalent, however, and none of his commitments is total. He recalls the beginning of his career as a militant as follows:

> At the beginning of the *mouvement associatif* [from 1989 onwards], I was mainly active in Akbou, with the *Amis de l'Art*. We moved around a lot: that's how I

came to know the universities of Béjaïa, Tizi Ouzou, Algiers, Boumerdes, all the universities and educational institutes in the region. We took the car, went off to meet people, exchange ideas.... When the *association culturelle* [in Ighil Oumsed] had to send a representative to Tizi Ouzou to take a training course in Berber [organised by the Berber movement in 1991], everybody suggested that I should go, maybe because I already had a certain experience of outside relations. We were put up at the student halls in Tizi Ouzou. That's where I met everybody, and where I learnt everything I know about Berber.

Arezqi's emphasis on his experiences outside the immediate surroundings of his village, and on his temporary access to the universities in the area, shows that participation in the cultural association not only conferred a certain degree of legitimacy on its members at village level. It also opened up access to new networks of solidarity and co-operation, linking the villages to the towns, and the towns to the larger cities and their universities, and ultimately to the universities of Paris. These networks often bypassed the hierarchy established by the national administration and the education system, and it is noticeable that the bulk of local militants consisted of the in-between class that had been created by the extraordinary rate of school failure. Thus, although a large part of the content of the Berber movement might seem to claim a *retour aux sources*, the Berber movement seen from its base in the villages and small towns appears also as an attempt to conquer the national and international centres of knowledge-production and decision-making, by villagers whose field of action had been massively reduced, due to the newly introduced visa restrictions, soaring unemployment, and the shortcomings of the national education system.

This double orientation is also exemplified by the reaction of the *association culturelle* to the discovery of a Roman statue and funerary stele near the village.[11] This discovery was made in 1991. The village soon approached the local authorities, who sent an archaeologist on a quick and unproductive assessment that nobody in the village seems to remember. It was only in 1997, when Arezqi himself took over the presidency of the *association culturelle*, that the discovery of the site led to a short period of glory for the village. As soon as he assumed the presidency of the association, Arezqi started to write letters to the 'authorities' at all levels. These letters expressed a double intention: to promote the archaeological site officially as an infallible sign of the village's participation in world history, while maintaining control over it, and to take the discovery of the site as an occasion to improve the village's infrastructure:

> We hope that our association will always be able to follow closely the discovery and the promotion of this site in order to be able to continue its cultural effort

[11] The Soummam valley abounds in Roman and pre-Roman sites, many of which have not yet been classified, analysed or even recorded (for a first and by now clearly dated survey of existing remains, see Gsell 1911). The statue and the stele found in Ighil Oumsed date from the first century AD, and mark the grave of a Roman veteran, whose name is likely to be of local origin. A relatively large area of village land is now classified as archaeological terrain, but the archaeologists who visited it were not sure that it necessarily contained a Roman settlement. In any case, settlement would not have been continuous. In addition to Roman traces, the archaeologists found traces of pre-Roman graves.

and to see to the preservation of the interests of the population, especially that of the landowners, as it has seen to the promotion and the protection of this hitherto totally unknown site for more than seven years by now ... In addition to this, we also hope that the locality will benefit from the promotion of the site through the creation of a communal museum and a cultural centre; through the opening of roads towards Chellata and Ifri-Ouzellaguen (already existent, but impracticable) that are suitable for motor vehicles; and that a telephone line will be installed at the post office of Ighil Oumsed.[12]

The *association culturelle* thereby positioned itself as the unique representative of the village to the 'authorities' and as the privileged intermediary of the 'authorities' to the village community and its heritage, even in matters that so far had been a prerogative of the *tajmaɛt*, such as the building of roads and the channelling of government funds towards the village.

As his letters were not answered, or only answered evasively, Arezqi decided to take things into his own hands. In April 1997, a delegation of archaeologists and their students arrived from the archaeological institute in Algiers. The archaeologist who was in charge of the student group, and who is himself of Kabyle origin, still rather fondly remembers this visit:

Ighil Oumsed? You should talk to my colleague, as soon as he hears this name, he laughs and says: *'urs al-qarya*, the village party [lit. village wedding]. We had taken a group of students to Bougie [Béjaïa] for an excursion, and the villagers had heard of our arrival – I have no idea how. When we got there, they were already waiting for us at the door of the museum, with two mini-buses, saying that they had an archaeological site in their village, that we absolutely had to come and see the site, and that they would take care of food and everything. There was no way we could have said no, so we went – it was very nice, the whole village was there to welcome us. Obviously, with all these people standing around, we couldn't see anything. Anyway, there wasn't much to be seen. In the Soummam valley, almost every village has got a site like that. And to make things even worse, they had destroyed everything – they are peasants, they don't know anything about archaeology, they think they just have to dig, and that's it. I would have preferred that everything remain underground; like that, we might have been able to do something at a later date.

The 'peasants' still carefully preserve the report produced by the archaeologists, and the site was one of the first places I had to visit. Like the Roman statue and the stele, the report is kept under lock and key in the office of the *association culturelle* (see Photo 6.2). In its oral version, the report has been slightly bent to fit a grander image of the village: whereas the main interest of the site archeologically lies apparently in its prehistoric traces, villagers generally describe it as 'Roman' or 'proto-Roman'. It thereby becomes a proof of their participation in a larger civilisation, but as an independent unit, the 'proto-Romans' or 'Romanised Numidians'.

The experience of the Roman site sums up several of the prominent features that were characteristic of the *association culturelle*: the importance of the interplay with outside sources of influence and legitimacy, here the national administration and the university, and of the ability to channel funds and prestigious visitors to the village; the attempts to monopolise the

[12] Letter from the *association culturelle* to the *commune*, 1997.

representation of the entire village to these 'authorities' and vice versa, and thereby to define the nature of the village or in this case its cultural heritage; and the importance of access to 'modern' and 'scientific' knowledge, of the possession of the written word and of a quasi-monopoly of knowledge of Berber matters. Taken together, these features led to the constitution of a new elite of modern notables and experts within the village community, responding to its own structures and networks. These and other features of the *association culturelle* were also present in the constitution of several other associations in the village, for which the *association culturelle* often served as inspiration and model, and whose memberships in any case often overlapped.

The religious association, the karate school and the pitfalls of collective action

The third association founded in the village was the *association religieuse*. The reason for its creation, according to its members, was the need to have a legal and more powerful representation of the village community to the Ministry of Religious Affairs. This was especially important as the last imam in and from the village had died in the 1980s (see Chapter 4), leaving the village without an imam for several years. All the attempts by villagers to ask for a new imam at the Ministry of Religious Affairs proved futile. As they had hoped, as soon as they organised themselves in an association, the village delegation to Béjaïa was more successful, and an official imam was dispatched to the village. He did not last long in his post, however, as he insisted on 'meddling' in village affairs: 'He didn't really understand what we wanted him to do, that an imam is supposed to go to the mosque or else he stays at home. Everything else is none of his business' (Mouloud Harkoun). The second imam was hardly any luckier: 'He was too young, he wasn't even married yet – that's why we went to Béjaïa to complain, and he left.' Nor the third:

> He was strange: he had friends from outside, strangers who came to see him, and he himself went into the forest, and he always came back via the back entrance of the village, and not the front. Sometimes he brought his friends in the middle of the night, and the next morning, they had already left.[13]

The fourth also had to leave, and it was only the fifth candidate who was widely accepted. At the time of writing, he still acts as the imam of the village. He is married and has several daughters, keeps quiet and sticks to his house and to the mosque. He has reduced his more radical opinions to preaching against Coca Cola. He speaks and preaches in Kabyle, not Arabic. He also seems happy to take on some of the more traditional functions of a village marabout, although in the eyes of the villagers he certainly does not have the *baraka* of the Ouhaddar family or other local marabouts. He lets his wife receive the village women, however, to a point where the women

---

[13] The imam is here implicitly accused of contact with the Islamist *maquis*.

of the village in particular say that he must be a marabout after all. He also agreed to bless the statue that was erected to the memory of one of the village's young people who was killed in 2001 by police. I do not know whether he was really selected in the way Mouloud, one of the younger members of the *association religieuse*, and currently its president, described it. In any case, Mouloud's story indicates how he conceived of the ideal relationship between the village and its imam-civil servant.

The *association religieuse* was founded at a time when the control of religion had to a large extent been taken away from the village community, and when religious matters had gradually been taken over by government officials. At the same time, ideas associated with the increasingly popular political Islam threatened the moral authority of the older generation as much as that of local institutions (Martinez 1998). The *association religieuse* appears as an attempt by the village community, or by some of its members, to (re)claim control over the religious activities in the village and of the villagers. Significantly, other projects of the *association religieuse* included the construction of a house for the imam, plans for the enlargement of the village mosque, and an attempt to rationalise and institutionalise the paying of *zakât* and other religious taxes in the village, thereby bringing it under the control of the imam and the *association religieuse*. The association thereby attempted to defend the village against too much outside influence, both by government officials and by 'Islamists', and to position itself as the privileged interlocutor where government influence seemed inevitable or beneficial. At the same time, it offered an opportunity for its younger members (indispensable in any association be it only for the amount of paperwork that is needed to 'officialise' it) to take over some of the religious legitimacy traditionally controlled by the village elders. It thereby also gave expression to a different, more scriptural and 'democratic' conception of religion, similar to that which is characteristic of modern political Islam (Kepel 1993; Starret 1998).

The membership of the *association religieuse* can be divided roughly into two groups: several older men known as representing the religious 'establishment' in the village, and who have always 'looked after the mosque', and a number of younger men, of Arezqi's generation, who are trying to 'modernise' religion in the village. As for the other associations, double mandates were very frequent among this younger generation. This is shown by the trajectory of Mouloud Harkoun, the association's current president:

> I was one of the founding members of the *association sociale*, one of the first members of the *association culturelle* – I am a good friend of Arezqi's. I was member of the *association des parents d'élèves* and even their president, even before I had any children at the school, and I had been active in the *association religieuse* for several years before I became its president. I like getting involved in village affairs: you should never leave others to decide for you, and besides, I have always been religious.

Similarly, the secretary of the *association religieuse*, Djamel Benhamidouche (the *trabendiste* and jeweller encountered in Chapter 5), was also president of the *association culturelle* during most of my stay, and he is one of the village's former delegates to the *aârouch* (see below).

Both Mouloud and Djamel spent considerable energy and time in furthering their economic position in the village. Mouloud, besides constructing his house, which is now almost as high as the mosque itself, runs one of the shops in the village, opened with profits said to have been made through his earlier activity as a *trabendiste*. He also plans to open a bakery, with help from the government. Djamel's trajectory was described in Chapter 5. For both, 'being active' (*activer*)[14] indicates a general attitude towards all aspects of life, without making an essential distinction between its economic, social and political aspects, or between theoretically opposed movements. All these aspects tend to be conflated in the notion of 'having a position' within the village community, and in life in general, 'being involved' in things, 'being informed', and, most importantly, being respected.

Since 1997, the activities of all of the village's associations have been reduced, the peaks generally coinciding with the presidency of an especially active and experienced member. As with any village organisation, their structure is prone to succumb to larger conflicts in the village. Projects are always read as part of a logic of personal interest, status or antagonism, which few seem to be able to resist (cf. Salhi 1999a: 38).[15] During my stay, some of the younger members of the *association culturelle* formed their own association (the *association sportive*) in order to run a karate school. This was interpreted by others as the result of their being lured away and 'used' by members of the social association, the FFS, the 'establishment', the MAK (*Mouvement pour l'autonomie de la Kabylie*, the only Kabyle 'movement' that clearly demands 'autonomy' from the rest of Algeria), or several of the above. All these accusations are probably true to a certain extent. They seem to be part of a larger struggle over power and influence in the village, leading to personal conflicts that might be explained on a variety of levels. All these struggles ultimately turn around one central issue: that of the right to act as intermediaries between the village and the outside, or the legitimacy to 'represent' the village both to the 'authorities' and to the village community itself. This legitimacy is never stable, as it carries within itself the suspicion of abuse. The village community is always ready to deny it to anyone as soon as it has been 'granted' – or 'usurped'. Similar issues of legitimate representation were at stake in the local development of political parties.

---

[14] In standard French, *activer* is a transitive verb and requires a direct object (e.g. *le vent active le feu*) or a reflexive pronoun (*s'activer* – to speed up). The derivative *activiste* tends to be pejorative (somebody who is committed to a political cause for the sake of being committed, rather than for the cause itself). In Algerian French (and Kabyle), *activer* has come to stand on its own, is generally seen as positive, and mainly refers to political commitment. It does not necessarily require any further precision as to the nature of this commitment.

[15] This logic of the inevitable manipulation of any successful political or social movement seems to run all the way through Algerian (and French) perceptions of politics (cf. Aggoun and Rivoire 2004). Indeed, it seems to be a standard feature of voluntary commitments in small communities, at least in Europe and the Middle East, see, for example, Frankenberg (1957) and the classic satire of French provincial life in *Clochemerle* (Chevallier 1934).

The politicians and the absent Islamists

Throughout Algeria, independent political parties were legalised after the riots of 1988. The first new party founded in the region was the *Rassemblement pour la culture et la démocratie* (RCD). Its foundation dramatically changed the village political landscape, which for years had been dominated by a rather lukewarm commitment to the FLN, then the *parti unique*:

> As soon as possible, everybody became RCD, that is to say everybody who wasn't FLN – and especially those who today are the most FFS in the village, like Mourad, they were straightaway a hundred percent RCD. (Arezqi Yennat)

With the 're-activation' of the second regional party, the FFS (*Front des forces socialistes*, see Chapter 2), political allegiances changed rapidly. The village soon became 'totally' FFS. The FFS has won all municipal elections held since the introduction of a multi-party system. Since 1997, it has held virtually all of the local town halls, although its legitimacy to do so was hotly contested by the *aârouch* movement (see below). In the village, the number of actual party members remained low, and several other parties, such as the FLN-offshoot *Rassemblement national pour la démocratie* (RND), had short moments of glory. These were mainly due to the personal commitment of some respected villager. As a general rule, commitments to parties were rarely clear and total, and could change surprisingly rapidly. Subsequent or even parallel membership in theoretically bitterly opposed groups was frequent. The important difference among villagers was not therefore their allegiance to opposed parties or other parapolitical groups, but between those who *activent* and those who, for various reasons, do not.

Mourad Hamlal, the 'village politician', resembles in his trajectory and age the members of the other associations, especially the *association culturelle*.[16] He was one of the founding members of both the social and the cultural associations. He refers to Arezqi as a 'friend'. In terms of schooling, he is more educated than the older generation, but not enough to make a career out of his education beyond the immediate area. His position as an intermediary between the village and the outside is reminiscent of that aspired to by members of the various village associations. He has been working in the branch of the town hall in Ighil Oumsed ever since it was opened, and he therefore provides the link between the 'authorities', as represented by the mayor of the *commune* and by the FFS party office in Akbou, and the village community. He describes his trajectory and his reasons for joining the FFS as follows:

---

[16] The most prominent politician from the village, the FFS's Djamel Zenati, has in more than one sense 'left' it, much as the 'real' intellectuals, based at universities in France or Algeria, only return for a short time and generally tend to stay outside village politics. Unfortunately, due to the increasingly tense political atmosphere in the whole country in the time leading up to the presidential elections, I did not manage to conduct an interview with Djamel Zenati himself.

Before the beginning of multi-party politics, nothing ever happened. Everything was managed by the 'revolutionary family' or those who said they were part of it. They never did anything for us, and they left no room for us. I started to be active as soon as the political parties were legalised, I even founded the RCD in the village, then I started to work for the MCB [*Mouvement culturel berbère*], and since 1989, the FFS. At that time, we were one hundred and fifty active members, and we would hold our meetings at *tajmaɛt*... The FFS is the only party with a certain legitimacy: they are fighting for the Berber cause, and [its president] Aït Ahmed is after all a historical figure of the revolution [the war of independence]. Since the FFS took over the *commune*, things are much better: they've installed a telephone line, an office of the town hall in the village, and they built the paved road.[17] They represent true democracy.

For Mourad, political legitimacy is thus a concoction of historical legitimacy derived from the war of independence, the improvement of the local infrastructure, commitment to the Berber cause and 'democracy'. Mourad also several times stressed the fact that the first FFS party meetings were held at *tajmaɛt*, and repeatedly emphasised the initial popularity of the meetings, much as he liked to underline the 'unity' of the village, lost but re-established by the villagers' homogeneous support for the FFS.

This re-found unity after the troubled years of the early 1990s was often stressed, by FFS activists and members of the 'establishment' alike. The latter, such as, for example, the school director and president of the *association sociale*, Mohand Ramdani, now often tend to be identified with the FFS. It appears as though the FFS locally, by taking over the positions and offices of the FLN, had also taken on its mode of functioning and its presumption not only to rule, but to be identical with 'society' or 'the village'. Similarly, the accusations of 'corruption', abuse of political power and vote-catching are now directed against the FFS with almost the same fervour as against the FLN. Seen from the village, the introduction of a multi-party system thus brought about a change of personnel and of style, but only a minor change in ways of conceiving and constructing political power.

Despite more or less openly expressed political conflicts within the village, villagers always agree on one point: as everywhere else in Kabylia, the most successful Algerian political party that emerged after 1988, the Islamist FIS (*Front islamique du salut*), remained excluded from village politics.[18] This does not mean that the FIS did not have an impact on the village: on the contrary, here as elsewhere in Algeria, it polarised opinions and changed notions of public morality. Political, social and moral arguments, even if they did not mention the 'Islamists' directly, tended to be constructed with reference to them, and 'Kabyle identity' became for many synonymous with

---

[17] The FFS took over the administration of the *commune* in 1997, i.e. several years after most of these improvements had been made (since the annulment of the electoral process after the landslide victory of the FIS in most Algerian *communes*, the *commune* of Chellata had been administered by an appointed mayor).

[18] In the 1991 elections, 13.8% of Kabyles voted for the FIS, as compared with 55.42% in Algeria as a whole, Kabylia included (Mahé 2001: 498).

'anti-Islamism'. The success of the FIS often strengthened local perceptions of being 'persecuted' by the government allied with their new 'Islamist friends'. Rather than being marked by an opposition between a secular FLN and an Islamist FIS, as often portrayed in the Western media (Roberts 2003), the FIS-years were seen locally by many as yet another in a long series of attacks by 'Arabo-Islamists' against Kabylia. Some people even interpreted the presence of veiled women in towns like Akbou as a 'government plot' to destabilise the region. This, rather than the 'innate secularism' of the Berbers, seems to have played an important role in the Kabyles' overall rejection of the FIS. Other reasons for the failure of the FIS to appeal to a majority of Kabyle voters seem to be the local perception of 'Islamists' as 'outsiders' or 'Arabs', the influence of a strong secular current especially among the post-war generation, and the existence of the region's own protest movement, which had already absorbed the local and locally bound elites who, according to Martinez (1998: 80), had largely been responsible for the success of the FIS elsewhere.

Despite the electoral failure of the FIS in the village itself, 'Islamists' were not totally unknown to villagers. Families originally from the village and now installed in Algiers have children counted among the *barbus* (the 'bearded ones'), and the small towns in the valley were apparently not as immune to the new political and cultural tendency as people liked to make out. Some members of the younger generation, especially girls, were very interested in Islam, and handed around brochures about 'true Islam' in the village. Others were secretly pointed out to me as 'one of them'. In general, however, people kept quiet on anything that might be connected with the subject of Islamism, partly because 'true Kabyles' are 'immune' to it, partly because it is identified with the unspeakably horrible events of the 1990s, and partly because of fear:

> You should never talk about the *barbus*, especially not in the fields (*laxla*). You never know who will hear what and to whom he will speak afterwards, and these people are everywhere. All these things, you mustn't ever talk about them, ever. (Fadila Yennat)

The years of violence following the annulment of the 1991 elections (see Chapter 2) appear to have had a rather indirect, but none the less powerful, impact on the village. The village appointed a patrol for defence against 'terrorist' attacks, about which I could never obtain any concrete information. I heard various stories about kidnapped villagers from the area, but not from the village itself, about 'requisitioned cars' and heroic deeds of villagers who managed to escape the 'terrorists'. Although I was voluntarily offered a whole series of explanations of the 'events' generally, nobody spoke about what had happened locally. The explanations offered all lacked conviction: they could change from one day to the next, and no coherent narrative ever seems to have been developed by the village community as a whole. The younger generation, however, convinced of the government's hostility and total ruthlessness and having lost all trust in state representatives, tended to blame the security forces for most of the violence.[19]

The death of the first villager to be killed during the 'events' of the 1990s forced the village to agree at least superficially on some kind of explanation, if only to decide how to arrange his funeral. The young man, like several others from the village after him, was killed during his military service, on its last day, in fact. His father, overcome with grief, buried him 'secretly and by night', as villagers say, but quite probably with the help of a substantial number of them, in the not yet inaugurated new graveyard of the *shuhadâ*, that had just been constructed next to the village *mairie*. By placing his son among the incontestable war heroes, the father's message was clear: his son had died to liberate his country, much as the *mujâhidîn* of the war of independence had done before him. Hence, his death had not been meaningless, but was part of a long Algerian national history of martyrdom and sacrifice, and it should be acknowledged as such. Clearly not everybody in the village agreed with his interpretation of the 'events', and both the leading members of the village council and the local representatives of the town hall refused to inaugurate the new war monument unless the 'intruder' was removed. Village morality declared the father to be 'mad', while the village council took him to court in Akbou. In 2005, after several years of deliberation, the court decided in favour of the village council. The 'intruder's' body, however, has not yet been removed. In any case, the answer to the questions this conflict really posed could not be found by the court in Akbou: how can sense ever be made of the deaths of those who were killed during the years of 'terrorism'?

The new generation of martyrs

Although Kabylia remained relatively calm during the 1990s, the beginning of the 2000s saw an unprecedented outbreak of violence in the area. In April 2001, the 'Black Spring' erupted, several months of rioting against the *gendarmerie* and other representatives of the government, to which the security forces responded by opening fire on the demonstrators, killing more than a hundred of them. As described in the Introduction, the riots had been set off by the death of an 18-year-old high school student in a *gendarmerie* in the district of Tizi Ouzou. His death immediately became a symbol of the *hogra* or disrespect that the younger generation in particular feel they are suffering at the hands of state representatives. The targets attacked by the demonstrators were similar to those destroyed during the 1988 riots in Algiers: the local FLN offices, but also the offices of the two Kabyle parties, FFS and RCD; cultural centres, *gendarmeries* and other

---

[19] Similar perceptions have lately also become fashionable in France. See, for example, Aggoun and Rivoire (2004). They are backed up by first-hand accounts by Algerians published in France, such as Yous (2000); Souaïdia (2001) and Samraoui (2003); cf. also Silverstein (2002).

symbols of state power and privilege, such as the offices of the state-run airline, *Air Algérie*, and various travel agents.[20] In the Soummam region, the riots were mainly confined to the towns of the valley. Most young male villagers from Ighil Oumsed took a more or less active part in them.

Kamel Ihamlalen, the only villager from Ighil Oumsed to be killed during the riots, died in Ighzer Amokrane. He had been a resident of Tiouririne, and a high school student in Ighzer Amokrane. He died after being shot by a *gendarme*. The village did not know how to react to his death, or how and where he should be buried. After three days of indecision, he was finally buried in the courtyard of the town hall of Ighzer Amokrane, as a 'martyr', although a grave had also been dug for him in the cemetery in Ighil Oumsed. Kamel was buried alongside three other victims of the riots, two of whom were from Ighzer Amokrane itself, and the third a 'foreigner' who had been killed while passing through (see photo 6.3). This outcome of the conflict was unusual, as Kamel was thereby made to remain in a town of which as a villager he had never quite been part. It showed that his body, at least at the time of the riots, was suddenly quite out of reach of the villagers, and that it had started to 'belong' to a new 'community': the rioting, town-based *jeunes*, who were publicly restyling themselves as a new generation of 'martyrs' or *shuhadâ*.

Kamel's body was also claimed by a very different kind of 'community', namely, the regional parties and para-political movements. Although many villagers, among them the *ikhwân* (village Sufis) and the village imam, attended the funeral, it was organised not by the family or the village community, but by the freshly created citizens' committee and the RCD mayor of Ighzer Amokrane. Some time after Kamel's burial, a statue – which did not look even vaguely like him – was erected in his memory, following a proposal by the FFS mayor of Chellata. The statue was set up next to the town hall in the village, just above the new, and still unused, graveyard of the *shuhadâ*. This solution was condemned by most villagers. It was seen as a depersonalisation of the victim, as political profiteering by the two regional parties, and, more importantly, as the dispossession of the village community of their 'new martyr' and of the political and moral legitimacy he carried within him.[21]

The conflicts over Kamel's burial site were some of the many signs that the riots had left everybody helpless, and had laid open a seemingly irreversible lack of communication between the generations:

[20] Overseas travel, and the possibility of obtaining visas and foreign currency had long been among the most salient advantages of the privileged groups of Algerian society (cf. Bentaleb 1984).

[21] Throughout the region, the places of burial of the 'new martyrs' were different from one town to the next, but none of them was lacking in symbolism. Some were situated within the enclosure of the official war monuments; some were buried in the courtyard of the town halls; some were buried where they had died; some had their own little monument constructed for them; and some were simply and quietly buried in the graveyards of their home villages. Whatever happened at the end, their place of burial was always controversial, and involuntarily expressed conflicting attempts to make sense of the riots, which the prevailing official ideology of a united Kabyle 'front' prevented from being expressed otherwise (cf. Scheele 2006a).

In Akbou, we knew who they were, thugs, riot specialists, who never said anything and never listened to anybody or anything. Like aliens. People say that
when the *gendarmes* threw tear-gas at them, they caught the bombs, breathed in
deeply with a big smile, and threw them back. And then they got shot.

In order to bridge this gap, and somehow control an increasingly uncon-
trollable situation, town-quarter or village committees sprang up all over
the area. These committees were referred to, depending on their location,
as *aârouch* ('tribes'), *comités de citoyens, comités populaires, comités de soutien* or
comités de suivi.[22] Every locality produced its own kind of committee,
following existing patterns of local organisation or 'natural' or 'co-opted'
leadership. These committees mainly had in common the fact that they
were all an immediate response to an acute crisis. Some based their claims
to political representation on their resemblance to the still functional
tijmaɛtin; others emphasised their members' active past within the Berber
movement, their reputation as important members of society independent
of state institutions, their proven capacities as 'mediators', or their representation of 'civil society'. They derived much of their legitimacy from their
eclecticism, and from their capacity to combine regionally recognisable
symbols with internationally valid categories such as democracy and human
rights. The definition of what a 'delegate' was and should be, how he should
be selected and to what extent he could represent and bind his village or
quarter to decisions were issues that were never resolved, however. After
the first months of urgent and direct action had passed, this led to continual
conflicts within the movement and to its denial by a large part of its 'con-
stituency'.

The population of Ighil Oumsed reacted to the events initially by calling
for village assemblies, organised by members of the *association culturelle* at
tajmaɛt. They produced the first official 'communiqué' (dated 27 April 2001)
after Kamel Ihamlalen's death and signed it in the name of the *association
culturelle*. After a citizens' committee had been constituted in Chellata, these
meetings became more formalised and distinct from the activities and the
personnel of the cultural association. Delegates were sought by written
announcements signed by the *comité de suivi de la commune de Chellata* and
displayed at the door of *tajmaɛt* and in the public square. About twenty vol-
unteers presented themselves:

> When the Black Spring started, we were literally paralysed. Kamel had been
> killed; it was as if a war had started; and we didn't know what to do. We started
> to get organised, the people from the *association culturelle* met every day, and then
> the committee in Chellata asked us to send delegates. The delegates were volun-
> teers suggested by the village. I suggested myself, just like maybe twenty others.
> (Djamel Benhamidouche)

---

[22] Despite this variety of terms chosen by the actors themselves, and although all the local
delegates whom I was able to interview liked to stress that they preferred the term '*mouvement
citoyen*' to '*aârouch*', the latter generally imposed itself. This is so despite the fact that it seems
to have been invented by the media. In what follows, in order to follow the local usage (and
for brevity's sake) I shall use the term *aârouch* to refer to any grouping that identifies itself with
the 2001 citizens' movement.

When it all started, I really felt I ought to do something. I had already been active in the *association culturelle*, and people knew me as somebody who was reliable. And I was practically unemployed, which meant that I had some spare time. We held meetings in the village, then in other villages in the *commune*; usually, two of us would go to represent our village. We were also in charge of the good conduct of the demonstrations, we had badges and professional cards to identify ourselves. (Yacine Yennat)

The delegates were exclusively young men, roughly ten years younger than Arezqi and the generation that had founded the *association culturelle*. They had been to high school, but had never obtained their baccalaureate. They survived on odd jobs in and about the village, but did not consider themselves *fellahin* (peasants). Most of the delegates had been active in village activities before. Many came from families already known for political commitment in more established groups. Yacine Yennat's eldest brother, for instance, is a senior officer in the army, his second brother is seen as one of the main representatives of the FLN in the village, and has also been involved with the *tajmaɛt*. As mentioned above, Djamel Benhamidouche was delegate and president of the *association culturelle*, and also secretary of the *association religieuse*. Similarly, Saïd Bouyennat, one of the few delegates who is still active within the committee, jokingly noted that

> in my house, we have almost all of political Algeria: my father, who has always been FFS, my elder brother, who has always leaned towards the RCD and who has at some point even been a militant, and my younger brother who is studying in Algiers, who is very active in the RND. (Saïd Bouyennat)

The citizens' committee in Ighil Oumsed was organised on the initiative of the citizens' committee of the *commune* of Chellata, which had asked every village in the area for representatives. This committee of the *commune* of Chellata in turn located itself in the larger structure of the citizens' committee of the *daïra d'Akbou*, which corresponded to the council at the level of the *wilâya*. The movement had thus organised its own administrative hierarchy to mirror that of the state. For the delegates, to move up in the hierarchy of the *aârouch* therefore meant travelling to the regional centres of decision-making, and literally gaining access to the centres of administrative power. Many of the delegates from Ighil Oumsed tended to sum up their activities in the itineraries they had travelled, the time they had spent in official centres of decision-making, and the new, generally town-based networks of support they had thereby established:

> At the beginning, we went to Chellata for the meetings, then to the other villages in the *commune*, then to Akbou. We went as far as Sidi Aïch, Béjaïa, and even Algiers for the demonstrations... except there we would usually be stopped by the cops in Nasiriyya [halfway between Akbou and Algiers], they always let us get as far as that, but never further. (Yacine Yennat)

The importance that was thereby accorded to the small administrative centres and towns seems to have been more than just a concession to administrative convenience and habit. Most places that came to fame during the events, and those where the *aârouch* still seem to be present and influential, were not remote villages, but small towns that had tripled or quadrupled their number of inhabitants since the 1980s. The *aârouch* movement was not merely a rural phenomenon, but also an expression of a semi-urban or recently urbanised population. It appears as an attempt by a young, disillusioned generation that quite literally cannot find its place in contemporary Algerian and Kabyle society to 'conquer' urban public space and signs of state power and legitimacy, and to 'domesticate' the rapidly growing small towns, where much of their life takes place nowadays, but where they are still considered as 'villagers'.

The first and only regional meeting of the *aârouch* in Ighil Oumsed took place in August 2002, that is to say, more than a year after the beginning of the 'Black Spring'. By then, the first and immediate need for action had been replaced by a parapolitical structure that had developed its own elite, its own idiom, internal debate and ritual:

> Scheduled for 16h00, the beginning of the working session at the conclave of Chellata was delayed by about five hours because of some delegations' [lack of] punctuality; it should be mentioned that on the fringes of this conclave which assembled twenty-five *communes*, flowers were deposited in front of the monument to Ihamlalen Kamel, born in Ighil Oumsed... after this a meeting was led by the delegates of the inter-communal delegation in the primary school Ben-mouhoub Bachir... while twelve parents of martyrs sanctioned their agreement by a solemn declaration calling for the rejection of the elections, it is after this that the working session started, that was at exactly 20h30, after the observation of a minute's silence accompanied by the national anthem by M. Lounès.[23]

The ability to organise a 'conclave' in the local primary school in Ighil Oumsed bore witness to the temporary consensus that prevailed among all groups in the village and between the village and the local administration during the Black Spring. By summer 2002, however, this consensus was already on the verge of breaking down. The conclave was not supported by all villagers, and was interrupted by villagers hostile to the *aârouch*, as some say, in the name of the FFS:

> I was very active until we organised the conclave, when very many people came to the village. At that time, there were already people in the village who were against us. Mourad for example came [to the conclave] and started to shout, he threatened to kill us. After that, every time I went to the coffee-house for example, everybody told me that I should be careful, and I decided to stop. (Djamel Ben-hamidouche)

Today, only three villagers still publicly identify with the *aârouch*. Most villagers claim that they no longer represent the village community – if they ever did – but rather only a fraction of it acting in their own personal interest and 'usurping' the name of the village. They are therefore heavily criticised, especially by members of the *association sociale* (who, as seen above, have themselves been condemned in similar terms):

> The *aârouch*? I don't even know what that means. Why do you want to talk to them? These lads, they don't have any legitimacy, if there is an *aεrc* [tribe], that's

---

[23] *Rapport de synthèse du conclave CICB*, 22–23 August 2002. Matoub Lounès is probably the most famous Kabyle singer and a radical opponent both of Islamism and of the government. He was shot in 1995.

us, not them, and we never said that one shouldn't vote. They are children, nobody listens to them, and they are looking for trouble, that's all. (Yahia Benallaoua)

They are also criticised by the older members of the *association culturelle*, who themselves might have been the first to get involved with the citizens' committee three years earlier. Regionally, the *aârouch* – like every political organisation before them – are now generally accused of having been instigated or at least taken over by the national government. The politics that they had tried, at least nominally, to avoid at any cost have finally caught up with them. As a new 'elite' with a claim to represent the village community, they thus appear as less successful than that which emerged during the Berber movement, and which, despite constant quarrels and criticism, still maintains parts of its legitimacy, at least in Berber or cultural matters.

During the 2004 presidential elections, both the *aârouch* and the FFS called for a boycott. It was largely observed, although more out of general desperation, frustration and a total lack of trust in the elections, I felt, than as a proof of the lasting influence of either of the two groups. The election results, widely seen as faked, seem to have been interpreted as the end of a period that began in the late 1980s, during which certain changes within the constitutional framework had seemed possible.[24] Whether this pessimism is justified, only the coming years will tell.

Ighil Oumsed abounds in political institutions, ranging from the 'traditional' village council through the various associations and political parties to the *aârouch* movement. They are seen as both essential to and potentially destructive of village society. On closer inspection, however, these various political institutions are strikingly similar, in terms of their personnel, their objectives and their practice. Although they reflect gradual changes in village society, they also bear witness to continuities in the notion of political legitimacy and power, namely, the recurrent accumulation of titles, the emphasis on mediation and 'closeness' to outside resources, and the exclusive claim to represent the 'village', construed as a homogenous community, to the outside world, and vice versa. Several writers have argued that these features account for many of the peculiarities of the Algerian political system as a whole (Harbi 1980; Martinez 1998; Roberts 2003). Whether this is true or not, they show the inherent difficulties associated with rightful political representation and power, which are by no means limited to Kabylia or Algeria. Although local political institutions as encountered in Ighil Oumsed thus only faintly resemble the *tajmaɛt* of nineteenth-century ethnography, they certainly remain crucial to the existence of the village as a community, and provide keys to understanding Algerian society as a whole.

---

[24] The boycott of the elections, although rather violent in Akbou itself, was totally peaceful in Ighil Oumsed. 132 out of the 915 villagers listed in the election register, that is to say, 14.42 % of villagers, mainly old men, voted. 45 votes (34%) went to the FLN's candidate, Ali Benflis, 33 (25%) to the nation-wide winner of the elections, Abdelaziz Bouteflika, 29 (22%) to the RCD's candidate Saïd Sadi, 21 (16%) to the Socialist Party's and only woman candidate Louisa Hanoun, and 2 each (1.5%) to the moderate Islamist Abdullah Djebellah and the 'joker' Rabiaïne.

Conclusion

As the hare arrived at the other end, Mrs Hedgehog shouted: 'I got here already!' The hare was amazed. 'Once more', he said', 'back the other way!' And he ran as fast as he could. Once he got to the top, Mr Hedgehog shouted: 'I got here already!' The hare cried: 'Back again!' and started running. And once more Mrs Hedgehog was standing at the other end and shouted: 'I got here already!' The hare ran up and down the field seventy-three times, and every time, the hedgehog got there before he had done. The seventy-fourth time the hare could not make it to the end. He dropped dead. (Grimm and Grimm 1915)

I used to tell villagers during my stay that I very much liked being there, and that I thought Ighil Oumsed very beautiful, and its people very welcoming, nice and interesting. This, though true, became a running joke. Women especially, when introducing me to their relatives and friends, would never fail to make me repeat these judgements, which never failed to get an incredulous laugh back. People felt flattered at my observation, as they generally did at my 'scientific' interest in their village, but they never quite believed that I was not just being polite, seeing that I had quite clearly come from the one place – Europe – where everybody wanted to go. Village girls, in particular, liked to stress that people might be nice to me now while I was still a foreigner, but that I should just wait a bit until I became truly Kabyle and lost the prestige attached to me (and my considerable naivety): then I would see how 'nice' people really were...

The general consensus in the village remained that the truly 'beautiful', 'interesting' and valuable things – including 'true Berber traditions' and knowledge about Berber matters – come from the outside, be it only from the nearest town in the valley. Outside ideas and goods have always been crucial to the village's intellectual and economic survival. The village has never been bounded, independent and autarchic, and the ability of the village community and of individual villagers to establish connections with the outside and to mediate outside ideas and resources has always been fundamental to village life. This does not mean, however, that the village is a mere passive receptacle of 'foreign' ideas and goods. On the contrary, on their arrival in the village, these outside ideas are scrutinised, reinterpreted, and submitted to village norms and rules, until they become virtually undistinguishable from their new surroundings.

Thus, on my arrival in the village, the general German-ness of all Kabyles, and the more particular German-ness of Ighil Oumsed, was quickly asserted (after all, it was maintained, the road just uphill was not called the 'road of the Germans' for no reason). However, much as I was admired for being German, interest in the circumstances of my life in Germany remained very low. My German-ness was admired because it had taken on a certain value within the village, and strictly according to village norms and rules. To make me 'even more beautiful', I was quickly dressed up in a Kabyle dress, my hair was (very painfully) pulled back, and I was told how to sit and how to walk, how not to look at people, how and where to eat and which foods to like. This attitude, I soon felt, was not particular to my circumstances – 'foreigners', as much as foreign values, ideas, goods, and languages, are by definition ambivalent, and although the village community as a whole is eager to obtain them and to establish 'connections' with them, it is equally keen to insert them into village categories and deal with them according to village logics and norms.

This emphasis on outside connections means that internal village struggles tend to appear as fought out in terms of larger political groupings and ideologies, while political struggles within the village might be regarded by villagers as personal antagonism or as the result of internal village affairs. This is doubly true for Kabyle villages, which are historically situated at the crossroads of various 'civilisations', and which, as a model as much as a demographic and geographical entity, are still at stake in various, often violent, conflicts between ideas and interest groups that are all too easily identified with clashing 'world civilisations'.

This emphasis placed on outside connections was one of the reasons why at first it seemed impossible to define the village, and why, like the hare in the fable, I seemed to be running from the 'local' to the 'global', only to be sent back empty-handed: while villagers would send me to Paris and Algiers to find out the 'truth' about them, city-dwellers would point to the village as the only possible source of legitimate information. This, however, was not the only reason for the elusiveness of the 'village'. Rather, this elusiveness seemed in itself fundamental to the villagers' self-definitions. Village society, most villagers maintained (thereby echoing much anthropological literature on the area), is organised according to rules and fixed categories, which are represented in village space, village history and family relations, and which in turn feed into the moral absolutes that govern Algerian society as a whole. Yet all of these categories and boundaries are in actual fact flexible, and are transgressed daily. Some of these tensions between discourses of fixed boundaries and factual flexibilities appears as the result of the long series of political and social upheavals that Kabylia and Algeria as a whole have undergone over the last few centuries. Yet they may also point to a more permanent feature of social life in the region. From a local point of view, boundaries are indeed essential to social order and to the establishment of 'civilised' moral spaces, even though everybody knows that these boundaries are disputed and vary from one situation to the next – as if, without the notional rigidity of these boundaries, the practical flexibility that characterises village society would be impossible.

This tension, as much as the 'mixing' of inside and outside categories, is not particular to village society. It characterises Kabylia as a whole: the basic features of 'Kabyle-ness' derive from French nineteenth-century thought, that is to say, from a tradition that has shaped our own way of thinking about society until today. 'Kabyle-ness' is thus as much internal to the European social sciences as it is to Kabylia itself, and separations of 'local' and 'global' truths make little sense. At the same time, 'Kabyle-ness', although branded as an unquestionable label in political protest, subscribed to by thousands of Kabyles, and seen as self-explanatory by many, is in itself elusive: Kabylia, much as the village studied, has only badly defined boundaries; 'Kabyle-ness' tends to be defined through oppositions that often disappear on closer scrutiny and, according to circumstances, give way to innumerable local differences or to an overreaching Algerian nationalism.

Algerian political history itself seems to be characterised by the same emphasis on absolute distinctions and neat boundaries combined with an astonishing lack of coherence and transparency on the ground. This is as true of the Algerian war of independence as it is of the 1990s, and, at least from a contemporary point of view, it can probably also be applied to the muddled history of the French conquest and subsequent rebellions. The implicit assumption of field-work-based anthropology – that 'things' will become clear once they are analysed from a 'local' point of view – thus here proves to be erroneous. The 'truth' about what really happened in Algeria remains elusive on all levels, and is certainly not to be found in the village, where people tend to be (almost) as much in the dark as the various political theorists puzzling over Algeria, and are (almost) as ready to ascribe sweeping explanations in terms of world-historical clashes and conspiracy theories to obscure multi-layered series of events.

In a sense, then, the preceding chapters mainly describe a failed search for the 'village' – from a space that could not be defined via a history that could not be written to a village council that had multiplied or disappeared over night. This search can be seen as symptomatic of the impossibility of defining 'Kabylia' as much as of finding the 'truth' behind what 'really happened' in Algeria, from the nineteenth century to the 'events' of 2001. It shows the interdependence and fuzziness of all the categories used, including those of 'local' and 'global', to the point where their heuristic value seems questionable (although the effects of 'global' power relations are certainly felt in the village, and rarely to the village's advantage). Yet inasmuch as this search forced me to debate the questions that were and still are central to village life, and unwillingly to take part in power struggles within the village, generally expressed as struggles over definition and representation of the village community, it appeared as a first step towards understanding what this 'community' might be about, and why – and this remained the one thing that all villagers agreed on – villages do indeed matter, even in countries as resolutely 'modern' as Algeria.

Appendix 1: Tables & Figures

A Marriages concluded in Ighil Oumsed 1891-2003

Married within geographical range

	Family	Adrum	Village	Illoula	Ouzella-guen	Akbou	Other	Total
< 1914	20 (8%)	62 (23%)	76 (29%)	65 (25%)	24 (9%)	1 (0.3%)	17 (6%)	265 (100%)
1914–29	20 (11%)	44 (25%)	62 (35%)	26 (15%)	15 (8%)		10 (6%)	177 (100%)
1930–54	27 (10%)	55 (20%)	117 (43%)	35 (13%)	27 (10%)	3 (1%)	7 (3%)	271 (100%)
1955–63[1]	8 (10%)	27 (33%)	26 (31%)	13 (16%)	4 (5%)	2 (2%)	3 (4%)	83 (100%)
1985–2002	25 (14%)	19 (10%)	79 (43%)	18 (10%)	18 (18%)	21 (11%)	5 (3%)	185 (100%)

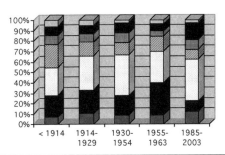

Mixed marriages between maraboutic and non-maraboutic families

	<1914	1914–29	1930–54	1955–63	1985–2003
Number	6	6	9	6	20
	2%	3%	3%	7%	11%

[1] Records for 1964-1984 were not accessible.

Marriages with villagers resident in France

	<1914	1914–29	1930–54	1955–63	1985–2003
Number			19	5	
Percent			7%	6%	

Number of marriages per year

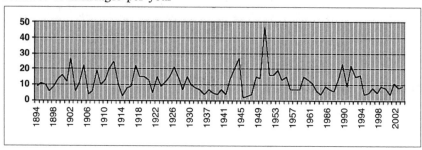

Average age at marriage

(Based on *Registre des mariages, Commune mixte d'Akbou* 1891-1963 ACA and *Sijill al-zawâj baladiyya shallâta* 1985-2003, ACC)

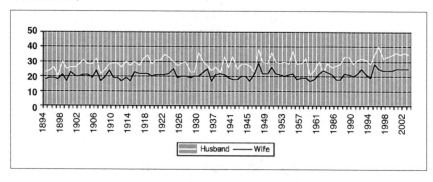

B Contents of Shaykh Tahar's library

Number of manuscripts/books/documents: ca. 200   Sample: 69

Subject/Kind

Tafsîr	Fiqh	Hagiography	Mysticism	Numerology	Quran	Hadith
7	12	5	10	3	3	3

Grammar	Contracts/Letters	Poetry	Agriculture	Medicine	Amulets
6	7	4	1	1	7

Subject/Kind

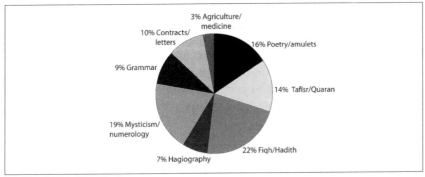

Origin (author or book)

Béjaïa	Algeria	Tunisia	Morocco	Egypt
6 (44%)	3 (21%)	2 (14%)	1 (7%)	2 (14%)

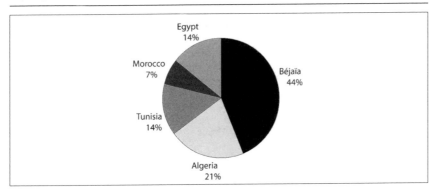

Date

Hijrî	1100–1150	1150–1200	1200–1250	1250–1300	1300–1350	1350–1400
Milâdî	1680–1730	1730–1780	1780–1830	1830–1880	1880–1930	1930–1980
Number	1	2	3	11	4	2

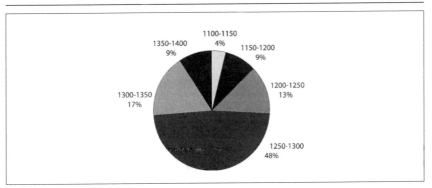

C Land division in 1924

In 1924, the Ben Aly Chérif consortium had to sell two pieces of land in the Soummam valley, one of an overall surface of 6 hectares which formerly was part of Ighil Oumsed's lands, and one former colonial property called the farm of St Julien further down the valley, which had originally consisted of land belonging to the neighbouring tribe Ouzellaguen, of an overall surface of 97 hectares and 18 *ares*. Seventy-one buyers, all from Ighil Oumsed, jointly acquired the land, which was subsequently divided into 660 shares of equal value, each amounting roughly 15 *ares* of arable land. The repartition among village *iderma* (extended families) and within the largest *adrum* was made as follows:

	At Boudjmaa	At Sliman	At Hamimi	Ouhaddar
Shares	321	108	207	24
%	49	16	31	4
Surface	48 ha 15 ares	16 ha 20 ares	31 ha 5 ares	3 ha 60 ares

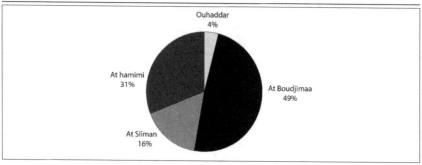

	Ihamlalen	Imessaouden	Yennat	Other
Shares	66	66	48	141
%	21	21	15	43
% of total	10	10	7	21
Surface	9 ha 90 ares	9 ha 90 ares	7 ha 20 ares	21 ha 15 ares

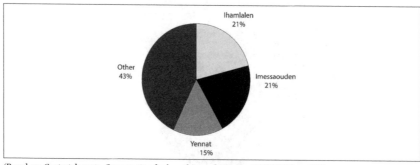

(Based on *Contrat de vente. Conservation des hypothèques de Bougie.* 14/08/1924. CDC)

D Emigration

Number of 20-year-olds absent from the village (according to the French military registers), 1912–1953

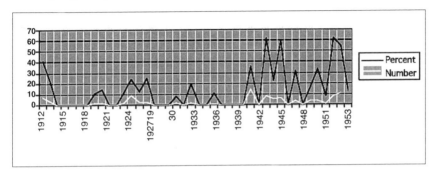

Destination of emigrants

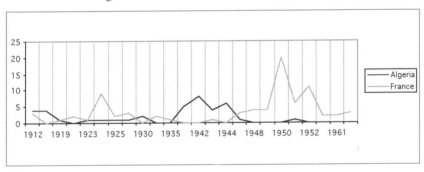

Distribution of new emigrants to France (1950–62)

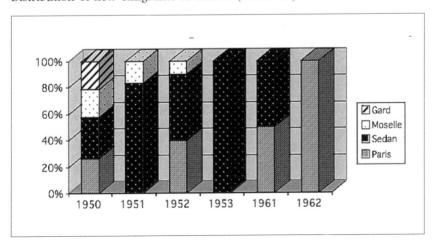

Emigration by family division

(Based on *Tableau de Recensement, Commune mixte d'Akbou* 1912-1953, ACA and *Registre des Mariages, Commune mixte d'Akbou* 1950-1962, ACA)

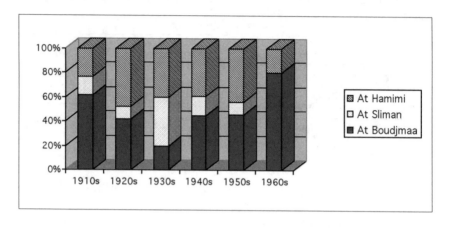

Appendix 2: Texts

A List of claims put forward by the *aârouch*

Plate-forme commune de revendications issue de la réunion Inter-wilaya du 11/06/2001 à El-Kseur (BGAYET)

Nous, représentants des wilayas de Sétif, Bordj-Bouareridj, Bouira, Boumerdes, Bgayet, Tizi-Ouzou, Alger ainsi que le Comité Collectif des Universités d'Alger réunis ce jour lundi 11/06/2001 à la maison de jeunes « Mouloud FERAOUN » d'El-Kseur (W) Bgayet, avons adopté la plate-forme commune de revendications suivante:

1/ Pour la prise en charge urgente par l'Etat de toutes les victimes blessées et familles des martyrs de la répression durant ces événements.

2/ Pour le jugement par tribunaux civils de tous les auteurs, ordonnateurs et commanditaires des crimes et leurs radiations des corps de sécurité et des fonctions publiques.

3/ Pour un statut de martyr à chaque victime de la dignité durant ces événements et la protection de tous les témoins du drame.

4/ Pour le départ immédiat des brigades de gendarmerie et des renforts de C.R.S.

5/ Pour une annulation des poursuites judiciaires contres tous les manifestants ainsi que l'acquittement de ceux déjà jugés durant ces événements.

6/ Arrêt immédiat des expéditions punitives, des intimidations et des provocations contre la population.

7/ Dissolutions des commissions d'enquête initiées par le pouvoir.

8/ Satisfaction de la revendication AMAZIGH dans toutes ses dimensions (identitaire, civilisationnelle, linguistique et culturelle) sans référendum et sans conditions et la consécration de TAMAZIGHT en tant que langue nationale et officielle.

9/ Pour un Etat garantissant tous les droits socio-économiques et toutes les libertés démocratiques.

10/ Contre les politiques de sous-développement, de paupérisation et de clochardisation du peuple Algérien.

11/ La mise sous l'autorité effective des instances démocratiquement élues de toutes les fonctions exécutives de l'Etat ainsi que les corps de sécurité.

12/ Pour un plan d'urgence socio-économique pour toute la région de Kabylie.

13/ Contre TAMHEQRANIT (la HOGRA) et toutes les formes d'injustice et d'exclusion.

14/ Pour un réaménagement au cas par cas des examens régionaux pour les élèves n'ayant pas pu les passer.

15/ Institution d'une allocation de chômage pour tout demandeur d'emploi à hauteur de 50% du S.N.M.G.

Nous exigeons une réponse officielle, urgente et publique à cette plate-forme de revendications.

ULAC SMAH ULAC / COORDINATION DES AARCHS, DAÏRAS ET COMMUNES

(Source: http://membres.lycos.fr/aarchs/)

Translation:

Joint list of claims resulting from the inter-wilaya meeting of 11 June 2001 in El-Kseur (Bgayet [Béjaïa])

We, the representatives of the *wilâyas* of Sétif, Bordj-Bouareridj, Bouira, Boumerdes, Bgayet, Tizi-Ouzou, Algiers, and the Collective Committee of the Universities of Algiers who came together this day Monday 11 June 2001 at the Youth Club 'Mouloud Feraoun' in El-Kseur, *wilâya* of Bgayet, have adopted the following list of claims:

1/ The state is to take care immediately of everybody injured and of the families of the martyrs of the repression during the events.

2/ All authors, instigators and commanders of the crimes are to be judged in civil courts, expelled from the security forces and barred from public posts.

3/ Everybody whose dignity has been attacked during the events is to be accorded the status of martyr, and all witnesses of this tragedy protected.

4/ All *gendarmerie* squads and riot police reinforcements are to leave immediately.

5/ All judicial charges against the demonstrators are to be dropped, and those who have already been judged during the events acquitted.

6/ All punitive expeditions, intimidations and provocations to the population are to be stopped immediately.

7/ The investigating committees initiated by the government are to be dissolved.

8/ The AMAZIGH [Berber] demands are to be satisfied in all their aspects (pertaining to identity, civilisation, language and culture) without a referendum or any further conditions, and Tamazight [Berber] is to be consecrated as a national and official language.

9/ The state is to guarantee all socio-economic rights and all democratic liberties.

10/ No to the politics of underdevelopment, pauperisation and reduction to vagrancy of the Algerian people.

11/ All executive functions of the state and of the security forces are to be placed under the effective authority of democratically elected institutions.

12/ A socio-economic emergency plan for the whole of Kabylia is to be implemented.

13/ No to TAMHEQRANIT (the HOGRA) and to all forms of injustice and exclusion.

14/ The regional exams are to be rescheduled case by case for the pupils who have not been able to sit them.

15/ An unemployment benefit of 50% of the minimum wage is to be instituted for every job-seeker.

We demand an official, urgent and public answer to this list of claims.

ULAC SMAH ULAC [There is no pardon].
    COORDINATION OF THE *AARCH, DAÏRAS* AND *COMMUNES*.

B Social Convention of the commune de Chellata

PACTE SOCIAL RELATIF AUX CEREMONIES ET FETES

– Vu l'initiative de la convention régissant les fêtes en vigueur à Felden.
– Vu l'enrichissement et l'adoption de la convention par l'ensemble des comités du village et de la commune de Chellata présents à la réunion du: 27 juillet 1995.
– Vu la conjoncture économique et ses répercussions sur la vie sociale.
– Vu les dispositions générales du présent pacte et de statu quo de son champ d'application.

Titre 1: MARIAGE

Chapitre 1: Cérémonie fiançailles (*tahbult*)
Art. 1: Après consentement préalable des parents, l'officialisation se fera au domicile de la fiancée, avec office religieux au cours de cette cérémonie dite *tahbult* qui sera sanctionnée par une réception (thé, café, limonade et gâteaux).
Art. 2: Le fiancé est astreint d'apporter 07 articles en guise de présents énumérés ci-après:
deux ensembles ainsi que deux coupons de tissu
une paire de chaussures
un flacon de parfum
un paquet de henné
six savonnettes
une bague de fiançailles.
Ces articles ne doivent en aucun cas faire l'objet d'une exposition durant cette cérémonie de fiançailles.
Art. 3: Le couscous et la chorba desservis habituellement sont supprimés, ainsi que les exigences (*chouroutes*) en matière de moutons et autre. *Taamamt* (dot) est fixée à 250 DA.
Ticakimt, les sœurs et la chargée du henné sont fixés à 50 DA. La quête d'argent et *lwaada* (l'offrande) sont facultatives.

Chapitre 2: Cérémonies nuptiales (*assensi*)
Art. 4: A cet effet le futur époux doit préalablement approvisionner ses futurs beaux parents en viande et en légumes (*nafaka*) et remettre lors de la visite de sa famille à la mariée sept articles vestimentaires ci-après désignés :
un tailleur
une robe kabyle
un déshabillé
une paire de chaussures blanches
une valise blanche
un foulard
une paire de claquettes.
Art. 5: A la même occasion la future épouse est tenue de préparer le trousseau ci-après désigné:
deux paires de draps
deux oreillers avec traversins
deux couvertures
deux couvertures en laine (*ajlal, asaku*)
un couvre lit

dix kilos de friandises (*laâda*)

deux valises pour le trousseau.

<u>Art. 6:</u> Le cortège nuptial (*tikli*) à l'intérieur et à l'extérieur du village est réglementé selon les coutumes et traditions du village ainsi que les capacités du futur époux d'offrir une réception ou un dîner à tous les citoyens du village ou uniquement à ses proches et invités.

<u>Art. 7:</u> En outre, l'utilisation des armes à feu durant et après la cérémonie est supprimée ainsi que *tounticines* et *idelaan* qu'on offre respectivement aux voisins et aux invités ayant assisté à cette fête.

<u>Art. 8:</u> Le lendemain du mariage (*aqueses*), la mariée est tenue à assister à cette cérémonie en gardant la même tenue, l'exhibition de tout son trousseau est supprimée.

<u>Art. 9:</u> Le septième jour (*seboua*) le coupla rendra visite aux beaux parents.

<u>Titre 2:</u> AUTRE CEREMONIES ET FETES

<u>Chapitre 1:</u> Naissances et Circoncisions

<u>Art. 10:</u> Les parents de la femme ayant accouché sont tenus seulement d'apporter de la viande et des fruits le lendemain de la naissance, le septième jour, un cadeau pour le nouveau-né et sa mère plus cent œufs.

<u>Art. 11:</u> Les parents du nouveau-né peuvent donner une réception restreinte selon leurs capacités en faveur de leur famille, leurs amis et proches.

<u>Chapitre 2:</u> Circoncision (*lextana*)

<u>Art. 12:</u> En cette honorable occasion, le père ou le tuteur de l'enfant circoncis peut donner une réception idem à celle citée en article 11, et néanmoins celui-ci peut recevoir des dons et cadeaux.

<u>Chapitre 3:</u> Fêtes traditionnelles et religieuses

<u>Art. 13:</u> Concernant les fêtes traditionnelles et religieuses (*Yenayer, Rbie, Aid el fitre, Aid el adha...*) il est souhaitable de les marquer avec toute la ferveur et ambiance pour mieux les perpétrer et les ancrer dans la mémoire collective, l'offre de cadeaux en se rendant mutuellement visite est toléré mais *taghrout* est supprimée.

<u>Titre 3:</u> DISPOSITIONS TRANSITOIRES

<u>Art. 14:</u> Les dons et les cadeaux pour les hadjis sont supprimés, mais ils sont libres de donner des réceptions afin de fêter leur hidj.

<u>Art. 15:</u> La participation de toute personne en guise de solidarité (*lahr thimzalines*) est tolérée pour un montant inférieur ou égal à 50 DA.

<u>Art. 16:</u> Lors d'un décès les repas en couscous et viandes au cimetière sont supprimés et par conséquent les coutumes et traditions de chaque village entrent en vigueur.`

Ce présent pacte sera soumis aux comités des villages de la Daira d'Akbou pour étude, modification, complément et approbation.

Le président de l'association sociale FELDEN

Translation:

Social pact concerning ceremonies and celebrations

in view of the initiative of a convention regulating celebrations in force in Felden
in view of the enrichment and adoption of the convention by the totality of the
villages of the district of Chellata that were present at the meeting of July 27th, 1995
in view of the economic situation and its repercussions on social life
in view of the general disposition of the present pact and the status quo of its field
of application

Heading 1: Marriage

Chapter 1: Engagement ceremony (*tahbult*)
Art. 1: Following the parents' prior consent, the engagement will be made official
at the fiancée's house by a religious office during this ceremony called *tahbult* that
will be sanctioned by a reception (tea, coffee, lemonade and biscuits).
Art. 2: The fiancé is asked to bring seven items by way of presents as listed below:
two suits as well as two pieces of cloth
one pair of shoes
one bottle of perfume
one packet of henna
six small bars of soap
one engagement ring.
These objects should under no circumstances be subject to exhibition during the
engagement ceremony.
Art. 3: The *couscous* and the *chorba* [meat stew] that are usually served are
abolished, as are the demands (*chouroutes*) in matters of sheep and so on. *Taamamt*
(dowry) is fixed at 250 DA. *Ticakimt*, the collection for the sisters and the henna
lady is fixed at 50 DA. The collection of money and *lwaada* (offerings) are optional.

Chapter 2: Wedding ceremonies (*assensi*)
Art. 4: For this purpose, the future husband has to supply his future parents-in-law
with meat and vegetables (*nafaka*) and hand over, on the occasion of his family's
visit to the bride, the following seven articles:
a woman's outfit
a Kabyle dress
a negligee
a pair of white shoes
a white suitcase
a headscarf
a pair of flip-flops.
Art. 5: At the same time, the future bride is obliged to prepare the trousseau
indicated below:
two pairs of sheets
two pillows with bolsters
two covers
two woollen blankets (*ajlal, asaku*)
one bedspread
ten kilos of sweets (*laâda*)
two suitcases for the trousseau.
Art. 6: The wedding procession (*tikli*) inside and outside the village is regulated by
the customs and traditions of the village as well as according to the ability of the
groom to offer a reception or a dinner to all the citizens of the village, or only to
his relatives and guests.

Art. 7: In addition to this, the use of firearms during and after the ceremony is abolished, as are *tounticines* and *idelaan* that are offered respectively to the neighbours and guests who attended the celebration.

Art. 8: The day after the wedding (*aqueses*), the bride is obliged to attend this ceremony wearing the same dress as before; the display of her whole trousseau is abolished.

Art. 9: The seventh day (*seboua*), the couple will visit their parents-in-law.

Heading 2: Other Ceremonies and Celebrations

Chapter 1: Births and Circumcisions
Art. 10: The parents of the woman who has given birth are only obliged to bring meat and fruit the day after the birth, and, on the seventh day, a present for the newborn baby and his mother plus a hundred eggs.

Art. 11: The newborn's parents may hold a small reception for their family, friends and relatives, according to their means.

Chapter 2: Circumcision (*lextana*)
Art. 12: On this honourable occasion, the father or the tutor of the circumcised child may hold a reception like the one mentioned in article 11, and he may receive gifts and presents.

Chapter 3: Traditional and religious festivals
Art. 13: As regards the traditional and religious festivals (*Yenayer, Rbie* [Berber new year and Spring celebrations], *Aid el fitre, Aid el adha...*), it is desirable to celebrate them with all possible fervour and commitment in order to perpetuate them and establish them firmly in the collective memory. Offering of presents during mutual visits is allowed, but *taghrout* is abolished.

Heading 3: Transitory Dispositions

Art. 14: The gifts and presents for the *hadjis* are abolished, but they are free to hold a reception in order to celebrate their *hidj*.

Art. 15: Anybody's participation by way of solidarity (*lahr thimazalines*) is allowed for a sum less than or equal to 50 DA.

Art. 16: At the time of death, the meal of couscous and meat at the cemetery is abolished; consequently, the customs and traditions of each village come into force.

The present document will be presented to the village committees of the *daïra* d'Akbou for examination, modification, completion and approval.

The president of the social association of Felden

Bibliography

Archival sources

AAF: Archives de l'Armée Française, Château de Vincennes, Paris, France.
1H1684 D2 *Zone militaire Grande Kabylie Est*
ACA: Archives de la Commune d'Akbou, Akbou, Wilâya de Béjaïa, Algeria.
Registre des mariages de la commune mixte d'Akbou, 1891-1963
Tableau de recensement de la commune mixte d'Akbou, 1912-53.
ACC: Archives de la Commune de Chellata, Chellata, Wilâya de Béjaïa, Algeria
Etat-civil de la commune mixte d'Akbou, douar de Chellata, 1892
Projet de développement et d'aménagement urbain (PDAU), douar de Chellata, 1997.
Sijill al-zawâj baladiyya shallâta, 1985-2003.
ACED: Archives du Centre d'Etudes Diocésain d'Alger, Algeria
L'Enseignement privé réformiste et l'Association des oulémas d'Algérie, n.d. (after 1950).
ANA: Archives Nationales d'Alger, Algiers, Algeria.
SAS Ighil Oumsed.
AOM: Archives d'outre-mer, Aix-en-Provence, France.

62K2	*Situation des tribus/ personnel indigène. Cercle d'Akbou, 1874-80.*
62K8	*Rapports annuels du cercle d'Akbou, 1873-9.*
67K1	*Rapports trimestriels, commune indigène d'Akbou, 1873.*
70K2	*Organisation des tribus dans le cercle d'Akbou, 1873.*
70K7	*Séquestres cercle d'Akbou, 1872-3.*
93/1393	*Ecoles coraniques, Akbou, 1912-36.*
93/1415	*Rapport sur l'émigration dans l'arrondissement de Bougie, 1938.*
93/4244	*SLNA Famille Ben Aly Chérif* (restricted access).
93/4332	*Rapports mensuels de la commune mixte d'Akbou, 1947-60* (restricted access).
93/5329	*Dossier sécurité Akbou, 1919-20.*
93/20033	*Rapport communes mixtes, 1921.*
93/20066	*Commune mixte d'Akbou. Questions de sécurité, 1914-16.*
Akbou	Various administrative documents and reports, 1937-52 (non-classified).
B3 150	*Tableaux concernant les confréries religieuses (Bougie), 1916.*
B3 246	*Zaouïas autorisées, arrondissement de Bougie, 1912-25.*
Sidi Aïch//5	*Monographie de la commune mixte d'Akbou,* n.d. (after 1951).

CDC: Cadastre du Département de Constantine, Constantine, Algeria.
Contrat de vente, 14/08/1924.
Sénatus-consulte de la tribu Illoula Asammeur, 1893.

Published works

Abdelfettah-Lahri, N. 2000. 'La ville, l'urbanité et l'autochtonie: analyse des représentations dans les discours sur Béjaïa. Mémoire de Magistère en langue et culture amazighes', University of Béjaïa. Béjaïa.

Addi, L. 2002. *Sociologie et anthropologie chez Pierre Bourdieu*. Paris: La Découverte.

Ageron, Ch.-R. 1968. *Les algériens musulmans et la France (1871–1919)*. Paris: PUF.

—. 1979. *L'Histoire de l'Algérie contemporaine*. Paris: PUF.

Aggoun, L. and J.-B. Rivoire. 2004. *La Françalgérie. Crimes et mensonges d'Etats*. Paris: La Découverte.

Aïssani, D. 2002. 'Timɛemmert n'Ichellaten. Un institut supérieur au fin fond de la Kabylie'. Unpublished manuscript.

Aïssani, D. and D. E. Mechehed. 1998. Manuscrits de la Kabylie: catalogue de la collection Ulahbib. Unpublished manuscript.

Aït Ahmed, H. 1983. *Mémoires d'un combattant*. Paris: Messinger.

Aït Ali, B. 1962. *Les cahiers de Bélaïd ou la Kabylie d'antan*. Fort National: Fichier de Documentation Berbère.

al-Ahnaf, M., B. Botiveau and F. Frégosi. 1991. *L'Algérie par ses islamistes*. Paris: Karthala.

al-Fâsî, H. 1956 [1550]. *Description de l'Afrique* (trad. A. Epaulard). Paris: Adrien-Maisonneuve.

al-Hafnawi, A. al-Q. 1907. *Kitâb ta'rîf al-khalâf bi-rijâl al-salâf*. Algiers.

al-Halim, I. A. 1996. *Kitâb Mafâkhir al-Barbar*. Madrid: Consejo Superior de Investigaciones Científicas.

al-Mili, M. 1963. *Tarîkh al-jazâ'ir fîl-qadîm wal-ḥadîth*. Algiers: Maktabat al-Nahda al-Jazâ'iriyya.

al-Wartîlânî, H. 1908. *Nuzhat al-anṣâr fî faḏl 'ilm al-târîkh wa-l-akhbâr*. Algiers: Bencheneb Editions.

Alilat, F. and S. Hadid. 2002. *Vous ne pouvez pas nous tuer, nous sommes déjà morts. L'Algérie embrasée*. Paris: Editions n° 1.

Alleg, H. 1958. *La question*. Paris: Editions de Minuit.

Altorki, S. 1986. *Women in Saudi Arabia*. New York: Columbia University Press.

Amrouche, F. 1982. *Histoire de ma vie*. Paris: Maspero.

Amrouche, J. 1985. *L'éternel Jugurtha*. Marseille: Archives de la Ville de Marseille.

Amrouche, T. 1976. *Le grain magique, contes, poèmes et proverbes berbères de Kabylie*. Paris: Maspero.

Anderson, B. 1983. *Imagined communities: reflections on the origin and spread of nationalism*. London: Verso.

Anderson, L. 1991. 'Legitimacy, identity and the writing of history', in *Statecraft in the Middle East* (eds) E. Davis and N. Gavrieldis, 71–91. Miami, FL: Florida International University Press.

Andezian, S. 1993. 'De l'usage de la dérision dans un rituel de pélérinage', in *Etre marginal au Maghreb* (eds) F. Colonna and Z. Daoud, 283–300. Paris: Editions du CNRS.

—. 2001. *Expériences du divin dans l'Algérie contemporaine: adeptes des saints de la région de Tlemcen*. Paris: Editions du CNRS.

Association des ouléma. 1937. *Statuts et bases fondamentales de l'Association des ouléma d'Algérie*. Constantine: Imprimerie algérienne.

Aucapitaine, H. 1860. 'Un kanoun ou code kabyle', *Revue de l'Orient, de l'Algérie et des Colonies* (N. S.) **11**, 187–93.

—. 1863. 'Kanoun du village de Taourirt Amokran, chez les Ait Iraten', *Revue Africaine* **7**, 279–85.

Aussaresses, P. 2001. *Services spéciaux, Algérie 1955-1957*. Paris: Perrin.

Bargaoui, S. 1999. 'Sainteté, savoir et autorité en Kabylie au XVIIIᵉ siècle: la *rihla de Warthîlânî*', in *L'Autorité des saints* (ed.) M. Kerrou, 249–71. Paris: Editions Recherches sur les civilisations.

Barrès, A. M. 1897. *Les déracinés: roman de l'énergie nationale.* Paris: Nelson.

Barret, S. 1997. 'Les sections administratives spécialisées en Grande Kabylie 1955-1962. Ambiguïtés et échecs d'une politique de pacification. Mémoire de Maîtrise d'histoire, Université de Provence, Aix-en-Provence.

Barth, F. 1953. *Social Organization in Southern Kurdistan.* Oslo: Brodrene Jorgensen.

Basagna, R. and A. Sayad. 1974. *Habitat traditionnel et structures familiales en Kabylie.* Algiers: CRAPE.

Basset, R. 1887. *Manuel de langue kabyle.* Paris: Maisonneuve et Leclerc.

—. 1920. *Essai sur la littérature des Berbères.* Algiers: J. Carbonel.

Bayart, J.-F. 1990. *L'état en Afrique: la politique du ventre.* Paris: Fayard.

Behar, R. 1986. *Santa María del Monte. The presence of the past in a Spanish village.* Princeton, NJ: University Press.

Bel, A. 1938. *La religion musulmane en Berbérie.* Paris: Geuthner.

Ben Jelloun, T. 1984. *Hospitalité française: racisme et immigration maghrébine.* Paris: Editions du Seuil.

Benabdallah, S. 1982. *La justice du FLN pendant la guerre de libération.* Alger: SNED.

Benghabrit-Remaoun, N. 1998. 'L'école algérienne: transformations et effets sociaux', in *L'école en débat*, 5–30. Algiers: Casbah Editions.

Benkheira, H. 1990. 'Un désir absolu: les émeutes d'octobre 1988 en Algérie', *Peuples méditerranéens* **52-3**, 7–18.

Bennoune, M. 1986. *El-Akbia. Un siècle d'histoire algérienne 1875–1975.* Alger: OPU.

Bentaleb, F. 1984. 'La rente dans la société et dans la culture en Algérie', *Peuples méditerranéens* **26**, 75–104.

Bernard, A. 1894. 'Emile Masqueray', *Revue Africaine* **38**, 350–71.

Bernard, A. and L. Milliot. 1933. 'Les qânûns kabyles dans l'ouvrage de Hanoteau et Letourneux', *Revue des études islamiques* **7**, 1–44.

Berque, J. 1974. 'Qu-est-ce qu'une 'tribu' nord-africaine?' in *Maghreb: histoire et société*, 22–34. Gembloux: Duculot.

Bertrand, L. 1921. *Le sang des races.* Paris: G. Crés.

Bessaoud, M.-A. 1991. *Heureux les martyrs qui n'ont rien vu. La vérité sur la mort du Colonel Amirouche et de Abbane Ramdane.* Paris: Editions Berbères.

Blin, L. 1990. *L'Algérie, du Sahara au Sahel.* Paris: L'Harmattan.

Bloch, M. 1971. 'Decision-making in councils among the Merina of Madagascar', in *Councils in Action* (eds) A. Richards and A. Kuper, 29–62. Cambridge: Cambridge University Press.

Bouaziz, M. and A. Mahé. 2004. 'La Grande Kabylie durant la guerre d'Indépendance algérienne', in *La guerre d'Algérie: 1954–2004. La fin de l'amnésie* (eds) M. Harbi and B. Stora, 227–66. Paris: Robert Laffont.

Boulifa, S. A. 1904. *Recueil de poésies kabyles.* Algiers: Jourdan.

—. 1925. *Le Djurdjura à travers l'histoire.* Algiers: J. Bringau.

Bourdieu, P. 1963. 'Statistiques et sociologie', in *Travail et travailleurs en Algérie* (eds) P. Bourdieu, A. Darbel, J.-P. Rivet and C. Seibel. Paris: Mouton.

—. 1965. 'The sentiment of honour in Kabyle society', in *Honour and shame* (ed.) J.G. Peristiany, 191-242. London: Weidenfeld and Nicolson.

—. 1972. *Esquisse d'une théorie de la pratique.* Geneva: Droz.

—. 1977. *Algérie 1960: structures économiques et structures temporelles.* Paris: Editions de Minuit.

—. 1980. *Le sens pratique.* Paris: Editions de Minuit.

Bourdieu, P. and A. Sayad. 1964. *Le déracinement. La crise de l'agriculture traditionnelle en Algérie.* Paris: Editions de Minuit.

Bousquet, G. H. 1950. 'Un culte à détruire. L'adoration de Hanoteau et Letourneux', *Revue de la Méditerranée* **8-9**, 491–54.

Braudel, F. 1975 [1949] *The Mediterranean and the Mediterranean world in the age of Philip II* (2nd edition). Glasgow: Fontana Press.

—. 1986. *L'identité de la France.* Paris: Artaud, Flammarion.

Breman, J. 1988. *The shattered image. Construction and deconstruction of the village in colonial Asia.* Dordrecht: Toris Publications.

Brett, M. 1998. *Ibn Khaldûn and the Medieval Maghrib.* Aldershot: Ashgate.

Bugeaud, T. R. 1948. *Par l'épée et la charrue.* Paris: PUF.

Burgat, F. 1988. *L'islamisme au Maghreb.* Paris: Karthala.

—. 1995. *L'islamisme en face.* Paris: La Découverte.

Burke, P. 1989. 'French historians and their cultural identities', in *History and ethnicity* (eds) E. Tonkin, M. McDonald and M. Chapman, 157–67. London: Routledge.

Camus, A. 1994. *Le premier homme.* Paris: Gallimard.

Carette, A.-E.-H. 1848. *Études sur la Kabilie proprement dite.* Paris: Imprimerie nationale.

—. 1853. *Recherches sur l'origine et les migrations des principales tribus de l'Afrique septentrionale et particulièrement de l'Algérie.* Paris: Imprimerie nationale.

Carlier, O. 1984. 'La production de l'image de soi. La "crise berbériste" de 1949', *Annuaire de l'Afrique du Nord* **23**, 347–73.

—. 1995. *Entre nation et Jihad: histoire sociale des radicalismes algériens.* Paris: Presses de la Fondation Nationale des Sciences Politiques.

Cassen, B. 2005. 'Un monde polyglotte pour échapper à la dictature de l'anglais', *Le Monde Diplomatique* **610**, 22–3.

Chachoua, K. 2001. *L'Islam Kabyle.* Paris: Maisonneuve et Larose.

Chaker, R. 1982. 'Journal des événements en Kabylie en 1980', *Les Temps modernes* **39**, 383–438.

Chaker, S. 1999. *Berbères aujourd'hui, Berbères dans le Maghreb contemporain.* Paris: L'Harmattan.

Chapman, M. 1978. *The Gaelic Vision in Scottish Culture.* London: Croom Helm.

Charef, A. 1994. *Algérie: le grand dérapage.* La Tour d'Aigues: Editions de l'Aube.

Chevallier, G. 1934. *Clochemerle.* Paris: PUF.

Chitour, F. 1990. 'Réflexions d'une femme après octobre', *Peuples méditerranéens* **52-3**, 25–35.

Clark, T.N. 1973. *Prophets and Patrons: The French university and the emergence of the social sciences.* Cambridge, MA: Harvard University Press.

Colonna, F. 1975. *Instituteurs algériens.* Paris: Presses des Sciences Po.

—. 1977. 'Les débuts de l'Islah dans l'Aurès, 1936–38', *Revue algérienne des sciences politiques, juridiques et économiques* **2**, 277–80.

—. 1983. 'Présentation' in *Formation des cités chez les populations sédentaires de l'Algérie* (ed.) F. Colonna, i-xxv. Aix-en-Provence: Edisud.

—. 1995. *Les versets de l'invincibilité. Permanence et changements religieux dans l'Algérie contemporaine.* Paris: Presses des Sciences Po.

Colonna, F. and C. Haïm Brahimi. 1976. 'Du bon usage de la science coloniale', in *Le mal de voir* (ed.) Université de Paris VII, 221–41. Paris: Union générale d'éditions.

Coordination des Aarch, Daïras et Communes 2001a. 'Plate-forme de revendications. Réunion inter-wilaya du 11/06/2001' (http://membres.lycos.fr/aarchs/).

—. 2001b. '1956-2001: Le combat continue' (http://membres.lycos.fr/aarchs/).

Cornell, V. 1998. *Realm of the Saint. Power and authority in Moroccan Sufism.* Austin, TX: University of Texas Press.

Dakhlia, J. 1990. *L'oubli de la cité: la mémoire collective à l'épreuve du lignage dans le Jérid tunisien.* Paris: La Découverte.

Darasse, V. 1885. 'Paysans en communauté et colporteurs émigrants de Tabou-Douchd-el-Baar (Grande Kabylie)', *Les Ouvriers des deux mondes* **5**, 23–32.

Daudet, A. 1872. *Tartarin de Tarascon.* Paris: Flammarion.

Daumas, E. 1864. *Mœurs et coutumes de l'Algérie: Tell, Kabylie, Sahara.* Paris: Hachette.

Davis, J. 1989. 'The social relations of the production of history', in *History and Ethnicity* (eds) E. Tonkin, M. McDonald and M. Chapman, 104–20. London: Routledge.

Deheuvels, L.W. 1992. *Islam et pensée contemporaine en Algérie.* Paris: CNRS.

Depont, O. and X. Coppolani. 1897. *Les confréries religieuses musulmanes.* Algiers: Jourdan.

Dermenghem, E. 1982 [1954]. *Le culte des saints dans l'Islam maghrébin.* Paris: Gallimard.

Devaux, C. 1859. *Les Kebaïles du Djerdjera, études nouvelles sur le pays vulgairement appelé la Grande Kabylie.* Marseilles: Camois frères.

Direche-Slimani, K. 1997. *Histoire de l'émigration kabyle en France au XXe siècle.* Paris: L'Harmattan.

—. 2004. *Chrétiens de Kabylie 1830–1954. Une action missionnaire dans l'Algérie coloniale.* Paris: Bouchène.

Doutté, E. 1908. *Magie et religion dans l'Afrique du Nord. La société musulmane du Maghrib.* Paris: Maisonneuve-Geuthner.

Dresch, P. 1986. 'The significance of the course events take in segmentary systems', *American Ethnologist* **13**, 309–24.

—. 1989. *Tribes, Government and History in Yemen.* Oxford: Clarendon Press.

—. 2000. 'Wilderness of mirrors: truth and vulnerability in Middle Eastern field-work', in *Anthropologists in a Wider World: Essays on field research* (eds) P. Dresch, W. James and D. Parkin, 109–28. Oxford: Berghahn.

—. 2006. *The Rules of Barat. Texts and translations from tribal documents in Yemen.* San'â: CEFAS.

Du Boulay, J. 1974. *Portrait of a Greek Mountain Village.* Oxford: Clarendon Press.

Dubois-Thainville. 1927 [1809]. 'Sur Alger', in *Reconnaissance des villes, forts et batteries d'Alger* (ed.) G. Esquer, 122-50. Paris: Champion.

Dumont, L. 1957. 'Village Studies', *Contributions to Indian sociology* **1**, 23–41.

—. 1966. 'Village Studies', *Contributions to Indian Sociology* **9**, 67–89.

Dupuis, J., E. Mandonnet and S. Dekeirei. 2002. 'Match France-Algérie. Contre-enquête sur un fiasco'. *L'Express* 14/02/2002. Paris.

Durkheim, E. 1893. *De la division sociale du travail.* Paris: Alcan.

Economist Intelligence Unit. 2006. *Country Profile Algeria* (available on-line http://www.economist.com/countries/Algeria).

Eickelman, D.F. 1977. 'Ideological change and regional cults: maraboutism and ties of "closeness" in Western Morocco', in *Regional Cults* (ed.) R.P. Werbner, 3-28. London: Academic Press.

Eisenhans, H. 1995. 'Du malentendu à l'échec? Guerre d'Algérie et tiers-mondialisme français entre ajustement capitaliste et engagement libéro-socialdémocrate', *Maghreb Review* **20**, 38–62.

Emerit, M. 1954. 'L'état intellectuel et moral de l'Algérie en 1830', *Revue d'histoire moderne et contemporaine* **1**, 199–212.

Enfantin, B.-P. 1843. *Colonisation de l'Algérie.* Paris: Bertrand.

Étienne, B. 1989. *La France et l'islam.* Paris: Hachette.

—.1995. 'Adieu Cancun', *Peuples méditerranéens* **70-1**, 31–40.

Fanon, F. 1959. *L'an V de la révolution algérienne.* Paris: Maspero.

—. 1961. *Les damnés de la terre.* Paris: Maspero.

Favret, J. 1972. 'Traditionalism through ultra-modernity', in *Arabs and Berbers: from tribe to nation in North Africa* (eds) E. Gellner and C. Micaud, 307–24. London: Duckworth.

Feraoun, M. 1950. *Le fils du pauvre. Mourad, instituteur kabyle.* Paris: Les cahiers du nouvel humanisme.

—. 1953. *La terre et le sang.* Paris: Éditions du Seuil.

—. 1954. *Jours de Kabylie.* Alger: Editions Baconier.

—. 1962. *Journal 1955–1962.* Paris: Editions du Seuil.

168 Bibliography

Ferchiou, S. 1993. 'La possession, forme de marginalité féminine', in *Etre marginal au Maghreb* (eds) F. Colonna and Z. Daoud, 191–200. Paris: Editions du CNRS.

Filali, K. 2002. *L'Algérie mystique: des marabouts fondateurs aux khwân insurgés, XVᵉ-XIXᵉ siècles*. Paris: Publisud.

Flaubert, G. 1863. *Salammbô*. Paris: M. Lévy.

Frankenberg, R. 1957. *Village on the Border. A social study of religion, politics and football in a North Wales community*. London: Cohen and West.

Frémeaux, J. 1993. *Les bureaux arabes dans l'Algérie de la conquête*. Paris: Denoël.

Fromentin, E. 1857. *Un été dans le Sahara*. Paris: Plon.

—. 1858. *Une année dans le Sahel*. Paris: Plon.

Fustel de Coulanges, N.D. 1864. *La cité antique: étude sur le culte, le droit, les institutions de la Grèce et de Rome*. Paris: Durand.

Gallouedec, L. and F. Maurette. 1922. *Enseignement primaire supérieur. La France et ses colonies. Troisième année, nouveaux programmes de 1920*. Paris: Hachette.

Gautier, E. 1927. *L'islamisation de l'Afrique du Nord: les siècles obscurs du Maghreb*. Paris: Payot.

Gellner, E. 1969. *Saints of the Atlas*. Chicago: Chicago University Press.

Gilsenan, M. 1996. *Lords of the Lebanese Marches. Violence and narrative in an Arab society*. London: I.B. Tauris.

Goodman, J. 2005. *Berber Culture on the World Stage: From village to video*. Bloomington, IN: Indiana University Press.

Grandguillaume, G. 1983. *Arabisation et politique linguistique au Maghreb*. Paris: Maisonneuve et Larose.

Grimm, J. and W. Grimm. 1915. *Kinder- und Hausmärchen* (ed.) C. Helbling. Zurich: Manesse.

Gsell, S. 1911. *Atlas archéologique de l'Algérie*. Algiers: Jourdan.

Guenoun, A. 1999. *Chronologie du mouvement berbère. Un combat et des hommes*. Algiers: Casbah Editions.

Guentari, M. 1990. 'Organisation politico-administrative et militaire de la Révolution Algérienne de 1954 à 1962'. Thèse de doctorat, Université Paul Valéry, Montpellier III.

Haddab, M. 1979. *Education et changement socio-culturel: les moniteurs de l'enseignement élémentaire en Algérie*. Algiers: OPU.

Hadibi, M. A. 1999. 'Sainteté, autorité et rivalité: le cas de Sidi Ahmed Wedris en Kabylie', in *L'Autorité des saints* (ed.) M. Kerrou, 273-86. Paris: Editions recherches sur les civilisations.

—. 2002. *Wedris: une totale plénitude. Approche socio-anthropologique d'un lieu saint en Kabylie*. Algiers: Editions Zyriab.

Hadj Ali, S. 1992. 'Algérie: le premier séminaire national des zaouias', *Maghreb, Machreq, Monde Arabe* **135**, 53-62.

Hadjeres, S. 1998. 'La crise du PPA de 1949 et l'actualité algérienne'. Quatre articles pour la presse algérienne, à partir d'extraits d'un ouvrage à paraître. Unpublished manuscript.

Haëdo, D. de. 1998 [1612]. *Topographie et histoire générale d'Alger*. Paris: Bouchène.

Hammoudi, A. 1974. 'Segmentarité, stratification sociale, pouvoir politique et sainteté', *Hespéris – Tamuda* **16**, 147-80.

Hamoumou, M. 1993. *Et ils sont devenus harkis*. Paris: Fayard.

Hamoumou, M. and A. Moumen. 2004. L'histoire des harkis et des français musulmans: la fin d'un tabou? In *La guerre d'Algérie: 1954-2004. La fin de l'amnésie* (eds) M. Harbi and B. Stora, 317-44. Paris: Robert Laffont.

Hanoteau, A. 1858. Une charte kabyle. *Revue Africaine* **3**, 75-80.

—. 1867 *Poésies populaires de la Kabylie du Jurjura. Texte kabyle et traduction*. Paris: Imprimerie Impériale.

Hanoteau, A. and A. Letourneux. 1872-3. *La Kabylie et les coutumes kabyles*. Paris: Challamel.

Hanoteau, M. 1923. 'Quelques souvenirs sur les collaborateurs de "La Kabylie et les coutumes kabyles"', *Revue Africaine* **64**, 134–49.

Harbi, M. 1975. *Aux origines du Front de libération nationale.* Paris: Bourgeois.

—. 1980. *Le FLN mirage et réalité.* Paris: Edition j.a.

Harvey, D. 1996. *Justice, Nature and the Geography of Difference.* Oxford: Blackwell.

Henni, A. 1990a. 'Le shaykh et le patron', *Peuples méditerranéens* **52-3**, 219–32.

—. 1990b. 'Qui a légalisé quel trabendo?', *Peuples méditerranéens* **52-3**, 233–44.

Herzfeld, M. 1985. *The Poetics of Manhood: Contest and identity in a Cretan mountain village.* Princeton, NJ: University Press.

—. 1987. *Anthropology through the Looking-glass. Critical ethnography in the margins of Europe.* Cambridge: Cambridge University Press.

Hirsch, E. and M. O'Hanlon (eds) 1995. *The Anthropology of Landscape.* Oxford: Clarendon Press.

Hugo, V. 1979 [1874]. *Quatre-vingt-treize.* Paris: Gallimard.

Ibazizen, A. 1979. *Le pont de Bereq'mouch ou le bond de 1000 ans.* Paris: Table ronde.

Ibn Khaldûn, A. 1847. *Histoire des Berbères et des dynasties musulmanes de l'Afrique septentrionale. Texte arabe publié par le baron de Slane.* Algiers: Imprimerie du Gouvernement.

INSEE. 2005. *Valeur d'achat du franc français 1900–1963.* Paris.

Jeanson, C. and F. Jeanson. 1955. *L'Algérie hors la loi.* Paris: Éditions du Seuil.

Jenkins, T. 1999. *Religion in English Everyday Life.* New York: Berghahn.

Kadri, A. 1999. 'Intellectuels algériens: aux fondements de la division', in *Parcours d'intellectuels maghrébins. Scolarité, formation, socialisation et positionnements*, 61–98. Paris: Karthala.

Katz, J.-G. 1996. *Dreams, Sufism and Sainthood. The visionary career of Muhammad al-Zawawi.* Leiden: Brill.

Kauffer, R. 2002. *L'OAS. Histoire d'une guerre franco-française.* Paris: Editions du Seuil.

Kemp, J. 1988. *Seductive Mirage: the search for the village community in Southeast Asia.* Dordrecht: Toris Publications.

Kepel, G. 1993. *Le Prophète et Pharaon: aux sources des mouvements islamistes.* Paris: Editions du Seuil.

Kerrou, M. (ed.) 1999. *L'Autorité des saints.* Paris: Editions recherches sur les civilisations.

Khadda, N. and M. Gadant. 1990. 'Mots et gestes de la révolte'. *Peuples méditerranéens* **52-3**, 19-24.

Kinzi, A. 1998. 'Tajmaât du village Lequelaa des Ait-Yemmel: étude des structures et des fonctions'. Mémoire de Magistère, Institut de langue et de culture amazighes, University of Tizi-Ouzou.

Kuper, A. 1988. *The Invention of Primitive Society: Transformations of an Illusion.* London: Routledge.

Lacoste-Dujardin, C. 1992. Démocratie kabyle. Les Kabyles: une chance pour la démocratie algérienne? *Hérodote* **65–6**, 63–74.

Lacoste-Dujardin, C. and Y. Lacoste (eds) 1991. *L'état du Maghreb.* Paris: La Découverte.

Lamchichi, A. 1991. *Islam et contestation au Maghreb.* Paris: L'Harmattan.

Lancaster, W. 1981. *The Rwala Bedouin today.* Cambridge: Cambridge University Press.

Launay, M. 1963. *Paysans algériens: la terre, la vigne et les hommes.* Paris: Éditions du Seuil.

Lazreg, M. 1983. 'The reproduction of colonial ideology: the case of the Kabyle Berbers', *Arab Studies Quarterly* **5**, 380–95.

Le Sueur, J. 2001. 'Decolonising "French Universalism": reconsidering the impact of the Algerian War on French intellectuals', in *North Africa, Islam and the Mediterranean world* (ed.) J. Clancy-Smith, 167–86. London: Frank Cass.

Leach, E. 1961. *Pul Eliya, a village in Ceylon: a study of land tenure and kinship.*

Cambridge: Cambridge University Press.

Lefebvre, H. 1991. *The Production of Space*. Oxford: Blackwell.

Lefeuvre, D. 2004. 'Les pieds-noirs', in *La guerre d'Algérie: 1954–2004. La fin de l'amnésie* (eds) M. Harbi and B. Stora, 267–86. Paris: Robert Laffont.

Leroy-Beaulieu, P. 1887. *De la colonisation chez les peuples modernes*. Paris: Guillaumin.

Lewis, B. 1990. *Race and Slavery in the Middle East: an historical enquiry*. Oxford: Oxford University Press.

Liauzu, C. 2004. 'Ceux qui ont fait la guerre à la guerre', in *La guerre d'Algérie: 1954–2004. La fin de l'amnésie* (eds) M. Harbi and B. Stora, 161–70. Paris: Robert Laffont.

Llamo, R.-C. 1956. *Essai sur le peuplement européen de l'Algérie. Euralgérie, ou la naissance d'un peuple original*. Algiers: Imprimerie moderne.

Lorcin, P. 1995. *Imperial Identities: Stereotyping, prejudice and race in colonial Algeria*. London: I.B. Tauris.

Lucas, P. and J.-C. Vatin. 1975. *L'Algérie des anthropologues*. Paris: Maspero.

Mahé, A. 1993. 'Laïcisme et sacralité dans les qanûns kabyles', *Annales Islamologiques* **27**, 137-56.

—. 2001. *Histoire de la Grande Kabylie, XIXᵉ–XXᵉ siècles*. Paris: Bouchène.

Maine, H. S. 1861. *Ancient Law: Its connection with the early history of society and its relation to modern ideas*. London: John Murray.

—. 1876. *Village-communities in the East and West: Six lectures delivered at Oxford*. London: John Murray.

Majumbar, M. 2005. 'The "New Man" at the dawn of the twenty-first century: challenges and shifts in Algerian identity', in *Transition and Development in Algeria: economic, social and cultural challenges* (eds) M. Majumbar and M. Saad, 113–30. Bristol: Intellect.

Malley, R. 1996. *The Call from Algeria. Third Worldism, revolution and the turn to Islam*. Berkeley, CA: University of California Press.

Mammeri, M. 1965. *L'Opium et le bâton: roman*. Paris: Plon.

—. 1985. *L'Ahellil du Gourara*. Paris: MSH.

—. 1989. *Shaykh Mohand a dit*. Algiers: CERAM.

—. 1991. *Culture savante, culture vécue. Etudes 1938–1989*. Algiers: Tala.

—. 1992 [1957]. *La colline oubliée*. Paris: Gallimard.

Manuel, F. E. 1962. *The Prophets of Paris*. Cambridge, MA: Harvard University Press.

Martinez, L. 1998. *La guerre civile en Algérie*. Paris: Karthala.

Masqueray, E. 1880. *Rapport sur l'état de l'instruction primaire française en Kabylie et sur les moyens de la développer*. Paris: Dupont.

—. 1893. *Souvenirs et visions d'Afrique*. Paris: Dentu.

—. 1983 [1886]. *Formation des cités chez les populations sédentaires de l'Algérie: Kabyles du Djurdjura, Chaouïa de l'Aourâs, Beni Mezâb*. Aix-en-Provence: Édisud.

Massignon, L. 1930. 'Centres de répartition des Kabyles dans la région parisienne', *Revue des études islamiques* **4**, 161–9.

Maunier, R. 1927. 'Recherches sur les échanges rituels en Afrique du Nord', *Année Sociologique* (N. S.) **2**, 11–97.

Maupassant, G. de 1884. *Au soleil*. Paris: A. Havard.

—. 1890. *La vie errante*. Paris: P. Ollendorff.

McDonald, M. 1989. *We are not French! Language, culture and identity in Brittany*. London: Routledge.

McDougall, J. 2006. *History and the Culture of Nationalism in Algeria*. Cambridge: Cambridge University Press.

Meneley, A. 1996. *Tournaments of Value: Sociability and hierarchy in a Yemeni town*. Toronto: University of Toronto Press.

Merad, A. 1967. *Le réformisme musulman en Algérie de 1925 à 1940*. Paris: MSH.

Merah, A. 1998. *L'affaire Bouyali. Comment un pouvoir totalitaire conduit à la révolte*. Algiers: A. Merah.

Messick, B. 1993. *The Calligraphic State: Textual domination and history in a Muslim society*. Berkeley, CA: University of California Press.

Meynier, G. 1981. *L'Algérie révélée. La guerre de 1914–1918 et le premier quart du XXᵉ siècle*. Geneva: Droz.

—. 2002. *Histoire intérieure du FLN, 1954-1962*. Paris: Fayard.

Mimouni, R. 1982. *Le fleuve détourné*. Paris: Robert Laffont.

Mollat de Jourdin, M. 2005. *Les explorateurs du XIIIᵉ au XVIᵉ siècle. Premiers regards sur des mondes nouveaux*. Paris: Editions du CTHS.

Monbeig, P. 1991. 'Le FFS et Hocine Aït Ahmed: parti kabyle et leader national?' Mémoire de DEA, Université Aix-Marseille 1.

Montagne, R. 1930. *Les Berbères et le Makhzen dans le sud du Maroc: essai sur la transformation politique des Berbères sédentaires*. Paris: Alcan.

Morizot, J. 1962. *L'Algérie kabylisée*. Paris: Peyronnet.

Mundy, M. 1995. *Domestic Government: Kinship, community and polity in north Yemen*. London: I.B. Tauris.

Musset, A. de 2002 [1834]. *La confession d'un enfant du siècle*. Paris: Maxi-Livres.

Norris, H. T. 1982. *The Berbers in Arabic literature*. London: Longman.

Nouschi, A. 1961. *Enquête sur le niveau de vie des populations rurales constantinoises de la conquête jusqu'en 1919*. Paris: PUF.

Oulebsir, R. 2004. 'Petite histoire d'une grosse restitution', *La Dépêche de la Kabylie* 7 January 2004.

Ourad, M. 2000. 'Jugurtha symbole de la résistance berbère', in *Actualités et culture berbères* **34**, 21–8.

Péan, P. 2004. *Main basse sur l'Algérie. Enquête sur un pillage*. Paris: Plon.

Pervillé, G. 2004. 'La guerre d'Algérie: combien de morts?' in *La guerre d'Algérie: 1954–2004. La fin de l'amnésie* (eds) M. Harbi and B. Stora, 477–94. Paris: Robert Laffont.

Peters, E. 1990. *The Bedouin of Cyrenaica. Studies in personal and corporate power*. Cambridge: Cambridge University Press.

Peyronnet, R. 1930. *Livre d'or des officiers des affaires indigènes*. Algiers: Sanbiton.

Peysonnel, J. A. 1987 [1724–5]. *Voyage dans la régence de Tunis et d'Alger*. Paris: La Découverte.

Philippe, A. 1931. *Missions des Pères Blancs en Tunisie, Algérie, Kabylie, Sahara*. Paris: Dillon et Cie.

Quandt, W. 1972. 'The Berbers in the Algerian political elite', in *Arabs and Berbers: From tribe to nation in North Africa*, (eds) E. Gellner and C. Micaud, 285–303. London: Duckworth.

Quemeneur, T. 2004. 'La discipline jusque dans l'indiscipline. La désobéissance de militaires français en faveur de l'Algérie française', in *La guerre d'Algérie: 1954–2004. La fin de l'amnésie* (eds) M. Harbi and B. Stora, 171–86. Paris: Robert Laffont.

Renan, E. 1873. 'La société berbère', *Revue des deux mondes* **107**, 138–57.

—. 1882. *Qu'est-ce qu'une nation? Conférence faite en Sorbonne, le 11 mars 1882*. Paris: Calman Lévy.

Rey-Goldzeiguer, A. 1977. *Le royaume arabe: la politique algérienne de Napoléon III, 1861-1870*. Algiers: SNED.

Richards, A. and A. Kuper (eds). 1971. *Councils in Action*. Cambridge: Cambridge University Press.

Rinn, L. 1884. *Marabouts et Khouan. Etude sur l'Islam en Algérie*. Algiers: Jourdan.

—. 1891. *Histoire de l'insurrection de 1871 en Algérie*. Algiers: Jourdan.

Roberts, H. 1981. *Algerian Socialism and the Kabyle Question*. Norwich: University of East Anglia School of Development Studies.

—. 1993. 'The FLN: French conceptions, Algerian realities', in *North Africa: Nation, state and region* (ed.) E.G.H. Joffé, 111–41. London: Routledge.

—. 2001. 'Co-opting identity. The manipulation of Berberism, the frustration of democratisation, and the generation of violence in Algeria'. London: LSE Working Papers.

—. 2003. *The Battlefield of Algeria 1988–2002*. London: Verso.

Robin, J. N. 1873. 'Notes sur l'organisation militaire et administrative des Turcs dans la Grande Kabylie', *Revue Africaine* **17**, 132–40 and 196–207.

Roy, O. 1994. *The Failure of Political Islam*. London: I.B. Tauris.

Sainte-Marie, A. 1976. 'Aspects du colportage à partir de la Kabylie du Djurdjura à l'époque contemporaine', in *Commerce de gros, commerce de détail dans les pays méditerranéens*, 103–19. Nice: Centre de la Méditerranée moderne et contemporaine.

Salhi, M. B. 1999a. 'Modernisation et retraditionnalisation à travers les champs associatif et politique: le cas de la Kabylie', *Insaniyât* **8**, 21–42.

—. 1999b. 'Entre subversion et résistance: l'autorité des saints dans l'Algérie du milieu du XXᵉ siècle', in *L'Autorité des saints* (ed.) M. Kerrou, 305–22. Paris: Editions recherches sur les civilisations.

—. 2002. 'Le local en contestation: citoyenneté en construction. Le cas de la Kabylie', *Insaniyât* **16**, 55–97.

Salinas, M. 1989. *Voyages et voyageurs en Algérie: 1830/1930*. Toulouse: Privat.

Samraoui, M. 2003. *Chronique des années de sang. Algérie: comment les services secrets ont manipulé les groupes islamistes*. Paris: Denoël.

Sayad, A. 1977. 'Les trois "âges" de l'émigration algérienne', *Actes de la recherche en sciences sociales* **15**, 59–79.

—. 2004. *The Suffering of the Immigrant*. Cambridge: Polity Press.

Schacht, J. 1966. *An Introduction to Islamic Law*. Oxford: Clarendon Press.

Scheele, J. 2006a. 'Algerian graveyard stories', *Journal of the Royal Anthropological Institute* (N. S.) **12**/4, 859–79.

—. 2006b. 'Generating Martyrdom: forgetting the war in contemporary Algeria', *Studies in Ethnicity and Nationalism* Special Issue **6**/2, 180–94.

—. 2007a. 'Recycling *baraka*: knowledge, politics and religion in contemporary Algeria', *Comparative Studies in Society and History* **49**/2, 304–28.

—. 2007b. 'Revolution as a convention: rebellion and political change in Kabylia', in *Creativity and Cultural Improvisation* (eds) T. Ingold and E. Hallam, 208–28. London: Berg.

Séminaire de Yakouren. 1981. *Algérie: quelle identité?* Paris: Imedyazen.

Servier, J. 1962. *Les portes de l'année. Tradition et civilisation berbères*. Paris: Robert Laffont.

Shryock, A. 1997. *Nationalism and the Genealogical Imagination. Oral history and textual authority in tribal Jordan*. Berkeley, CA: University of California Press.

Silverstein, P. 2002. 'An excess of truth: violence, conspiracy theorizing and the Algerian civil war', *Anthropological Quarterly* **75**/4, 643–74.

Souaïdia, H. 2001. *La sale guerre: le témoignage d'un ancien officier des forces spéciales de l'armée algérienne*. Paris: La Découverte.

Starret, G. 1998. *Putting Islam to Work*. Berkeley, CA: University of California Press.

Stendhal. 1854. *Le rouge et le noir: chronique du XIXᵉ siècle*. Paris: Michel Lévy Frères.

Stora, B. 1985. *Dictionnaire biographique des militants nationalistes algériens. ENA –PPA – MTLD, 1926-1954*. Paris: L'Harmattan.

—. 1986. *Messali Hadj: pionnier du nationalisme algérien, 1898-1974*. Paris: L'Harmattan.

—. 1992. *La gangrène et l'oubli: la mémoire de la guerre d'Algérie*. Paris: La Découverte.

—. 1993. *Histoire de la guerre d'Algérie*. Paris: La Découverte.

—. 1994. *Histoire de l'Algérie depuis l'indépendance*. Paris: La Découverte.

Stora, B. and Z. Daoud. 1995. *Ferhat Abbas, une utopie algérienne*. Paris: Denoël.

Strathern, M. 1981. *Kinship at the core*. Cambridge: Cambridge University Press.

Tailliart, C. 1925. *L'Algérie dans la littérature française: Essai de bibliographie méthodique et raisonnée jusqu'à l'année 1924*. Paris: E. Champion.

Taleb Ibrahimi, A. 1973. *De la décolonisation à la révolution culturelle, 1962–1972*. Algiers: SNED.

Tocqueville, A. de 1988. *De la colonie en Algérie*. Paris: Complexe.

Touati, H. 1990. 'Essor et fonction du saint homme', *Peuples méditerranéens* **52–3**, 145–54.

—. 1997. 'Algerian historiography in the nineteenth and early twentieth centuries: from chronicle to history', in *The Maghrib in question* (eds) M. Le Gall and K. Perkins, 84-94. Austin, TX: University of Texas Press.

Trautmann, T. R. 1987. *Lewis Henry Morgan and the Invention of Kinship*. Berkeley, CA: University of California Press.

—. 1997. *Aryans and British India*. New Delhi: Vistaar.

Tristan, F. 1980 [1844]. *Le tour de France: état actuel de la classe ouvrière sous l'aspect moral, intellectuel et matériel*. Paris: La Découverte.

Trumelet, C. 1881. *Les saints de l'islam. Légendes hagiologiques et croyances algériennes*. Paris: Didier.

Turin, Y. 1983. *Affrontements culturels dans l'Algérie coloniale. Ecoles, médecines, religion, 1830–1880*. Algiers: Entreprise Nationale du Livre.

Urvoy, D. 1993. 'Effets pervers du ḥajj, d'après le cas d'al-Andalus', in *Golden Roads: migration, pilgrimage and travel in mediaeval and modern Islam* (ed.) I.R. Netton, 43–56. Richmond: Curzon Press.

Vaïsse, M. 1983. *Alger le putsch*. Paris: Complexe.

Valensi, L. 1969. *Le Maghreb avant la prise d'Alger*. Paris: Flammarion.

—. 1984. 'Le Maghreb vu du centre. Sa place dans l'école sociologique française', in *Connaissances du Maghreb*, 227–44. Paris: CNRS.

Vidal-Naquet, P. 1972. *La torture dans la République*. Paris: Editions de Minuit.

Von Oppen, A. 2003. 'Bounding Villages. The enclosure of locality in Central Africa, 1890s to 1990s'. Habilitationsschrift, Humboldt-Universität, Berlin.

Warnier, A. 1865. *L'Algérie devant l'Empereur*. Paris: Challamel-Aîné.

Weber, E. 1976. *Peasants into Frenchmen*. Stanford, CA: Stanford University Press.

Wilaya de Béjaïa. 2000. *Annuaire statistique de la wilaya de Béjaïa*. Béjaïa.

Wolf, E. 1982. *Europe and the People without History*. Berkeley, CA: University of California Press.

Yacine, K. 1956. *Nedjma*. Paris: Editions du Seuil.

Yous, N. 2000. *Qui a tué à Bentalha? Chronique d'un massacre annoncé*. Paris: La Découverte.

Newspapers consulted

La Dépêche de la Kabylie
Liberté
Le Matin
Le Monde
El Moudjahid
Le Quotidien d'Oran

Index